Designing Language Courses: A Guide for Teachers

Kathleen Graves
School for International Training

A TeacherSource Book

Donald Freeman
Series Editor

Australia · Brazil · Japan · Korea · Mexico · Singapore · Spain · United Kingdom · United States

Designing Language Courses: A Guide for Teachers
Kathleen Graves

Senior Editor: Erik Gunderson

Market Development Director: Charlotte Sturdy

Production Services Coordinator: Michael Burggren

Assistant Development Editor: Jill Kinkade

Project Manager and Compositor: Jessica Robison

Production Manager: Su Wilson

Cover Designer: Ha. D. Nguyen

Credits appear on page 308, which constitutes an extension of this copyright page.

ISBN-13: 978-0-8384-7909-4

ISBN-10: 0-8384-7909-X

Heinle
25 Thomson Place
Boston, MA 02210
USA

Cengage Learning is a leading provider of customized learning solutions with office locations around the globe, including Singapore, the United Kingdom, Australia, Mexico, Brazil, and Japan. Locate your local office at: **international.cengage.com/region**

Cengage Learning products are represented in Canada by Nelson Education, Ltd.

Visit Heinle online at **elt.heinle.com**

Visit our corporate website at **cengage.com**

Printed in Canada
15 16 17 18 13 12 11 10

Dedication

To my father, Thomas Graves, whose belief in the power of education has been a source of inspiration and support.

Thank You

The series editor, authors and publisher would like to thank the following individuals who offered many helpful insights throughout the development of the TeacherSource series.

Jo Ann Aebersold	Eastern Michigan University
Linda Lonon Blanton	University of New Orleans
Tommie Brasel	New Mexico School for the Deaf
Jill Burton	University of South Australia
Margaret B. Cassidy	Brattleboro Union High School, Vermont
Florence Decker	University of Texas at El Paso
Silvia G. Diaz	Dade County Public Schools, Florida
Margo Downey	Boston University
David E. Eskey	University of Southern California
Alvino Fantini	School for International Training
Sandra Fradd	University of Miami
Jerry Gebhard	Indiana University of Pennsylvania
Fred Genesee	University of California at Davis
Stacy Gildenston	Colorado State University
Jeannette Gordon	Illinois Resource Center
Else Hamayan	Illinois Resource Center
Sarah Hudelson	Arizona State University
Joan Jamieson	Northern Arizona University
Elliot L. Judd	University of Illinois at Chicago
Donald N. Larson	Bethel College, Minnesota (Emeritus)
Numa Markee	University of Illinois at Urbana Champaign
Denise E. Murray	San José State University
Meredith Pike-Baky	University of California at Berkeley
Sara L. Sanders	Coastal Carolina University
Lilia Savova	Indiana University of Pennsylvania
Donna Sievers	Garden Grove Unified School District, California
Ruth Spack	Tufts University
Leo van Lier	Monterey Institute of International Studies

ACKNOWLEDGMENTS

This book is the result of extensive collaboration with many language teachers, especially the twenty-eight teachers who took my course design seminar in 1997. While not all of their voices are featured in the book, they all worked with me to articulate the kinds of things a teacher needs to know and be able to do in order to design a course:

Kay Alcorn, Dylan Bate, Toby Brody, Iris Broudy, Michelle Carr,
Chris Conley, Akemi Fujimoto, Jessica Gahm, Michael Gatto,
Amy Ginsburg, Derica Griffiths, Jeremy Hedge, J. D. Klemme,
Jon Kmetz, Carole Knobloch, John Kongsvik, Denise Lawson,
Ann Leonard, Denise Maksail-Fine, David Markus, Patricia Naccarato,
Ali Pahlavanlu, Brooke Palmer, Mary Patten, Sharon Rose-Roth,
Jennie Steele, Cyndy Thatcher-Fettig, and David Thomson.

When I was in São Paulo, Mônica Camargo, Simone Camillo, Eliana Pinto, Andrea Porchia, Rosa Silva, Wagner Veillard, and Lauro Gisto Xavier were some of the early testers of the ideas in the book.

I had the good fortune to be Sally Cavanough's outside evaluator for her M.A. thesis on learner-centred assessment. I wish I could have used more of Carolyn Layzer and Judy Sharkey's material—next book! I was pleased to finally use some of Valarie Barnes' work.

My spring 1998 independent study group used the book in draft form and asked me numerous questions, not all of which I have been able to answer! Thanks to Meredith Askey, Kate Carney, Mark Hansen, Tom Kuehn, Jennifer Meese, Joanne Richman, Dan Riney, Roshani SenGupta, Leigh Anne Sippel, Wendy Wen, and Pam Woodward.

I would like to thank the teachers at Queensland University of Technology who so graciously agreed to review the first draft of the book and gave me insightful feedback: Melitsa Apostolos, Julie Barff, Kim Griffin, Shirley Martin, and Bella Sandelin.

Thanks to Markus Greutmann for his feedback on Chapter 9.

Five reviewers, including series editor Donald Freeman, gave me valuable feedback on the book. I would like to thank the two anonymous reviewers for their encouraging comments. I would especially like to thank Penny McKay for her thorough and thoughtful review of the book. As I revised, I felt that I was in a professional dialogue with her. I would also like to thank Karen Johnson for her suggestions and particularly her timely help with Chapter 9.

Finally, I would like to thank my daughters, Emily and Laura, for being willing to wade through a very messy study to get to their e-mail. They have promised to remind me to write my next book during a sabbatical. And a lasting thank you to Donald Freeman, spouse and colleague, for convincing me that I really did want to write this book.

Series Editor's Preface

As I was driving just south of White River Junction, the snow had started falling in earnest. The light was flat, although it was mid-morning, making it almost impossible to distinguish the highway in the gray-white swirling snow. I turned on the radio, partly as a distraction and partly to help me concentrate on the road ahead; the announcer was talking about the snow. "The state highway department advises motorists to use extreme caution and to drive with their headlights on to ensure maximum visibility." He went on, his tone shifting slightly, "Ray Burke, the state highway supervisor, just called to say that one of the plows almost hit a car just south of Exit 6 because the person driving hadn't turned on his lights. He really wants people to put their headlights on because it is very tough to see in this stuff." I checked, almost reflexively, to be sure that my headlights were on, as I drove into the churning snow.

How can information serve those who hear or read it in making sense of their own worlds? How can it enable them to reason about what they do and to take appropriate actions based on that reasoning? My experience with the radio in the snow storm illustrates two different ways of providing the same message: the need to use your headlights when you drive in heavy snow. The first offers dispassionate information; the second tells the same content in a personal, compelling story. The first disguises its point of view; the second explicitly grounds the general information in a particular time and place. Each means of giving information has its role, but I believe the second is ultimately more useful in helping people make sense of what they are doing. When I heard Ray Burke's story about the plow, I made sure my headlights were on.

In what is written about teaching, it is rare to find accounts in which the author's experience and point of view are central. A point of view is not simply an opinion; neither is it a whimsical or impressionistic claim. Rather, a point of view lays out what the author thinks and why; to borrow the phrase from writing teacher Natalie Goldberg, "it sets down the bones." The problem is that much of what is available in professional development in language-teacher education concentrates on telling rather than on point of view. The telling is prescriptive, like the radio announcer's first statement. It emphasizes what is important to know and do, what is current in theory and research, and therefore what you—as a practicing teacher—should do. But this telling disguises the teller; it hides the point of view that can enable you to make sense of what is told.

The TeacherSource series offers you a point of view on second/foreign language teaching. Each author in this series has had to lay out what she or he believes is central to the topic, and how she or he has come to this understanding. So as a reader, you will find this book has a personality; it is not anonymous. It comes as a story, not as a directive, and it is meant to create a relationship with you rather than assume your attention. As a practitioner, its point of view can help you in your own work by providing a sounding board for your ideas and a metric for your own thinking. It can suggest courses of action and explain why these make sense to the author. And you can take from it what you will, and do with it what you can. This book will not tell you what to think; it is meant to help you make sense of what you do.

The point of view in **TeacherSource** is built out of three strands: **Teachers' Voices, Frameworks,** and **Investigations.** Each author draws together these strands uniquely, as suits his or her topic and more crucially his or her point of view. All materials in **TeacherSource** have these three strands. The **Teachers' Voices** are practicing language teachers from various settings who tell about their experience of the topic. The **Frameworks** lay out what the author believes is important to know about his or her topic and its key concepts and issues. These fundamentals define the area of language teaching and learning about which she or he is writing. The **Investigations** are meant to engage you, the reader, in relating the topic to your own teaching, students, and classroom. They are activities which you can do alone or with colleagues, to reflect on teaching and learning and/or try out ideas in practice.

Each strand offers a point of view on the book's topic. The **Teachers' Voices** relate the points of view of various practitioners; the **Frameworks** establish the point of view of the professional community; and the **Investigations** invite you to develop your own point of view, through experience with reference to your setting. Together these strands should serve in making sense of the topic.

In *Designing Language Courses: A Guide for Teachers*, Kathleen Graves argues for the central role of teachers in course design and curriculum planning. For those in classrooms, designing language courses is a process that is anchored in students' learning geared towards distinct ends within a particular context. When teachers approach planning and teaching in such a grounded way, they draw on their rich experiences of practice, animated by reflection and scrutinized through careful analysis. Thus, Graves notes, "Course design requires teachers to make reasoned choices... so that they can convert what they know about teaching and learning languages into a coherent course plan." Course design and teaching go hand-in-hand as the teacher builds and acts on knowledge in and from classroom practice.

Throughout the book, Graves eschews the more technical and technicist approaches to curriculum planning which are well represented in the professional language-teaching literature. While recognizing the value in many of the concepts and models they propose, she points out that such approaches often depend on having time and access to information and resources which many teachers do not. This fact can disconnect many teachers from the course design literature. When course design is framed in these terms—things that they often cannot do—teachers can be alienated from the very processes of conceptualizing, planning, and reflecting which are at the heart of comprehensive and integrative thinking about teaching. By refocusing course design on what teachers can—and do—do as they teach, Graves makes the central point that "teachers are the best people to design the courses they teach." She thus argues for a more integrated view of course design, one which blends theory and newly acquired skills with the basic processes of teaching.

This book, like all elements of the **TeacherSource** series, is intended to serve you in understanding your work as a language teacher. It may lead you to thinking about what you do in different ways and/or to taking specific actions in your teaching. Or it may do neither. But we intend, through the variety of points of view presented in this fashion, to offer you access to choices in teaching that you may not have thought of before and thus to help your teaching make more sense.

— Donald Freeman, Series Editor

1

A Systems Approach to Course Design

1.1 *Before you read the chapter, complete the following sentence:*

Designing a language course involves _____.

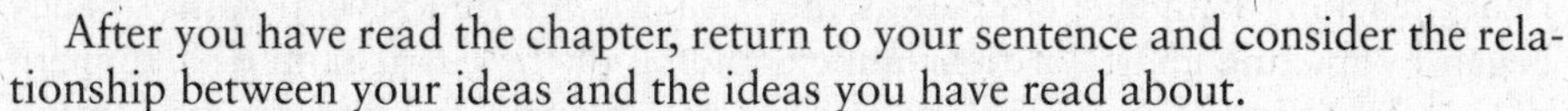

After you have read the chapter, return to your sentence and consider the relationship between your ideas and the ideas you have read about.

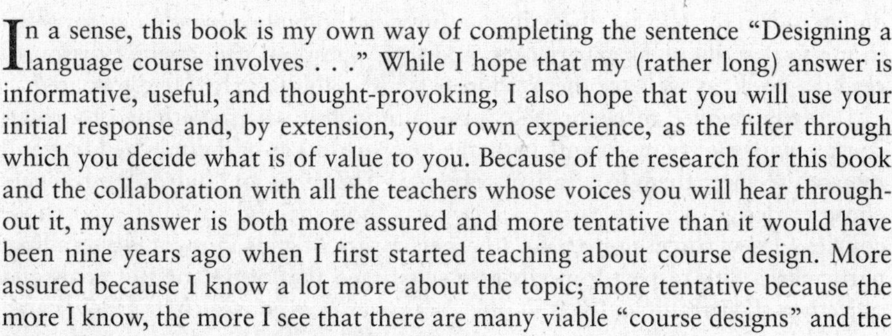

In a sense, this book is my own way of completing the sentence "Designing a language course involves . . ." While I hope that my (rather long) answer is informative, useful, and thought-provoking, I also hope that you will use your initial response and, by extension, your own experience, as the filter through which you decide what is of value to you. Because of the research for this book and the collaboration with all the teachers whose voices you will hear throughout it, my answer is both more assured and more tentative than it would have been nine years ago when I first started teaching about course design. More assured because I know a lot more about the topic; more tentative because the more I know, the more I see that there are many viable "course designs" and the less inclined I am to give definitive answers.

I first became interested in the topic of course design because of my experience co-authoring an EFL textbook series for adult learners, *East West* (1988), for which my co-author, David Rein, and I had to make decisions about what should be taught in each level, in what order, and how. Our decisions were based on our collective experience as teachers and materials developers as well as our research of other textbooks and literature on course design. Writing a textbook forced me to be explicit about what I knew and believed about how people learn languages, in ways that had been implicit in my teaching up to then. The publication of the books, with their tables of contents organized into charts with categories of topics, functions, grammar, vocabulary, culture, and pronunciation, provided me with a useful credential as an authority on language curriculum design. These tables of contents seemed a far cry from my previous "output" as a language teacher: handwritten (this was before personal computers) lesson plans organized in manila file folders, with after-teaching comments and ideas scribbled on them; handouts I had prepared for my classes; mimeographed tests. The relationship between those file folders of lesson plans, handouts, and tests, and the printed tables of contents of our books did not become apparent until I later started teaching about course design.

I had to organize my thinking about course design when I agreed to teach a course on it to a group of teachers in 1990. In preparation for teaching my course I ordered David Nunan's book *Syllabus Design* (1988) as the course text. The book had come out two years before, the same year as the first level of *East West,* and had provided me with food for thought about how to go about designing a language course and why. Because I didn't have much lead time to order the books, there was some anxiety about whether they would arrive in enough time for me to design course activities around them. Fortunately, they arrived the week I was to begin teaching the course. However, when I opened the carton of books for my class, I discovered that the publisher had sent me instructional manuals for health care workers in rural areas! (I still wonder what the health care workers did with their books on syllabus design.) While I didn't see it that way at the time, not having the books as the course began was fortunate because it forced me to ask the teachers in the course to use their own experience teaching language courses as the basis for the first several classes. They began by making charts of their understanding of the curriculum development process and drawing up a list of questions they wanted to answer by the end of the course. The core of the classes became a course that each teacher chose to design. When the text finally arrived, it provided common terminology for them to use to describe their experiences, and their questions gave them a reason to read the book, as well as other resources from a bibliography I had prepared.

I greatly enjoyed teaching the course, although it was something of a roller coaster, with me trying to anticipate the teachers' needs and do the reading and research to meet them in a satisfactory way. The range of courses the teachers chose to design was wide, and I felt I was more helpful to those who chose courses I knew something about. I became aware of gaps in my understanding, particularly with respect to needs assessment and the formulation of goals and objectives. For example, I wasn't able to answer questions such as "How can a needs assessment tool serve as a learning assessment tool?"

As I set out to deepen my understanding, a few things nagged at me. The first was that in the published resources on language course design with which I was familiar, the voices and experiences of the teachers who could make practical use of the ideas were conspicuously absent. There were plenty of examples from published material like the EFL series I had co-authored, and from academic specialists, but there was little from teachers' own accounts. Additionally, course design tended to be portrayed as a more-or-less systematic process with results that did not resemble the messy, multi-faceted, two-steps-forward one-step-back process that I had experienced in my own designing of courses and recognized in that of teachers I worked with. The process had been idealized into something that made some teachers feel inadequate because they were not doing things the "right way" and getting the "right results." The reality the teachers were dealing with was how their manila folders of lesson plans, handouts, and tests could become a coherent course. What they needed was a coherent understanding of how the parts fitted together into a whole. However, the whole was not a result like the tables of contents of my books, nor was it a unitary, linear process. Rather it was an interrelated set of processes and products, which I have now come to see as a system.

Processes of Course Design

Designing a language course has several components. Classic models of curriculum design as well as more recent models agree on most of the components, although they may subdivide some of them and give them slightly different names. These components comprise setting objectives based on some form of assessment; determining content, materials, and method; and evaluation. The model I use in this book, which I call a framework, draws on the work of others, as well as my own work. In 1996, when I set out a course development framework in the book I edited, *Teachers as Course Developers* (1996), it was a list of components with questions as a way of explicating them. For example, the first component was called Needs Assessment, and the accompanying questions were *What are my students' needs? How can I assess them so that I can address them?* The framework in Figure 1.1 is largely the same, with two differences. The framework is no longer a linear list, but a flow chart, and the processes are described as verbs, not nouns.

For classic models see Stenhouse (1975), Taba (1962), Tyler (1949); for recent models see Brown (1995), Johnson (1989), Nunan (1988), Richards (1990), Yalden (1987).

Figure 1.1: A Framework of Course Development Processes

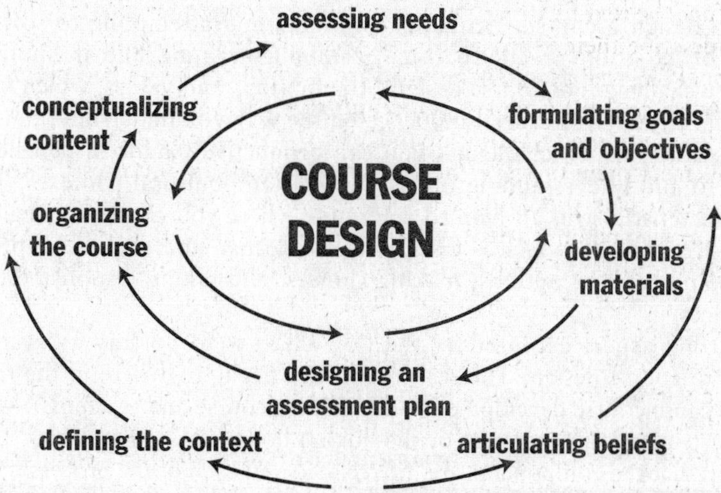

By changing the framework to a flow chart I hope to capture two aspects of course design. The first aspect is that there is no hierarchy in the processes and no sequence in their accomplishment. As a course designer, you can begin anywhere in the framework, as long as it makes sense to you to begin where you do. What makes sense to you will depend on your beliefs and understandings, articulated or not, and the reality of the context and what you know about your students. For that reason, articulating beliefs and defining one's context are on the bottom of the chart to serve as the foundation for the other processes.

Deciding where to begin will depend on how you problematize your situation, that is, how you determine the challenges that you can most productively address within the context. This view of the role of the teacher as course designer is captured in Zeichner and Liston's list of features that characterize reflective teaching. They write that a reflective teacher:

For more on problematizing, see Chapter 2, pages 20–21.

- examines, frames, and attempts to solve the dilemmas of classroom practice;
- is aware of and questions the assumptions and values he or she brings to teaching;
- is attentive to institutional and cultural contexts in which he or she teaches;
- takes part in curriculum development and is involved in school change efforts; and
- takes responsibility for his or her own professional development.

(Zeichner and Liston 1996 p. 6)

When you design a course, examining, framing, and attempting to solve the dilemmas of classroom practice become examining, framing, and attempting to address the challenges of course design. Assumptions and values, which in this book I call beliefs, are a crucial influence on the way you understand the challenges. Deciding which challenges you can productively address depends on attention to and understanding of institutional and cultural contexts. These three characteristics will all help to determine where you choose to begin the course-design process, which is essentially a reflective and responsive process of understanding your options, making choices, and taking responsibility for those choices.

The second aspect captured by the flow chart is to portray a "systems" approach to course design. The reason you can begin anywhere in the framework is because course development—designing a course and teaching it—comprises a system, the way a forest or the human body is a system (Clark 1997). This means that the components are interrelated and each of the processes influences and is influenced by the other in some way. For example, if you begin with formulating goals and objectives, you will need to think about the content you are teaching. If you begin with designing an assessment plan, you will need to think about the objectives you are trying to reach and assess. If you begin with developing materials, you will need to think about what you are trying to teach and for what purpose.

Course design is a system in the sense that planning for one component will contribute to others; changes to one component will influence all the others. If you are clear and articulate about content, it will be easier to write objectives. If you change the content, the objectives will need to change to reflect the changes to the content, as will the materials and the assessment plan. If you are clear about your plan for assessing student learning, it will help you design appropriate materials. If you change your approach to assessment, it will have an impact on the content, the objectives, and so on.

The processes have been changed from nouns to verbs, for example from "needs assessment" to "assessing needs," in order to portray course design as a thinking process. I see this as similar to Shulman's idea that good teaching involves pedagogical reasoning (1987). Pedagogical reasoning means thinking through how to transform subject matter knowledge into something that can be taught and learned, which Shulman calls pedagogical content knowledge. Similarly, course design requires teachers to make reasoned choices about each of the processes in the framework so that they can convert what they know about teaching and learning languages into a coherent course plan.

See Karen Johnson's book in this series, *Understanding Language Teaching: Reasoning in Action* (1999).

I believe that teachers are the best people to design the courses they teach, and having the processes expressed as verbs such as "assessing needs" rather than nouns such as "needs assessment" means that each verb needs a subject. I see the teacher as the subject of these verbs, taking charge of the processes, rather than playing the role of recipient of the products. This doesn't preclude collaborating as much as is feasible and desirable with students, other teachers, and administrators. In fact, such collaboration is important, because a course is usually part of the larger system of a curriculum and an institution. Teachers who teach within explicit curriculum guidelines can be active agents in the courses they teach if they are clear about what the processes are and how they can take responsibility for them. For example, it is possible to assess students' needs as part of teaching.

One of the reasons I started teaching and writing about course design was because much of the literature about curriculum design portrayed the process as a logical, rational sequence: conduct a needs assessment; based on the needs assessment, develop objectives; based on the objectives, select content, and so on. My experience and research have not been at the level of the overall curriculum of a program, and so I cannot comment on how accurately the literature captures that reality. However, at the course level, this logical sequence is often impractical or unproductive and has the effect of making teachers feel that they are doing something wrong if they don't follow it.

If you take a systems view of course design and see that when you are working on one process, you are in fact working on others, then it becomes a more feasible process. For example, a clear set of goals and objectives will provide a framework for both assessment and materials development and thus make both of those processes easier. Because teachers often have little planning time, it is important that the process be manageable. Additionally, you may not really be able to complete one process before doing some work on another. Your goals and objectives may become clearer once you have begun to organize and sequence the course. You can then go back to the goals and objectives and refine them. It's not a question of getting one "right" before moving on to the next. Because course design is a grounded process in the sense that you design a course for specific students within a specific context, you can work on more than one process at once or move between processes within the system and still be connected to the context. Each of the processes in the flow chart in Figure 1.1 is the basis of a chapter and will be further elaborated there.

David Thomson

David Thomson is a teacher with experience in Saudi Arabia, Japan, and the US. He describes the way he used the framework in planning a course on writing using computers at an Intensive English Program in the United States.

> The development of goals and objectives came after content had been created. When I taught the first version of this course, I had goals and objectives in my head, but never formally wrote them down. . . . It felt strange to write goals and objectives after I had already determined the content. In my previous career prior to teaching, we determined what the goals would be and then built a program on that, using the goals as a base. I struggled with this issue—which element of the Course Development flow chart should come first—until we were reminded that we should decide for ourselves where to begin. In a freewriting exercise I wrote that ". . . it has boiled down to the interrelatedness of goals, objectives, content, and evaluation. There's a chicken-egg scenario and it really doesn't matter where I start my journey into this course which isn't a destination but itself a point along the way. It was pointed out that objectives are not etched in stone and hearing that freed me to start this trip." As I said, I had already started with content and could not see any reason to do any dramatic cutting to a course that I felt "had legs."

Products of Course Design

Course or curriculum "products" are the tangible results of the processes in the framework in Figure 1.1. For example, the actual list of goals and objectives is the product of formulating the goals and objectives. The activities and materials designed to assess needs are the products associated with assessing needs. A syllabus is the product of organizing a course. A mind map, grid, or flow chart is the product of conceptualizing content. Each chapter gives guidelines for producing these products with examples of the products of various teachers in various settings. The teachers also describe their reflections, dilemmas, and decisions with respect to each process and the resulting product.

The chapters are in an order that makes sense to me. However, my hope is that you can read the book by beginning with any chapter. Chapters 2 and 3 provide a foundation for the remaining chapters. Chapter 2 is about defining one's context, which means being as specific as possible about the students, setting, resources, and so on. Chapter 3 is about articulating one's beliefs and understandings about language, social context, learning, and teaching. These two chapters are foundational because they guide the decisions for the other chapters.

Chapters 4 and 5 are about somewhat abstract processes in the sense that you do not have to factor in "real" time—although you do have to consider students, purpose, needs, etc. Chapter 4 is about conceptualizing content, which means making decisions about what is most important for students to learn, given who the students are and the resources and constraints of the context. Chapter 5 is about formulating goals and objectives. The remaining chapters result in products that will actually be used in the classroom, and so have more concrete outcomes.

Chapter 6 is about assessing students' needs. This process usually comes first in most books on curriculum design and for good reason: if a course is to be responsive to students' needs, then needs should be assessed before other decisions are made. I have put it after content and goals and objectives because, in my experience, the majority of teachers do not have the opportunity to do a precourse needs assessment and so must do needs assessment once they start teaching. Additionally, needs assessment is more effective if you have some idea of what you want to assess and why, which depends on how you've conceptualized the content of your course.

Chapter 7 is about organizing the course, which means designing the actual syllabus so that it fits within the given time constraints. Chapter 8 is about developing materials. I use the term "developing materials" to include how the teacher will conduct the classes he or she teaches. This is sometimes referred to as "methodology" in other frameworks. Chapter 9 is about adapting a textbook. Chapter 10 is about designing an assessment plan, both to assess students' learning and to evaluate the effectiveness of the course.

Designing a Language Course Is a Work in Progress

1.2 *Before you read the next section, briefly write down or discuss with a colleague what you think this statement "designing a language course is a work in progress" means.*

Because it involves human beings, teaching—and the planning and thinking which are a part of it—is not an enterprise that can be easily quantified, codified, and replicated. Rather, teaching is an organic, unpredictable, challenging, satisfying, and frustrating process. It is not an imperfect craft, but a dynamic one. Any activity associated with teaching is in some respect a work in progress because it will be transformed by those involved in it. The teacher who is formulating objectives for a course will go through a few "drafts" as she tries to articulate what she wants her students to achieve in the course. They are her reasoned plan for the course based on what she knows about her context. Once she teaches the course, especially if it is the first time, it is likely that those objectives will change in some way as she determines their appropriateness for her students. The next time she teaches the course she will be "testing" the modifications to the objectives. The objectives will probably undergo fewer modifications, because the teacher will know more about what she hopes students will achieve. However, the students will be different and so the teacher may well want to modify the objectives to make them more responsive to that particular group. After teaching the course several times, the objectives may change because of changes in "knowledge in the field" or because of the students. In his book on curriculum design, *The Elements of Language Curriculum,* J. D. Brown gives the example of changes made to a curriculum for a program in China because the proficiency level of the students changed over time and thus the objectives needed to reflect those changes (1995).

The notion that course design is a work in progress means that it is not a good use of a teacher's time to try to get each detail of each aspect of a course "right" prior to actually teaching it. Once "course design meets students" and the course is underway, it will of necessity be modified. I would go even further to say that a course in which every aspect is decided and written up is doomed to fail because it has been done as though what the learners will do with it is predictable. One of the first lessons of teaching that most of us learn with some pain is that our carefully crafted lesson plans are fragile constructs once in the classroom, and that attachment to them may cause us to blame the students when the plans don't work. The lesson plan is not the lesson. The course design is not the course.

I observed a class in a seminar on "Curriculum and Materials Development" at Lancaster University taught by Alan Waters who is the co-author of another book on curriculum design that I admire, *English for Specific Purposes* (1986). He used the following diagram, which captures some of the tensions inherent between designing a course and teaching it.

Nature of Syllabus	*Nature of Language Learning*
serial/linear	holistic
segmental	developmental
pre-determined (in most cases)	unpredictable

How can a teacher do the preparation needed to produce a syllabus which is, to a greater or lesser extent linear, segmental, and pre-determined, and still be responsive to the learning processes of her students which are holistic, developmental, and unpredictable? One way to address the dilemma is to keep in mind that the plans for one's course are a "work in progress" that will change once the course is underway.

Iris Broudy

Iris Broudy, a teacher with experience in Vietnam and Mexico, writes about this tension between wanting to have a "finished product" prior to going into the classroom, and viewing course design as a work in progress. She is redesigning a course she taught at a University in Orizaba, Mexico, as part of a seminar on course development.

> I find myself struggling against my nature. My working style tends to be perfectionistic. When I was a journalist, I would rewrite a piece as many times as the deadline would allow, refining, fine-tuning, adding another clever twist or turn of phrase. It is tempting to treat this course design project similarly. Yesterday I spent a solid eight hours trying to revise the goals and objectives for my course, expanding and refocusing, consulting numerous books, even toying with the idea of changing the whole course.

At that point in her planning, Iris and I had a conversation during which I mentioned that a possible subtitle of this book was "Always a work in progress." She later writes about her reaction to the title:

> Always a work in progress. So never complete. *Never perfect.* How could it ever be perfect? Students are not machines, predictable in their abilities and responses. Each learning context is different. If my course design is so refined, my objectives so detailed, my materials so elaborate that nothing is left to chance, then I am creating a teacher-centered environment in which the learners are just pawns to be moved about the game board of curriculum.

She elaborates this further in recalling her experience when she taught the course she is redesigning.

> At the moment, I am still wrestling with a performance demon that wants control—over the material and the students—in order to ensure a perfect outcome. I watched it happen [when I taught the course]. . . . If I couldn't find an appropriate activity, I would design my own, often spending hours creating elaborate materials. These activities didn't always "work" according to plan, however. When they didn't, I found myself trying to steer the students to use them "properly," rather than allowing things to emerge from the material. And if a class wasn't a "success," I concluded that I wasn't either.

Designing a language course is a work in progress in its whole, in its parts, and in its implementation. Each aspect of course design, the content, objectives, needs assessment, materials, and evaluation are works in progress both in their conception and in their implementation. This does not mean that it is better to go into the classroom with no plan at all, although in some cases that is possible. I wouldn't have written this book if I didn't believe in the importance of planning a course. On the contrary, I have found that teachers who carry out the planning processes of course design are better prepared to let their plans go because they have thought through the whats, hows, and whys of the course and are better prepared to pay attention to their students. To me this is analogous to great conductors who can conduct without a score and pay attention to the musicians who are playing the music. But they can only do so because they know the music so intimately that they carry it in their bones.

From Conceptualization to Practice

1.3 *Conceptual processes are those that involve thinking and planning. Practice involves implementing the plans. Look at Figure 1.2. Where do you see conceptual processes taking place? Where do you see practice taking place?*

The plan or design of the course is not the course, but a part of course development. Course design is part of the complete cycle of course development, depicted in Figure 1.2, which includes planning the course, teaching it, evaluating it, and replanning it based on the evaluation, and then teaching it again in the replanned version, and so on. Conceptualization takes place at the first stage: everything up to actually teaching. Practice is the second phase: teaching the course. The third stage could be called "reconceptualization" based on what was learned while teaching the course. Stage 4 is again practice, and the cycle continues. However, during "practice," conceptualizing is also going on, because practice is not simply applying the design, but reshaping it as you go along.

Figure 1.2: The Cycle of Course Development

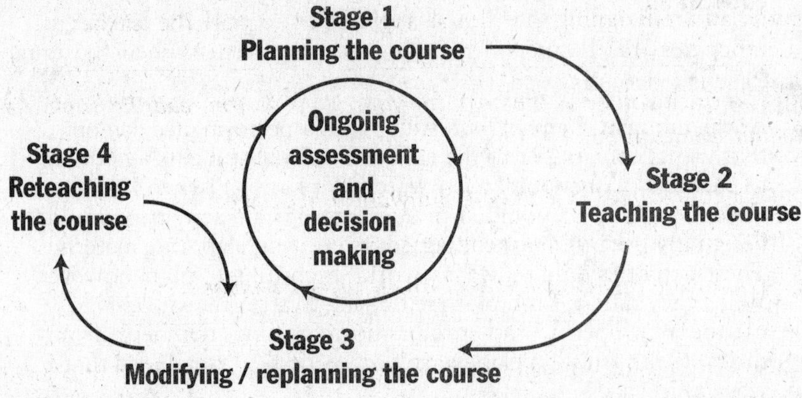

For six case studies of teachers going through the complete cycle, see Graves (1996).

This book focuses mainly on Stage 1, the conceptualization part of the cycle, planning a new course or redesigning one you have already taught. Not all the examples of teachers' curriculum products have been "tested" in practice, so we cannot know if they "worked" in practice. However, they are part of a redesign of a course the teacher had already taught, so she or he had a good idea of what would work in the context. My hope is that by doing the investigations you will receive enough guidance from them and from the frameworks to plan your course.

How to Use this Book as a Guide to Designing Language Courses

Ultimately, this book is intended to be what its title says: a guide for teachers who are designing a course. Each chapter includes three elements, common to all the books in the TeacherSource series: frameworks, teachers' voices, and investigations. The frameworks provide information and guidelines about what I think is important for teachers to know about each of the processes of course design. The teachers' voices provide reflections on how they carried out the processes, the dilemmas they faced, the decisions they made. The teachers also provide examples of curriculum products they developed for their courses. The investigations are a combination of reflective tasks which require thinking and responding to a question, a framework or a curriculum product; problem-solving tasks which require you to arrive at a solution that makes sense to you; and product tasks which ask you to design a curriculum product.

In effect, the investigations ask you to "co-author" the book by questioning and adding to the frameworks and developing your own examples. I strongly recommend that you, as the reader, choose a course to design, either one you have already taught and wish to redesign, or one you plan to teach, as the basis for the investigations. Teachers who work with a predetermined syllabus or textbook can also carry out the processes within the parameters of the syllabus or textbook. If you complete all the tasks, you will have the structure of a course in place. For teachers who are new to teaching and don't feel they know enough yet to design a course, I suggest using a language course in which you have been a learner and redesigning that course as though you were the teacher.

1.4 *Choose a course as the basis for your work as you read the book. As suggested above it can be:*

- a course you have taught and want to redesign
- a course you are planning to teach
- a course in which you are or have been a learner

I also strongly recommend that you work with a partner or in a group of three or four. The sociologist, Dan Lortie, in his seminal work *Schoolteacher* (1975) describes teachers as teaching in "egg crate schools" (p. 14) because they are separated in and by their classrooms. While this provides great autonomy, it also has the effect of "institutionally infantilizing" teachers (Erickson, 1986, p. 157) so that they have little say in the educational policies that affect their professional lives. Dialogue among teachers is a crucial step in giving teachers more power in their professions: it helps teachers to be more aware of their own practice and how it relates to that of their colleagues.

One teacher, Denise Maksail-Fine, whose voice we will hear throughout the book, writes about the importance of collaboration. She began to redesign a course for the third year of Spanish for high school students, a course she had already taught for several years and would teach again, in the rural part of upstate New York where she lived. When she returned home, she hadn't completed the redesign and had difficulty continuing to work on it. She writes:

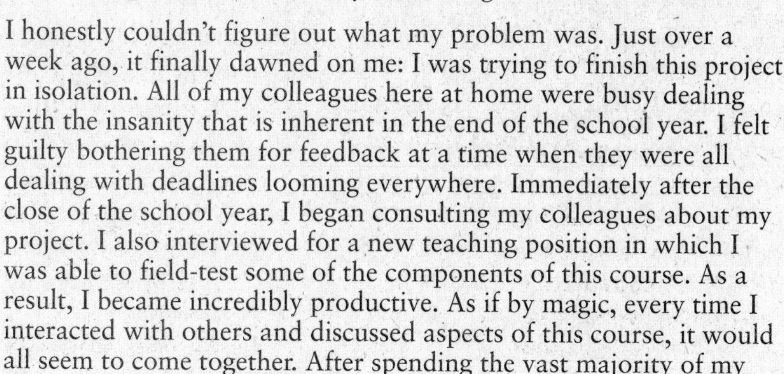

> I honestly couldn't figure out what my problem was. Just over a week ago, it finally dawned on me: I was trying to finish this project in isolation. All of my colleagues here at home were busy dealing with the insanity that is inherent in the end of the school year. I felt guilty bothering them for feedback at a time when they were all dealing with deadlines looming everywhere. Immediately after the close of the school year, I began consulting my colleagues about my project. I also interviewed for a new teaching position in which I was able to field-test some of the components of this course. As a result, I became incredibly productive. As if by magic, every time I interacted with others and discussed aspects of this course, it would all seem to come together. After spending the vast majority of my

academic training and professional life working in isolation, I am amazed at the impact that collaboration has had on how I work.

Some of the reflective tasks in the book ask you to react to various curriculum products (e.g., sets of goals and objectives, needs assessment activities) as a way of arriving at what will work best for you. Talking through your reactions and hearing others' will help you become clear about your own beliefs about what is important for your course. Pay attention when you react strongly either positively or negatively to something another teacher has done or said. It usually means your beliefs are being confirmed or challenged. Likewise, talking through your curriculum products and answering your colleagues' questions about them will help you to learn from your colleagues, and to reach greater clarity about your own work.

1.5 *Identify one or two colleagues to work with as you design your course. It is generally preferable to work with someone who is designing a similar course or working in a similar context and so is familiar with the issues you are facing. However, working with someone who is unfamiliar with your context can also be helpful because you will need to be more explicit about what you are doing and your reasons for doing so.*

Suggested Readings

"The Design Solution: Systems Thinking," the second chapter in Edwin Clark's book *Designing and Implementing an Integrated Curriculum: A Student-Centered Approach* (1997), was influential in helping me understand course design as a system. For another view of an interactive approach to course design, see Alvino Fantini's gemstone model, described in "At the Heart of Things: CISV's Educational Purpose" in *Interspectives: A Journal on Transcultural and Educational Perspectives,* Vol. 13, CISV (Children's International Summer Villages) International, Newcastle, England, 1995.

To extend the argument that teachers are producers and not just recipients of knowledge, see the first chapter from Donald Freeman's book in this series, *Doing Teacher Research: From Inquiry to Understanding* (1999).

For a clear and useful summary of more traditional views of language course design, see "Curriculum Development in Second Language Teaching," the first chapter of Jack Richards' book, *The Language Teaching Matrix* (1990).

2

Defining the Context

In a pedagogical grammar course I teach, I begin each unit by asking my graduate students to list questions they have about the focus of the unit. The units address subjects such as lexicon and phonology. I collect the questions to get a sense of their concerns and needs so that I can think about how to address them. The questions are largely about how to teach the subject we are about to study. Those kinds of questions do not have one answer because the answer will depend on the context in which the teacher teaches. For example, the answer to the following question about teaching pronunciation "What is the goal of our learners, to achieve native-like pronunciation (if we can define what that is) or to be intelligible?" will depend on the goals of the students, which in turn depend on the context. At one time I taught students from different countries in a high school program in the United States; the majority of those students wanted to sound like their American counterparts. A few years later I taught Japanese junior college students in Japan; sounding American was not a goal of most of those students.

The context is a key factor in answering questions like the one above. For this reason, it is important to define what you know about the context in order to know how to answer the question. The same is true for designing a course. You need to know as much as possible about the context in order to make decisions about the course. The two teachers below illustrate how different the contexts of teaching English as a second or foreign language can be. The first teacher, Patricia Naccarato, describes the program in which she taught for two summers.

Patricia Naccarato

> [The context is] a private language school with branches in Florida, California, and suburban Virginia, outside of Washington D.C. They recruit international students who come to the United States for a summer of English study and cultural exchange. The students range in age from 12 to 18 years and, while in the country, stay in a homestay situation with a local family. The components of the program are writing, grammar and conversation. This is the second summer I have taught the writing component of the program, at the Virginia site. There is no set curriculum and it is left up to the teacher to select what they will include, although a book is provided. Quite honestly, the people running the school don't seem the least bit concerned about what I will be doing with the students. They have assigned a book and are happy to have found a "real" teacher to teach at least one element of the course.

The second teacher, Michael Gatto, describes the context for his teaching practicum at a language institute in El Salvador.

Michael Gatto

> Mrs. B., the director, welcomed us and informed me that I would not be allowed to enter the building again without a tie. She then plopped three books down in front of me and said in a very serious tone of voice, "You start teaching tomorrow morning at 8:00. You will be teaching twenty-three students in the beginning level. You have one month to finish Units 1, 2, and 3. Don't deviate from this book. I know that students from [your MA program] like to try their own things. Don't. We have a method that works for us, so please follow it. Wear a tie and get a hair cut. See you tomorrow morning. Don't be late."

These two teachers' brief accounts illustrate not only two kinds of contexts, but two kinds of responsibilities with respect to designing a course. Patricia has complete freedom to design her course, which provides its own set of challenges in that she will have to make all the decisions relating to content and goals, organization, materials, and assessment. Michael, on the other hand, is expected to follow a prescribed text and methods, another type of challenge in that he will need to consider how to adapt the text to meet the needs of his students. In order to meet their respective challenges, each teacher needs to understand the context so as to work successfully within it. This chapter will address the following questions, *What is meant by "context"?* and *Why is it important to define one's context?*

WHAT IS MEANT BY CONTEXT?

Imagine that you are an architect and you have been commissioned to design a house. Where do you start? Do you start by sketching some designs of houses on paper? My father-in-law and brother-in-law are both architects. Having watched them design and oversee the building of houses over the years, I know that if you have to design a house you don't begin with sketches, because you have no basis for the design. You begin with specifications. For example, where is the site, how big is it, what are its particular features? How many people will live in this house? What are their interests or needs that will affect how they use the house, the kinds of rooms, and how the rooms relate to each other? What is the budget? What is the time line? What materials are available locally? And so on. Designing a course is similar to designing a house. You need to have a lot of information in order to design a structure that will fit the context. The first investigation in this chapter is designed to begin the process of outlining the kinds of information necessary to define the context of a course.

2.1a *The investigation will have two parts. You will begin it here and then add to it after you read the next section.*

You and a colleague have submitted a proposal to your local teachers' organization to give a workshop for teachers on course design. You plan to give the participants in the workshop three descriptions of three different teaching situations. The participants will choose one and use it as a basis for the course planning exercises in the workshop. Each description should provide relevant information about the context for the course. Your colleague has begun each of the descriptions and has asked you to finish them. Choose one of the contexts below with which you have some familiarity, and list the kinds of additional information you think the participants in the workshop will want to know so that they can begin to design a course for that context. If you do not have experience with contexts similar to those described below, choose one you are familiar with, either as a teacher or a language learner, and write a description of that context. The focus of the course does not have to be English; it can be another language.

> *Context #1: Adult education in an ESL setting.* There are twenty five students in the class, fourteen men and eleven women, ranging in age from 18 to 57. They are immigrants and come from Haiti, Russia, Poland, and China. They have been in the United States less than a year. The students are at a low to mid-intermediate level.
>
> *Context #2: English for teens at a language institute in their country (EFL setting).* There are 12 students, 5 boys, 7 girls, 13-14 years old. Class meets in the afternoon for two hours, two days a week, for 3 months.
>
> *Context #3: English for academic purposes course in Canada.* The students are from Italy, Japan, Korea, Mexico, and Colombia. They range in age from 18 to 25. They are taking the course to improve their writing skills so that they can enroll in courses in the university in which the ESL program is housed.

This investigation is meant to help you think about the information that you feel is important to have when beginning to design a course. I include it because whenever I give teachers examples of course design products—for example, a needs assessment activity, a set of goals and objectives, or a syllabus plan—they rightfully want to know the answers to questions such as *"What is the level of the students?" "How long is the course" "Where is the course taking place?"* Without that information it is difficult to evaluate the appropriateness or effectiveness of the product. Course design, like teaching, and like architecture, is a grounded process. This means that when you design a course, you design it for a specific group of people, in a specific setting, for a specific amount of time; in short, for a specific context. The more information you have about the context, the easier it will be for you to make decisions about what to teach and how. For example, if you are designing an EAP (English for Academic Purposes) course, you will probably choose one set of topics if the course is for high school students and somewhat different topics if the course is for adult postgraduates, although the academic skills in both cases may be similar. On the other hand, if you are teaching teenagers in a general English course, you may not focus on academic skills. If your course is an extensive thirty-hour course, you will make different choices than for an intensive course that meets for sixty hours. It doesn't mean that each time you teach a similar course you will redesign it from scratch, even though you teach it to a different group of students. However, you will adapt it to that group.

The chart below summarizes the various aspects of context that you can define: people, time, physical setting, teaching resources, and nature of the course and institution. Chapter 6, Assessing Needs, addresses the aspects of people and nature of the course and institution in greater depth.

Figure 2.1: Factors to Consider in Defining the Context

People	*Physical setting*
students	location of school: convenience,
how many, age, gender, culture(s),	setting
other language(s), purpose(s),	classroom: size, furniture
education, profession, experience,	light, noise
other stakeholders	always same classroom?
school administrators	
parents	
funders	
community	

Nature of course and institution	*Teaching Resources*
type/purpose of course	materials available
mandatory, open enrollment	required text?
relation to current/previous courses	develop own materials?
prescribed curriculum or not	equipment: cassettes,
required tests or not	video, photocopying
	clerical support

Time
how many hours total over what span of time
how often class meets
for how long each time
day of week, time of day
where fits in schedule of students
students' timeliness

2.1b *In the first part of Investigation 2.1, you completed the description of a context for a course. Go back to the description. Discuss it with a colleague. Which factors listed on the chart in Figure 2.1 did you include in your description? Did you include factors that are not on the chart? How would you modify the chart to include your ideas?*

Charts like the one in Figure 2.1 are meant to serve as tools for you to adapt to your own purposes and understanding. You may not be able to get all the information in Figure 2.1 about a given context prior to teaching in it; for example, you may not know the number of students, and you may not have information about their cultural backgrounds. You can find this information during initial or ongoing needs assessment, as outlined in Chapter 6. Some of the information listed on the chart may be more relevant to one context than another. For example, information about funders and the community is relevant in an adult education course, but may not be relevant in an English for academic purposes course.

Why Is It Important to Define One's Context?

The "givens" of one's context are the resources and constraints that guide our decisions. Knowing how long a course is, its purpose, who the students are, and how it fits in with other aspects of the curriculum helps us to make decisions about content, objectives, and so on. One teacher I worked with, David Markus, tried to design a "contextless" literature course for high school students. He initially thought that it would be easier to design a generic course, which he could later adapt to a specific high school context. He found the experience very frustrating. He writes:

> A few weeks into the process I felt as if I was floundering in a sea of ideas but had nothing concrete to hang on to. Each time a new idea came up, I would move in a different direction. At that point I realized that trying to create a course for a generic situation complicated the course development process needlessly. Though each situation has constraints and issues associated with them, these constraints can provide focus.

David Markus

David's description of how difficult it was to make decisions about his course illustrates why I suggested in Chapter 1 that when you use this book you do the investigations with a particular course in mind. Virtually every teacher has had the experience of planning a lesson that was unrealistic for the time frame, or unrealistic for the level of the students, or for which the equipment was not available. Similar challenges face the course designer. A clearer understanding of what is possible within a given amount of time will allow us to be realistic about what we—teacher and students—can accomplish. Knowing what equipment or support is available will help us make choices about how much and what kind of material to prepare. As David Markus points out, the constraints of our context can actually help us to focus on what is realistic and appropriate and thus plan for success. Information about time, for example, can help us make decisions about how many areas of content we can realistically address within the time frame of the course. Information about teaching resources will help us make decisions about the kinds of materials we choose or develop. The relationship of the course to other courses will help us make decisions about content, so that we build on previous content. Expectations of the students and stakeholders can help us make decisions about what is appropriate to cover and how students will be assessed.

An Iranian teacher, Ali Pahlavanlu, describes the way in which the stakeholders in his context in a language school in Iran constrained what he could realistically do in his course. Ali taught in a private language institute. His students were young adult men and women in segregated classes. They were largely from educated backgrounds, and their parents wanted them to pass a national university entrance exam called the Concours. The English portion of the exam focused on grammar and reading skills. Ali wanted to redesign the text used as the basis for his intermediate level course. The text focused on grammar and functions, with each unit targeting different grammatical points and functions. Ali wanted to develop a course that was more integrated and took the students' interests into account. He writes about how he tried to consider all the contextual factors that could have an impact on the acceptability of his course text:

Ali Pahlavanlu

> Creating an ideal course is absolutely out of the question. The conditions in Iran are far less than ideal for EFL teaching. The same conditions paralyze the course developer. What I have tried to accomplish is an attempt to consider all those factors involved in decision making and to create a relatively well-balanced text for my course which is acceptable under the current conditions ruling Iran.

In Ali's case, the stakeholders played a major role in his decisions about what was possible with respect to redesigning his course. The stakeholders included the investor who had put up the money for the school, the license holder who was licensed by the government to run the school, the religious leaders who ensured that nothing anti-Islamic or anti-government was allowed, the government officials, who enforced the rule of religion, and the parents, whose aim was for their children to pass the Concours. Ali knew that for a course to succeed in that setting, it had to be profitable, it had to meet religious codes, and it had to be geared toward passing the Concours. These constraints forced him to make choices about what to teach and how to teach it that were often in conflict with some of the beliefs he held about the nature of language and the purpose of language learning. Nevertheless, being very clear about the constraints of the context showed him where he could put his beliefs into operation. For example, his belief that students are more motivated to learn when they find the topics meaningful to their lives caused him to switch from the traditional grammar-based syllabus to a topic based syllabus, with functional and grammatical components. He chose the topics based on what he knew about the students, their age, educational background, and interests.

Most teachers who are in the position to design their own courses and course materials are not faced with constraints as explicit as the ones Ali faced. However, having information about the givens of your context—both the constraints and resources—is important because you can use that information to guide your decisions as you plan the course. The more information you have about your context the more able you will be to make decisions and to plan an effective course. It doesn't mean that decisions will necessarily be easier to make! Returning to the architect analogy, if an architect designs a house that is too big for the site or beyond the budget of the clients or with material that is not available, the house will not get built. If you design a course that covers too much material for the time given, or is built around topics that are inappropriate for your students, or depends on materials that are not readily available to the students, the course will be ineffective or, at best, require ongoing repair. Unlike architects, teachers can, to some extent, make the changes in the blueprint as they carry out the course.

Defining one's context can also be viewed as part of pre-course needs assessment. Information about the students and about the curriculum is clearly related to students' learning needs. Other information, such as time and setting, does not necessarily help define students' language learning needs, but has to be taken into account in order to design a course that can focus on the needs within the givens of the context. It is similar to what J. D. Brown calls "situational needs analysis," which pertains to information about a program's "human aspects, that is, the physical, social and psychological contexts in which learning takes place" and is related to "administrative, financial, logistical, manpower, pedagogic, religious, cultural, personal, or other factors that might have an impact on the program." (1995, p. 40) In Ali Pahlavanlu's case, students' learning needs were not directly shaped by the investors, license holders, and government officials. They were shaped to some extent by parents' demands that the course help their children pass the Concours and by the religious concerns of Iranian society. Reconciling competing demands, while difficult, is made easier when you know what they are.

See Chapter 6 on assessing needs.

Ann Leonard, a teacher who designed an EAP course for students in an intensive English program, writes about her struggle to build a rich definition of context:

Ann Leonard

> It may often be the case that one knows little about a context before teaching a course. But something to keep in mind is that people define "context" in various ways. I began very narrow and, as I continued with this project, quickly learned that to view the context in the very broadest sense can help one see more clearly further down the road. Factors that first influenced how much I could plan my course *a priori* included: information about the institution, as I had already taught there; what kinds of students made up the major portion of the institution's population, including country of origin, age, and reason for studying English.
>
> I now recognize the depth of information one can gather that is a relevant part of the course context and will inevitably inform the choices that one makes during the course. Some of my discoveries at various points during the course include: Knowing the students' age range tells you something about their motivation levels, interest levels, attention spans, and their ability to comprehend themselves on a meta-cognitive level, just to get started. And what factors about the course are going to influence material you can conceivably cover? How the particular course fits into the scheme of the entire program can help you avoid any redundant course content later on. . . .
> In my situation the total number of hours was also a pivotal factor: in that amount of time I was extremely limited as to what I could cover and what the students could be expected to produce.

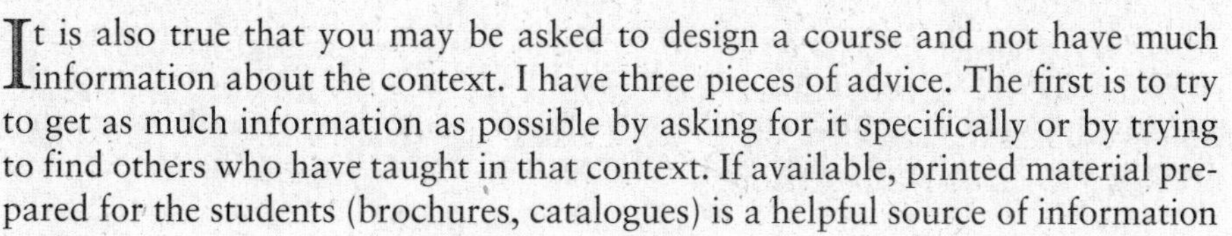

It is also true that you may be asked to design a course and not have much information about the context. I have three pieces of advice. The first is to try to get as much information as possible by asking for it specifically or by trying to find others who have taught in that context. If available, printed material prepared for the students (brochures, catalogues) is a helpful source of information since students' expectations may be based on what they find there. Talk to students who have taken the course or teachers who have taught it. Ask for information as though you were a student. The second is to design the course with a similar group in mind, if you have knowledge of such a group, so that you are not stymied when making decisions, as David Markus initially was when he tried to design his literature course for any group of high school students. The third is to work into your course design process flexibility so that you have more than one option at each step of the way. For example, you can develop a menu of possibilities (topics, tasks, materials) from which to choose as you know your students and your context better. A good example of this approach can be found in Carmen Blyth's (1996) account of designing an EAP course for Ecuadorian students in which she outlined inventories of academic tasks, skills, and materials which she had taught or used in past EAP courses and from which she was able to select once she started teaching in Ecuador.

2.2 *Consider the course you identified in Investigation 1.4 as the basis for this investigation.*

1. Using the chart in Figure 2.1, make a list of all the information you have about the context for your course.
2. Add information that occurs to you that is not on the chart. Make a list of information you would like to obtain.
3. Discuss your list with a colleague and brainstorm (make a list without evaluating each item on the list) ways to obtain the information you don't have.
4. Follow through on one or two of the ways for obtaining the information (e.g., interviewing teachers with experience with such courses, calling a school or institute that offers similar courses and asking for information, sitting in on a similar course). Report back to your colleague.

PROBLEMATIZING

Defining your context is an important step in problematizing your course. The term **problematizing** comes from Paulo Freire (1973). It means looking at something that is taken for granted—literacy, for example—and taking it apart to understand it, challenge it, and act on it. I use problematizing to mean looking at what you know about the context and defining the challenges you feel you need to and are able to meet in order to make the course successful. These challenges may involve class size, multi-levels, number of hours, lack of resources, your own lack of experience with the content of the course, and so on.

Problematizing is rooted in the assumption that the teacher who teaches the course is the best equipped to understand its challenges and to mobilize the resources available to meet those challenges. It is also based on my belief that there is not one way or "best way" to design a course. Rather, the course must work within the givens of the context and make use of the skills that the teacher brings to the course. For example, Lu Yuan, a teacher who taught Chinese to university exchange students in an immersion program in China, grappled with how to design her course so that she could make use of the world outside of the classroom as an integral part of the course. This became a key challenge that influenced her design of materials and course organization. Whenever her students learned an aspect of grammar, a function, or vocabulary items, they were given a task that required them to use the new aspect of language outside of class and then report back to class on what they encountered and what they learned. In designing his history of American literature course for high school students, David Markus at first followed the kind of syllabus the high school used: a chronological survey of American literature. He wasn't satisfied with this approach. When he problematized his situation he realized that his challenge was how to provide enough time and depth in the course for students to really understand the literature, while still covering a broad spectrum of the literature. Defining the challenge helped him to produce a solution: a syllabus based on themes in the literature.

For David Markus' description of the syllabus see page 33.

Problematizing helps you decide where to start and what to focus on in planning the course. The more information you have about the context, the more apparent the challenges will be, and the better you will be able to define and address the challenges as you design and teach the course. Problematizing is about making choices for action. A given course can be designed and taught in any number of ways. You need to make decisions about how you will design the course, based on what you know about your context.

Patricia Naccarato described some features of her context in the beginning of the chapter on page 13. Her experience provides another example of how problematizing shapes one's approach to designing a course. The curriculum had three components, grammar, conversation, and writing, each taught by a different teacher. She taught the writing component. She taught the course the first summer and was dissatisfied with it. In order to redesign it for the next summer, she problematized her situation. She didn't simply want to find another textbook or reorganize the syllabus. She wanted to figure out what hadn't worked. She was able to identify three main challenges that she felt she needed to meet in order to plan and teach a successful course. The first had to do with the subject matter, the second with the students, and the third with logistical factors. The first was how to improve the students' writing skills without being overly academic and boring. The second was how to deal with intercultural conflicts among students. The third was how to integrate students who arrived days or weeks late due to visa, school schedule, or transportation problems.

In relation to the first challenge, how to work on writing, she says,

Patricia Naccarato

> The students seemed to feel last summer that the "school" element of their summer in the United States was the least important and, most definitely, the least interesting. They were in the United States mostly as a vacation, and the few hours spent in the classroom every morning were an inconvenience, at best. I tended to sympathize with them to the extent that I found myself trying to make the classes "fun" at the expense of their learning.

Patricia realized that the challenge here was not simply to develop a set of "fun" activities, but to provide opportunities to learn writing skills in ways that the students found interesting.

In relation to the second challenge, how to deal with intercultural conflicts among students so that they could carry out the group work that she felt was crucial to learning, she says:

> The conflicts among the students were at times quite volatile. All the students came to us with a very strong sense of national pride. This created clashes and polarization that I, as the teacher, found difficult to bridge. I feel that only by addressing these issues directly, will we be able to get past them to reach a point where the students can comfortably work together.

In relation to the third challenge, how to integrate students who arrived late, she says,

> I want each student to feel that he or she is an integral member of the class whether they arrive on day one or day 15 of the overall program.

The challenges she defined guided her decisions in designing the course for the second summer. She resolved the first challenge of teaching writing skills in an interesting way by focusing on a specific writing skill each week, having students keep portfolios of their work, with the goal of having each student contribute to a class newsletter, to be published at the end of the course for the students to take home with them.

> I think that by working on a product wherein they can express themselves and have something to show for their summer's time in the classroom, they will be more motivated to do the work necessary to create a finished product they will be proud of.

She resolved the second challenge by designing activities that enabled students to talk about their cultures and learn from each other. She addressed the third challenge by having students who were there from the beginning brainstorm what the late-arriving students would need to know and do to fit into the class, and then develop activities accordingly.

Not every teacher has the freedom to create a course from scratch that Patricia Naccarato had. Many teachers teach with a syllabus that is part of a set curriculum within a specified period of time, as was the case with Michael Gatto in El Salvador (see page 14). Or, as in Ali Pahlavanlu's case in Iran (see page 18), teachers may have to develop a curriculum that is governed by economic, religious and legal factors. To continue the analogy with building a house, teaching within a prescribed curriculum and exam system is similar to working with an already developed blueprint. While the teacher may not be able to design the blueprint for the house/course, she can learn to adapt it or some aspect of it to the particular needs of her students.

Although the challenges may arise more in the actual teaching stage than in the designing stage of the course, it is nevertheless important to understand the context well enough to know how to work within it. Problematizing is one way for teachers to "bite off what they can chew" and assume control of some aspect of their course. In Michael Gatto's case, as we shall see in Chapter 9, this meant varying the order and ways in which he covered the material in the textbook unit. In other words, armed with a solid understanding of your context, you can define a challenge that you have some control over and can generate a means to address.

2.3 *Look over the information about your course context from Investigation 2.2. Does anything stand out that will be a major resource or constraint in developing your course? Can you identify particular challenges that you will need to address in order to design a successful course?*

To return to the analogy with designing a house, if the site for the house has particular problems associated with it, such as poor drainage, they must be accounted for in the design or there will be continual problems with the house. On the other hand, if there are particularly spectacular features of the site, such as a beautiful view, it makes sense to take advantage of them. By defining your context and the challenges it presents, you put yourself in a position to take advantage of the resources of the context and your own internal resources of common sense and creativity.

3

Articulating Beliefs

Some years ago I taught a beginning Chinese class. There were fifteen students in the class. I had them do a lot of work on pronunciation so that they would feel confident when speaking. I used a variety of techniques in which the students listened to each other and to me, and worked individually to produce the correct sounds. In a feedback session in which I asked students to discuss what was and wasn't effective in helping them learn in the course, one student asked me why I didn't conduct choral repetition drills. I told him that I was concerned that such drills—in which students repeat sentences after the teacher in chorus, over and over again—usually involved mechanical and mindless repetition which I thought resulted in little learning of the pronunciation. He explained that he liked such choral repetition because it enabled him to practice the new sounds anonymously without fear of making mistakes. Other students agreed that they felt as he did and would benefit from such drills. After that discussion, choral repetition drills became a part of the classroom repertoire.

The story about the Chinese class can help to illustrate the complex nature of the beliefs and understandings that guide a teacher. I knew that learning to speak a language involves learning how to pronounce its sounds. In the case of Chinese, learners often have the expectation it will be difficult to speak and to pronounce. I wanted to demystify this aspect of Chinese by having students feel comfortable with the pronunciation early on. I had a strong belief that teacher-led choral repetition drills were not conducive to learning. This belief was based on experience as a learner in high school when I would happily tune out during drills in German class. It was based on subsequent readings about, and philosophical disagreement with, the behaviorist principles of Audiolingualism, for example that learning was habit formation and language was learned through mimicry (Brown 1994). Additionally, in the institutional setting in which I worked, drilling was regarded as outdated and unproductive. Another reason I didn't like to use drills was because I had to play the role of drill master, which did not allow for student choice.

The role of drill master was also in conflict with other strong beliefs I held: that different students learn in different ways, and that students should learn to direct their own learning. My beliefs about student responsibility and choice prompted me to conduct regular feedback sessions in which students discussed what was and wasn't helping them to learn in the class. I believed that such discussions helped them become aware of how they learned. The information gathered in these sessions also helped me to make decisions about how to adapt the class to meet students' needs. The students' reasons for wanting choral repetition drills made sense to me. They wanted to use the drills attentively and not mechanically. I could see that the anonymity would in fact help them feel comfortable making the new sounds of Chinese and thus contribute to their learning. I was still uncomfortable in the role of drill master, but I was able to let go of my own antipathy toward the drills in response to their needs.

Beliefs are not necessarily something that teachers can easily articulate or are completely aware of (Johnson 1998). Most teachers don't have opportunities to make their beliefs explicit because the institutions in which they work do not generally ask them to articulate their beliefs nor do they place a value on such articulation. However, the more aware you are of your beliefs the easier it is to make decisions, or at least to know why you are making the decisions as in the Chinese class above.

To understand where beliefs come from you need to look at your past experience and the beliefs about learning and teaching that grow out of and guide that experience. Experience includes your education and its discourse. I mean discourse in Gee's (1990) sense of the way one learns to think, speak and act and what one learns to value in a given setting such as a school. In my case, my experience in high school as a learner with drills was not positive. When I first started teaching, however, I used drilling extensively both because it was what I had known as a learner and because that was a prevalent method at the time. Later in graduate school, a methods course helped me understand the theoretical basis for drills as a form of teaching and also why drilling had not worked for me in high school. Moreover, my professors advocated—and practiced—helping students take responsibility for their learning, which helped to shape my beliefs.

Beliefs also arise from work experience and the discourses of the workplace, what you feel constitutes success and "works" in each setting, what you perceive to be important or necessary or "the way things are done." In my case in the Chinese class, my colleagues would have felt that a teacher who used drills was taking the responsibility for learning away from her students. Finally, your ongoing professional development—readings, presentations, or courses can influence your beliefs. All of these influences—as a learner, as a teacher, as a colleague—provide the basis for your understanding of how languages are taught and learned and the beliefs that guide your choices.

The process of designing a course is one way in which you can learn to understand and articulate your beliefs, because those beliefs provide a basis for making choices. When I teach course design the question of choices always arises. *"There are too many choices! How can I decide?" "Did I make the right choice?" "What is the right choice?" "Is there a right choice?"*

In this book, you will hear teachers refer to their beliefs as either beliefs, principles, or precepts.

In fact there are multiple possibilities, multiple justifications, and multiple answers. I tell teachers that I don't have an answer to give them, but there is an answer for them to find. The answer they choose depends on the context, on their experience, and on their beliefs and understandings. Ann Leonard writes about the way that her beliefs helped her to make choices as she designed a reading and writing course:

Ann Leonard

The phrase "You have to make decisions and justify them," was made, and often repeated, in response to a tendency during the course design process to get stuck on one product or one component. I was often in this dilemma. . . . Whenever I found myself spending too much time over a decision, or lamenting too many choices, I would remember this phrase, and it forced me to stop and look at what I had for the moment, and to rationalize and justify these choices. I began to understand that more is not necessarily better, and that one aspect of designing a course is having the confidence in one's principles and experience to make decisions.

3.1 *Think of a language lesson you observed, took part in, or taught, that you thought was an excellent lesson. Imagine that after the lesson you run into a colleague who asks you "How was the lesson?" You respond that it was a great lesson. The colleague says, "Oh, really? What made it so great?" Explain in as much detail as possible why you thought it was a good lesson.*

The way you answer the question in this Investigation is a means of getting at what you feel is important in teaching and learning a language. What you feel is important is based on your understandings of how people learn languages and the beliefs you hold about language teaching that stem from those understandings. For example, let's suppose the lesson took place in a class for adult learners. The learners were comparing different letters to the editor taken from the local newspaper. The letters were written in support of (or against) candidates in forthcoming elections. The students were working in small groups to figure out how the candidates differed. I might say that one thing that made the class great was that students had an opportunity to do a problem-solving activity in small groups that required the use of the target language. Answering the question *"Why did that make the lesson 'great'?"* would help me to uncover some of my beliefs about learners' and teachers' roles in the classroom and how language is learned. I might say that problem solving as a way of learning requires learners to negotiate with each other, which stands in contrast to a way of learning in which learners receive knowledge from the teacher which they then memorize or internalize. When problem solving in the target language, learners are required to use the language they know and adapt it to the communication needs of the situation. When working in small groups, learners are usually more likely to participate because they feel less "on the spot" than in a large group and because there are fewer people. Responses such as these can help me arrive at what I feel is important, what I believe, about how people learn language.

One framework for sorting out your beliefs is Stern's framework, which he outlines in his books *Fundamental Concepts of Language Teaching* (1983) and *Issues and Options in Language Teaching* (1992). He proposes that any theory of language teaching needs to address the concepts of <u>language</u>, <u>society</u> (or social context), <u>learning</u>, and <u>teaching</u>.

> ". . . there are four concepts which are treated as fundamental, and not simply one. Time and time again language teaching has fallen into the trap of making a single belief, concept, or principle paramount, with a resulting loss of perspective." (1992, p. 23)

I would like to look at each one of these concepts in turn. One caveat is that the boundaries between them are very often blurred because they are all dealing with how people learn languages and you are likely to find that some of your beliefs lie in more than one category.

3.2 *Look over the following framework (Figure 3.1a) and note what you think each category means. Then make a list of possible examples to illustrate each category.*

Figure 3.1a: A Framework for Articulating Your Beliefs

1. Your view of language
2. Your view of the social context of language
3. Your view of learning and learners
4. Your view of teaching

Beliefs About Language

Your view of what **language** is or what **being proficient in a language** means affects what you teach and how you teach it. Language has been defined in many ways, for example as pronunciation, grammar, lexis, discourse (Bailey 1998), or as form, meaning and use (Larsen-Freeman 1990). Models of communicative competence which include grammatical, sociolinguistic, discourse and strategic competences have outlined what it means to be proficient in a language (Canale and Swain 1980; Omaggio Hadley 1993.)

Your beliefs about which view of language should be emphasized will translate into beliefs about how the language should be learned. An emphasis on language as rule-governed may translate into the belief that learning a language means learning to use it accurately, with no grammatical errors. To return to the example of a class of adult learners, a good lesson might have students analyze the grammatical errors in letters *they* had written to the editor and then correct the errors. An emphasis on language as meaning-based may be manifest in the belief that language in the classroom should be relevant and meaningful to the students in the class. A good lesson might have the students write a letter about issues that affect them. An emphasis on language as socially constructed among people in discourse communities may be manifest in the belief that learning a language requires an awareness of how language is used within a given community such as the classroom or neighborhood. A good lesson might have students compare two sample letters to the editor and determine which social factors accounted for the difference. It is possible to imagine the three lesson scenarios above taking place with the same group of learners, and, in fact, you may hold all three beliefs.

Beliefs About the Social Context of Language

In Stern's view, **society,** which he also refers to as **"social context,"** encompasses sociolinguistic, sociocultural, and sociopolitical issues in language teaching. **Sociolinguistic issues** bridge language and social context in that they are concerned with how language is adapted to fit (or not) the social context. A nonnative English speaking graduate student once began a letter to one of her professors to request a recommendation with *"I need a letter of recommendation for ___. Please write me a recommendation and send it to . . ."* Grammatically and lexically, the request was accurate; however it was not appropriate for the purpose or for her relation to the receiver of the request. An emphasis on the sociolinguistic aspect—that language cannot be separated from the context in which it is used—may translate into the belief that learning a language means learning how to adjust it to contextual factors such as roles and purpose. A good lesson might have students examine different ways to begin and end letters depending on the purpose for the letter and the person to whom it was being sent.

Sociocultural issues are concerned with the interaction between language and culture. They include different dimensions of culture such as social values (e.g., gender differences) attitudes (e.g., toward roles of men and women) norms (e.g., ways of greeting, eating), customs (e.g., marriage customs), and "products" (e.g., literature, art). A belief related to sociocultural issues would be that language learning involves understanding both one's own culture and that of the target language because attitudes one holds may be different or even in conflict with those held by some users of the target language. A good lesson might have students discuss the cultural values implicit in sending letters to the editor, and their own comfort level with doing so.

Sociopolitical issues are concerned with how a given language or social group (ethnic, gender, etc.) is viewed by other social groups, access to language and services, and a critical awareness of how language is used. The beliefs that learners need to know how to participate in the community and that language teaching involves helping learners gain access to social systems are both related to sociopolitical issues. A good lesson that stems from these beliefs might have students write a letter to the editor about an issue that affects them, in which they outline action that can be taken to address the issue. The belief that language learning involves analyzing the way in which language is used to gain, hold, and deny power could be manifest in a lesson in which students analyze the point of view of a newspaper story about a topic that affects them and decide how to respond.

Beliefs About Learning and Learners

I think the fundamental issue around learning is your view of how people learn and the roles that enable them to learn. In my experience, teachers can hold seemingly contradictory beliefs about the process, the roles, and the focus of learning and accommodate them in the classroom to some extent. In the Chinese class I described at the beginning of the chapter, my belief in students' taking responsibility for the direction of their learning conflicted with the practice of repetition drills, in which the students follow the teacher's lead.

Regarding the **process**, learning can be perceived as a process of problem solving and discovery by the learner—an inductive process. The learner is viewed as a maker of knowledge. In contrast, learning can be perceived as the process of applying received knowledge—a deductive process. The learner is viewed as an internalizer of knowledge. Learning can be viewed as a cognitive process, involving mental activity, an affective process, involving emotional connection and risk taking, and a social process, involving learning with others (Stevick 1998). Learning can be viewed as involving different intelligences such as visual, kinesthetic, auditory, and so on. (Gardner 1983). Regarding the **roles** of learners, learning may depend on individual effort in which the learner works alone. It may also depend on a group effort in which learners learn with and from each other. Learners may be the source of expertise or the recipients of it. They may be partners and decision-makers in the process or subordinates. Regarding the **focus** of learning, it may be acquiring new knowledge, mastering skills, developing awareness, or learning about attitudes. It may focus on how the language works or on using the language. It may focus on the development of metacognitive and critical thinking skills.

Some questions about learning and learners might be: Do learners learn better when they can discover their own answers or when they are given the correct answers? When they feel secure or when they are challenged? Individually or through interaction with others? Is the learner an expert? Is the learner a partner in the learning process? If you hold the belief that learners learn best when they feel secure, then a good lesson might have students first discuss the content of their letters to the editor in small groups prior to discussing them in the large group.

Beliefs About Teaching

Beliefs about teaching and the role of the teacher are connected to beliefs about learning, although this is an area in which what a teacher does is sometimes in contradiction to what he believes, or professes to believe. The process of teaching can be viewed on a continuum in which at one end the teacher transmits knowledge to the students, and at the other end the teacher and students negotiate the knowledge and skills and methods of learning. On the one end the teacher makes decisions about knowledge and skills to be learned, tells the students what to learn, or provides models or examples and expects or helps students to internalize them. As we move up the continuum, the process is viewed as providing problem-solving activities and actively helping students to negotiate them; learning may be viewed as a process of shared decision making with the students. Still further along the continuum, students determine the problems to be solved and use the teacher as a language and culture resource.

Some questions about teaching and the role of the teacher might be: Is the teacher the expert? Is the role of the teacher to provide answers or is it to provide structures for finding answers? Does the teacher make all the decisions or does she negotiate decisions with the learners? Is the teacher a collaborator in students' learning? Is the teacher a learner? If you hold the belief that the teacher should negotiate decisions with the learners because learning involves responsibility, then a good lesson might have the learners decide how to respond to an issue they had identified.

3.3 *In Investigation 3.2 you used the framework in Figure 3.1a to organize and write down your own ideas. Compare your ideas with those in the framework in Figure 3.1b below. Discuss the differences and similarities with a partner. Which areas overlap? What would you add to the framework below? To your own framework?*

Figure 3.1b: A Framework for Articulating Your Beliefs

1. Your view of language

   For example, language is rule governed, meaning-based, a means of self-expression, a means of learning about oneself and the world, a means of getting things done.

2. Your view of the social context of language

   For example, the social context of language includes sociolinguistic issues such as adapting language to fit the context, sociocultural issues such as cultural values and customs which may be in harmony or in conflict with those of the learners' own culture, and sociopolitical issues such as access to work and education.

3. Your view of learning and learners

   For example, learning is a deductive or inductive process; learning occurs in community or individually; learning is the acquisition of knowledge and skills; learning is the development of metacognitive and critical thinking skills.

   Learners have affective, cognitive and social needs; learners receive knowledge or construct knowledge; learners follow directions or direct their own learning.

4. Your view of teaching

   For example, teaching is knowledge transmission, management of learning, providing of learning structures, a collaborative process.

   The teacher is a decision maker, knowledge transmitter, provider of learning structures, collaborator, resource.

3.4 *In Investigation 3.1, you made a list of what made a particular lesson great. Look through your list and categorize your responses according to whether they involve a view of language, of the social context of language, of learners and learning, or of teaching. Is one category more prominent than another?*

An Example of a Teacher's Beliefs

Denise Lawson is a teacher who designed an advanced writing course for a university extension program in the United States. Three factors influenced her beliefs: her experience as a learner, her experience as a teacher and how the students responded to her and each other, and understandings from readings. Certain authors and readings as well as a presentation on the significance of sociocultural issues in writing in a second language were particularly influential in helping her understand what she felt was important. The following are her teaching beliefs and what each of them mean for her teaching and for the course:

Denise Lawson

Learner-centered curriculum

Development of a community of learners who support each other's learning process; emphasis on cooperation in place of competition; student participation in course content, process, and assessment; use of feedback as a means of course evaluation

Meaning-centered curriculum

Development of course content relevant to students' needs and interests; incorporation of sociocultural issues of second language learning

Process-centered curriculum

The five steps in the process: brainstorm, draft, revise, edit, publish.

Use of five step process writing model; use of self-assessment as well as assessment by peers and teacher; final assessment based on progress, participation, and performance

Clear articulation of roles of teacher and students

- Students as managers of their own learning (via learner strategy training), and as resources for their peers
- Teacher as curriculum designer and articulator of goals and objectives, enthusiast, resource, coordinator of class activities, participant in assessment process, and co-learner

3.5 *Which of the four categories, language, social context, learning, teaching are addressed in Denise Lawson's beliefs? How? If you were designing a writing course, would you change the list or add to it? What does this tell you about your beliefs?*

3.6 *Brainstorm an initial list of your beliefs that you feel are relevant to the course you are designing. You can write them as they occur to you or you can list them according to the categories in Figure 3.1 or you can use the triangle in Figure 3.2. At this point you do not need to worry about having too many or too few. The point of the investigation is to begin to articulate relevant beliefs. They will be refined later.*

Figure 3.2: David Hawkins' Elements of Teaching

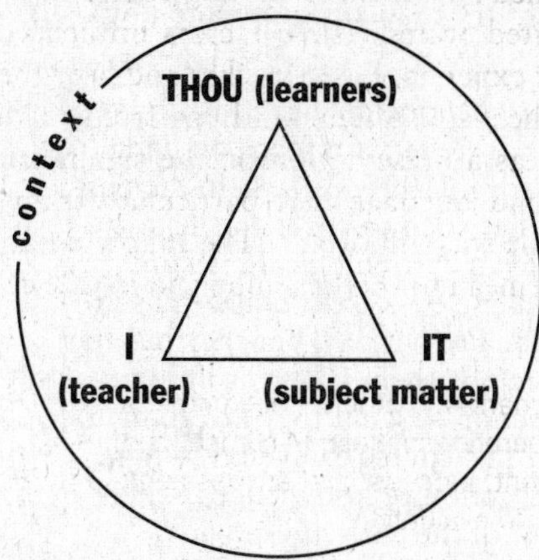

Figure 3.2 is drawn from the work of educator David Hawkins (1967). The triangle is a visual way of representing the same elements of teaching Stern proposes. *I* refers to the teacher. *Thou* refers to the learners. *It* refers to the subject matter. My colleague, Carol Rodgers, has added the circle of *context* which represents the environment in which the teaching takes place. You can note your beliefs about the teacher and teaching, learners and learning, subject matter, and context, as well as their relationships, on the visual itself, or you can use it as a trigger.

How Do Beliefs Affect the Actual Designing of a Course?

Your beliefs play a role at each stage of course design. They may not always be present in your thinking, but they underlie the decisions you make. David Markus designed a history of American literature course for high school students studying English in the United States. He writes about the way his beliefs influenced the course.

We first hear David Markus's voice in Chapter 2.

David Markus

> As I approached the course development process I had certain beliefs that helped me decide what was important to focus on. These personal values were not always in the forefront of my thinking, but at certain places in the project, I would return to them to assess how my course design incorporated these principles. If I found that I had strayed, I would revise the plan so it coincided with those principles.

David returns to his beliefs at a later point in the process, as a way to help him organize the content of the course.

> After deciding on goals and objectives for the course, I was ready to decide on a syllabus and some principles for course organization. It was at this point that I reminded myself that my original goal was to create a course that was based on certain educational beliefs I held. In the first few stages of curricular development, I had paid very little conscious attention to these principles since my first

instinct was to get a firm grip on *what* I was going to teach and then move to the *how*. Over the years, I have come to believe in a few principles of education that I try to incorporate into any class I teach.

The first precept comes from *Smart Schools* by David Perkins. He talks about the need to trade coverage for a focus on understanding and active use of knowledge. (1995, p. 164) In the past, St. Andrew's English department has tried to cover the history of American literature in 4 months in chronological fashion. The students feel that they are moving on a train that begins in the Colonial Period and ends in the Present day, but they only get a glimpse of the landscape whizzing by them. There is little time to apply lessons learned in one section to what they are going to encounter in a future section. For this course to live up to my standard of depth and active application of knowledge, I knew I would have to cut something out of the curriculum.

A change from a chronological syllabus to a thematic syllabus seemed to be the solution. This would make the connections from different time frames more explicit, but also give the students the opportunity to make some of the connections themselves. When I inquired whether I would be able to teach the course in this fashion, the English department chair gave lukewarm support for the idea. She agreed that the old syllabus skimmed over the content, but also expressed concern that the students would not be able to put the literature in historic context. I assured her that the class would consistently keep the historic context in mind through a timeline that they would be responsible for updating throughout the term as we read new authors.

A second key educational precept that I wanted to include in the design was the idea of student choice. The complaint in the past was that students did not seem interested in the books that were taught. I believed if students had a choice of materials (with some structure provided by the teacher) they would choose good literature that would be interesting for them. Just the investment that is inherent in choice would suggest this, but I believed that they would also choose themes that have personal significance for them. This principle of student choice can even be applied to organization of the course and classroom rituals.

From this belief in choice, I decided that the students would not only get to choose some of the readings in a theme, they would get to choose two of the three themes. This would help individualize instruction and to a certain extent allow us to deal with the coverage issue through the back door of literature response groups, where students discuss different readings. (This also prevents students who may have had different exposure to American literature from being made to read a book or story for a second time.)

> Hand in hand with the belief in student choice is a belief that the teacher needs to provide support and structure within which students work and learn. This idea derives from Stevick's concept of the balance between control and initiative (Stevick 1998, p. 31–35.) All students can feel safer in an environment where they know the rules and know what to expect. Having an organization keyed to the weekly or daily schedule provides them with advanced organizers that help LEP (limited English proficiency) students focus mainly on the language. The use of daily and weekly rituals also saves time in transitions. This is important since Saphier and Gower (1987) estimate that up to 25% of class time can be wasted each day in transitions. Based on these assumptions I decided to have certain constant ritual-like activities as a part of this course.

David Markus has articulated beliefs about the teacher's role, about student choice, and about learning, which he views as the understanding and active use of knowledge. Each of these beliefs has helped him make key decisions about the content and organization of his course. Earlier in this chapter, Denise Lawson articulated four main beliefs that guided her planning of an advanced composition course: her belief in a learner-centered curriculum, a meaning-centered curriculum, a process-centered curriculum and her belief that the roles of teachers and learners should be clearly articulated. She then explained what each belief meant. Both of these teachers have articulated rich and powerful beliefs that had important implications for how each designed his or her course. They both "boiled" their beliefs down to a few essential ones that they felt were key to their particular courses. They may have had other beliefs, but chose to focus on only a few that they considered essential. These became their core beliefs or principles.

See page 32.

Articulating a belief requires clarity about the experience from which it is drawn, and about the knowledge base that provides the language in which to express it. It is not always easy to identify these beliefs. Iris Broudy, a teacher whose voice we first heard in Chapter 1, expresses the challenge of identifying her beliefs this way: "I find myself struggling to sort out what I really believe about my course from what seems like a good idea (based on theory, examples from books, etc.)." There are a lot of good ideas to draw from, and it is important to be clear about their relevance to those core beliefs that will guide you in your particular context.

An image that captures what is meant by a core belief or principle is one provided by a former president of my university in a welcoming speech to our students. He talked about burning wood in a campfire and how the last and brightest to burn were the nodes in which the sap had gathered, sap from all parts of the tree. Identifying the core principles for a given course is akin to finding the nodes with the sap in them. A core belief or principle will carry within it elements of other beliefs you hold. Don't overwhelm yourself with too many beliefs, but look to the ones that you feel essential. Your essential beliefs are the nodes where the sap has gathered.

3.7 *Look over your initial list of beliefs. Choose the four that are the most important—the ones you feel you could not sacrifice, no matter what the constraints of your context. Now, look over the description of your context (Chapter 2). Do you see ways in which your beliefs can support the context? Do you see any potential conflicts? Problematize your situation—identify some of the potential challenges that designing your course will pose. Do you see some ways to meet the challenges?*

See page 12.

Throughout this book, you will see references to teachers' beliefs and principles and how they influenced the choices they made. Your own beliefs will play a role in the way you react to the reflections and decisions the teachers made. As mentioned in Chapter 1, your reactions will provide clues to your beliefs. If you feel strongly that something is missing, you are uncovering or articulating a belief. Conversely, the same is true if you really like something a teacher has done. I made an analogy between course context and architecture in Chapter 2. Two architects given the exact same specifications will design different houses. Each house will exhibit certain fundamental similarities based on fundamentals of architecture such as providing shelter, having a roof and a floor, letting in light, providing places to eat, sleep, and so on. If they both went to the same design school and had the same professors, it is likely there will be similarities in their designs. However, they will both be different in ways that range from small to striking. Similarly, two teachers asked to design the same course for the same students will design different courses because of differences in their experience, education, and beliefs. The courses will need to account for how language is dealt with, how the four skills of reading, writing, speaking, and listening are integrated or isolated, the roles learners are asked to take, how learning is assessed, and so on. However, they will both be different in ways that range from small to striking. How much a house bears the architect's individual imprint depends on how much freedom he or she had in designing the house. The best houses, however, marry the architect's imprint with the needs of those who will eventually live in the house. So, too, your course design should marry your beliefs with the needs of the students within the context of the course.

Suggested Readings

Earl Stevick's ideas in *Teaching Languages: A Way and Ways* (1980) and later in *Working with Teaching Methods: What's at Stake* (1998, in this series) have been particularly helpful to me in articulating my own beliefs. H. H. Stern's book, *Fundamental Concepts of Language Teaching* (1983), while dense, gives a comprehensive explanation, including a historical perspective, of the four areas of social context, language, learning, and teaching. Karen Johnson's book in this series, *Understanding Language Teaching: Reasoning in Action* (1999), describes the research on how teachers think about their teaching, and how beliefs function as one construct in that research.

4

CONCEPTUALIZING CONTENT

John Kongsvik

It was very difficult to conceptualize the content of my course. There were so many variables to take into account. I found myself lost several times during the process. At one point, I stepped back and focused on my educational precepts and then the goals and objectives of the course. This helped focus my attention on what was important but did not make the task any easier. I would so much like to design a course that is flexible enough to meet the needs and interests of my students and solid enough to be grounded in what I believe to be worthy principles. When I set out to give form to the situations and conversations, I found myself unable to envision what the entire course would look like. How can I guess what my students will want to cover? By the same token, how can I prepare myself to meet their needs on an ongoing basis? What skills can I develop to meet these dynamic groups? How do I conceptualize the whole?

John Kongsvik wrote the opening thoughts above after his first attempt to complete the process of conceptualizing the content of the communicative language course he was designing for beginners at a university in Mexico. He makes three important points. First, conceptualizing content involves making choices. The territory of language learning is vast and there are various ways to cover the territory. For a given course a teacher has to choose from among them. In this chapter we will look at ways the territory of language learning has been defined, which provide a basis for making choices about what to teach in a course. Second, it is a recursive process like writing. It usually takes several drafts to produce a finished piece of writing. Similarly, the way you conceptualize content will go through more than one iteration before you are satisfied with it. Unlike writing, however, the "drafting" process may continue, even as you are teaching the course. In this chapter we will hear the voices of teachers describing the drafting process and look at different ways they conceptualize the content of their courses. Third, any syllabus prepared prior to meeting the students will be transformed in its implementation, and thus it is worthwhile building room for students' responses into the syllabus itself.

WHAT DOES IT MEAN TO CONCEPTUALIZE CONTENT?

The process of conceptualizing content is a multifaceted one which involves:

- thinking about what you want your students to learn in the course, given who they are, their needs, and the purpose of the course;

- making decisions about what to include and emphasize and what to drop;
- organizing the content in a way that will help you to see the relationship among various elements so that you can make decisions about objectives, materials, sequence and evaluation.

The product of conceptualizing content is a kind of syllabus in that it delineates what you will teach. The form it takes—mind map, grid, list, flow-chart, how detailed it is, whether it is one that someone else can interpret and use—is up to you. If you are given a syllabus, either as specifications of what is to be taught or in the form of a textbook, it is still important to go through the process of conceptualizing content so that on the one hand you can understand how the syllabus is constructed, and on the other hand can become aware of your own priorities with respect to your students. Such a process can give you tools to manage and adapt the syllabus as a resource rather than be governed by it.

Chapter 9 looks at ways to adapt a textbook.

Conceptualizing content involves answering the questions listed in Figure 4.1:

Figure 4.1: Questions that Guide Conceptualizing Content

1. What do I want my students to learn in this course, given who they are, their needs, and the purpose of the course?
2. What are my options as to what they can learn?
3. What are the resources and constraints of my course that can help me narrow my options?
4. What are the relationships among the options I have selected?
5. How can I organize these options into a working plan or syllabus?
6. What is the driving force or organizing principle that will pull my syllabus together? (There may be more than one organizing principle, as we shall see in Chapter 7.)

One of the reasons that it is important to answer the questions in Figure 4.1 is that teachers have an array of options to consider in conceptualizing the content of the course they will teach. This was not always the case. When I first started teaching English in Taiwan in 1973, I was issued a textbook for my class and wished "good luck." I didn't think about content. I thought about getting through the lesson. The textbook provided the content, which in those days was fairly limited: grammar, vocabulary, and pronunciation (through repetition). The syllabus of the textbook was structural, with pattern drills accompanied by tiny pictures. A subsequent class I taught used a textbook which prepared Chinese students for study in a university setting in the United States. Each lesson consisted of a lengthy dialogue, which was followed by a breakdown of each line of the text with a translation into Chinese and notes about the vocabulary and about American culture. My role was to help with pronunciation and to answer questions about the vocabulary and culture. The real language learning in that class probably occurred in interaction with me about what was in the book, and not with the book itself. Ideas that are common today such as communicative competence, a notional-functional approach, and learning strategies, were not on my horizon. I was not aware that I had choices about what to teach, other than which textbook to use. If someone had asked me what content I was teaching, I probably would have said grammar and vocabulary.

Perhaps a useful analogy to conceptualizing content is that of making a map of a part of the planet earth. One map highlights the geological surface features of the territory such as mountains, valleys, and rivers. Another map highlights the natural resources such as minerals, lumber, natural gas. A third map shows the network of roads and towns. A fourth map shows population density. Some maps show a combination of these. They are all charting the same area of the planet, but in different ways and for different purposes. In a sense, they each have a different organizing principle—geological features, natural resources and so on.

Similarly, when designing a language course, there are a number of features which you can choose to highlight or to include in your map. What you choose depends on the constraints and resources of your context, who your students are, their needs, why they are taking the course, and whether and how the course has been described to students or the public, as well as your own experience and preferences. Choice is a key, because you cannot explicitly focus on or do everything. A map which tried to show all the features of the four maps listed above would be a mishmash that would be hard to make sense of.

Conceptualizing content, then, is a matter of articulating what you will explicitly teach or explicitly focus on in the course and knowing why you have made those choices. It also involves choosing the organizing principle or principles that will help to tie the content together. In my first teaching experience in Taiwan, the choices had been made for me. Grammar and vocabulary were the organizing principles for the courses I taught.

I have chosen the term "conceptualizing content" rather than the more traditional "syllabus design" for this process because I see it as a conceptual process that is really about figuring out how to chart the territory in a way that makes sense to each teacher individually. At the same time, the way a teacher charts the territory is influenced by current thinking, by his beliefs, by the way in which he was educated, and by the institution and community he works in. Thus it is an individual process influenced by the educational and work environment. For some teachers, for example, language learning may encompass more than language skills, it may also include skills related to affective areas, participation in the community, and learning strategies. As long as a teacher purposefully teaches that element as part of his or her syllabus, it is part of the content of the course. Syllabus design, in the sense of how you choose and organize specific content, is the subject of Chapter 7, "Organizing the content."

As outlined in Figure 4.1, the process of conceptualizing content involves answering a number of questions, the first of which is *What do I want my students to learn in this course, given who they are, their needs, and the purpose of the course?* I'd like to expand this question to include the third question, *What do I feel is most important for my students to learn, given the resources and constraints of my situation?* The expansion is, in effect, a way of limiting oneself. As much as we may want to teach many things, the resources and constraints of our situation will help us to narrow our choices to what is feasible. A further challenge is to figure out how to integrate what we do choose to teach into something coherent, so that we use our students' time well.

Here is how one teacher, Iris Broudy, navigated the process of conceptualizing the content for a class of adults at an intermediate level of proficiency offered to the community by the University of Orizaba in Mexico. Her students were mainly young professionals in their twenties.

Iris Broudy

> [When I started the process] it was a given that my syllabus should be communicative, but I wondered: how can I determine its shape, its content, its "personality"? To visualize what my course would contain, I had to at least consider what I wanted the students to get out of it. I already had a sense of what they wanted; I knew what the institution required; I knew I wanted it to be fun. That background gave some direction to my initial brainstorming. But once I "got it all out there," I faced a major hurdle: How could I organize all these elements into a coherent syllabus?

Iris then looked at a list of possible elements of a syllabus (See, for example, Figure 4.4, pages 52–53) to get ideas for her own syllabus. She did an initial "mind map" of her course content and found that it revolved around functions because she felt that "communication means doing things with the language in order to interact with others." However, when she consulted texts specializing in functions of English she felt that they focused on "stock phrases to be 'plugged in' to various contexts" and that was too limiting. She writes:

> Furthermore, functional language is so contextual that without a certain level of sociolinguistic and discourse competence, the student cannot always sense which language is right for a given situation.
>
> Clearly, if my classroom is to be an environment of real language use, I need to provide opportunities for my students to be exposed to authentic language and then produce it in a fashion that is both comfortable for them and acceptable to a native speaker. So I redid the mind map, this time putting topics at the center. When it came time to plan an actual unit, it was helpful to have a topic (dating/social relationships) around which to develop and sequence materials. It gave me a focus, and provided coherence for disparate curriculum elements. However, in laying out the syllabus—and later designing materials for one unit—I felt constrained by having the topics determined in advance.

She wonders if determining the topics in advance means that the learners, the ones who are learning to communicate, have been left out of the course.

> Uh-oh! Then were does that leave me? I have to throw away everything I've done and start over? *Whoa, Iris! Don't lose sight of the fact that right now the process is more important than the product.*
>
> That's true. What I am doing here is more than designing a course. I am translating my awareness of who I am as a teacher and my deepest beliefs about the learning process into something tangible and usable. So instead of jumping into a whole new syllabus at this

point, I need to ask myself: How can you use the syllabus and materials you have already developed in a more learner-centered way? In other words, how can you let go of the need to be in control, to let the students lead their own learning, even if the results are raggedy and imperfect?

Ideally, especially at the classroom level, the learners should be involved in "a process of consultation and negotiation." (Nunan, 1988) Okay, so that means working within a general framework but not having everything set in advance. It means trusting that I will be able to find and develop materials that fit the topics and communicative tasks that evolve from collaboration with the students. So maybe instead of planning around specific topics, I should think in broader modules or themes into which I can integrate various elements as needed. That would allow for more flexibility and allow the course to evolve more organically.

So that is where I am now. The visual representations should give a sense of where I've traveled through this process of conceptualizing content. There never really will be a "finished" syllabus, because without input from the students, a plan is just a skeleton, not a complex living—and changing—organism.

Figure 4.2: Iris Broudy's Final Mind Map

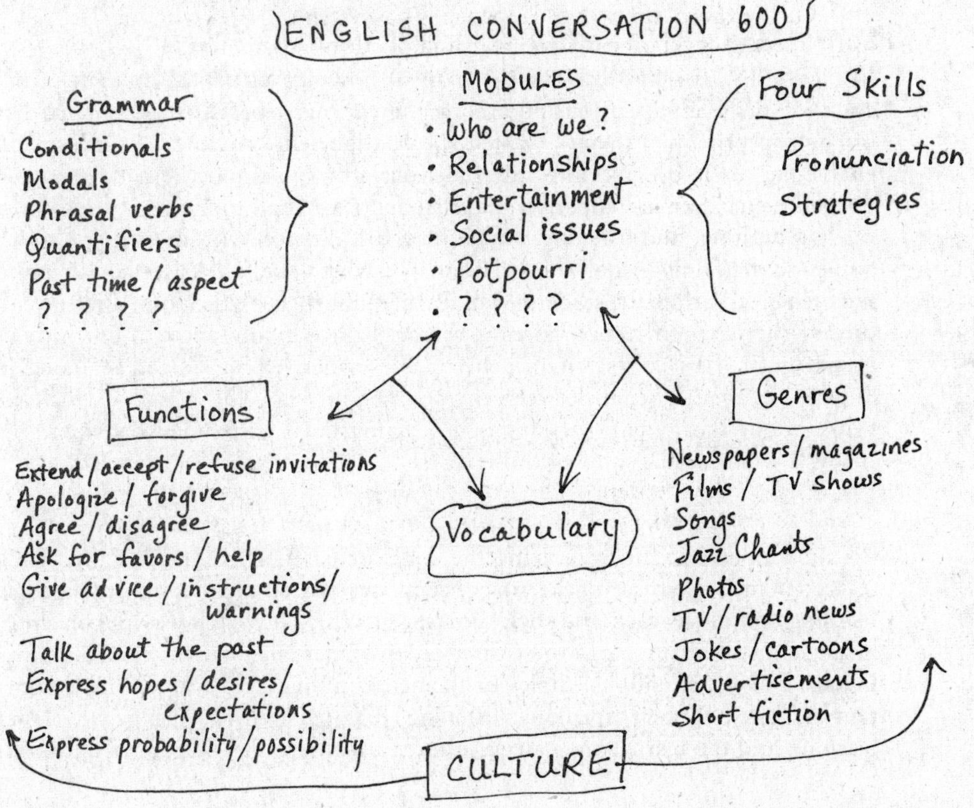

Iris has tried to capture the process she went through in conceptualizing the content of her course. The process she described was recursive—she made several drafts of her mind map syllabus based on different questions and considerations she grappled with as she planned. Major considerations were who the students were, what she believed they needed, and how she could involve them. She was acutely aware that she wanted the students to have some say in the syllabus itself. She was thus able to answer the questions John Kongsvik posed at the beginning of the chapter: How can I guess what my students will want to cover? By the same token, how can I prepare myself to meet their needs on an ongoing basis? What skills can I develop to meet these dynamic groups? How do I conceptualize the whole?

4.1 *Look at Iris Broudy's mind map in Figure 4.2. She has labeled different areas she wants to teach in her course. Those areas represent the way she conceptualized content. What are they? How do the areas interrelate? Does the mind map help you see a driving force or organizing principle for her course?*

4.2 *Think about your experience as a learner and teacher of languages. Brainstorm a list of how you would answer the question "What makes up the content of language learning?" Add to or modify the list as you read the next section.*

What Makes Up the Content of Language Learning?

In Figure 4.2, Iris has drawn up a map of how she views the content of her course and the interrelationship among the various aspects of its content. The organizing principle, themes (which she has labeled "modules" on the map), enable her to choose and integrate functions, grammar, and vocabulary related to each theme. She has chosen to have students learn all four skills of speaking, reading, writing, and listening, which they will develop with the aid of various authentic materials (listed under "Genres"), which she will select according to the theme. Additionally, students will learn about their own culture and the culture of the L2 with respect to each theme. Conceptually, there is much more going on in Iris's course than in my classes when I first started teaching in Taiwan. In the 25 years between my course and hers, the ways in which we think about the "what" of language learning have expanded considerably. Below, I will describe some of those ways.

See Chapter 8, "Developing Materials," for an example of how Iris fleshed out the theme of relationships (pages 169–170).

As a framework for organizing the ways or categories for conceptualizing content, I use three of Stern's concepts introduced in Chapter 2: **language, learning and the learner,** and **social context** (1992). Thus each way of conceptualizing content fits in one of these three areas. Under **language** the categories are: **linguistic skills, situations, topics or themes, communicative functions, competencies, tasks, content, speaking, listening, reading, writing,** and **genre.** Under **learning and the learner** the categories are: **affective goals, interpersonal skills,**

and **learning strategies.** Under **social context** the categories are: **sociolinguistic skills, sociocultural skills** and **sociopolitical skills.** These categories are represented in Figure 4.3 below. They are explained in the next section and summarized with examples in Figure 4.4.

Figure 4.3: Categories for Conceptualizing Content

Focus on Language

linguistic skills	situations	communicative functions
topics/themes	tasks	listening
competencies	speaking	writing
content	reading	genre

Focus on Learning and Learners

affective goals	interpersonal skills	learning strategies

Focus on Social Context

sociolinguistic skills	sociocultural skills	sociopolitical skills

Two points are important to keep in mind when reading and thinking about the next section. First, the boundaries of the categories are not fixed, but permeable. They overlap and connect with other categories. This is because all are an attempt to break down the complex phenomenon of language and what it is, how one learns and uses it, and for which purposes. This means that when deciding what to include in your syllabus, one component will, by its nature, include other components. For example, you cannot focus on *topics* without including *vocabulary* and probably some kind of *situation* or *communicative function*. You cannot focus on *speaking* without including *listening*. *Genre* will involve one or more of the *four skills* as well as *sociolinguistic* or *sociopolitical* skills. Some of the categories are, in effect, combinations of others. For example, *competencies* are a combination of *situations, functions,* and *linguistic skills.* Second, under the **language** section in the framework, the categories include both "what"—knowledge, and "how"—skills or activities. This means that when you think about the content of the course, you can think about both *what* students will learn and *how* they will learn it. For example, if your course is skills based, as in a writing course, the what and how are intertwined. You may conceptualize the content in terms of a "what"—types of writing they will learn, but learning how to produce those types of writing involves a how—the actual process of writing. If your course is task-based, the emphasis will be on "how," or students doing tasks together.

I have tried to use names for the different areas of content that are familiar to teachers either from textbooks or from the literature in our field. This was easiest in the focus on language, which is the area that has been most "explored" in our field and is also the section that has the most categories. Even in that area there are competing definitions for various terms, such as "tasks." For this reason, I have tried to give examples of what each category means. For the section

See list of suggested readings at the end in order to learn more about each area.

that focuses on learning and learners I drew on what I have seen in the syllabuses of teachers I work with as well as the work of Stern. In that section, "learning strategies" has received the most attention in our field. For the section that focuses on society and social context, I follow Stern's 1986 breakdown of sociolinguistic skills, sociocultural skills and sociopolitical skills.

Each category is followed by an example of how it might be implemented in a classroom. These examples are drawn from my most recent language learning experience, a course in American Sign Language (ASL), the language used by Deaf North Americans. As I have already pointed out, no language course can include all the categories explicitly. Therefore, when the ASL class did not address a given category, I explain how it might have addressed it.

Focus on Language

Linguistic Skills

Linguistic skills are those which focus on the systems that underlie the way language is structured: its **grammar, pronunciation,** and **lexicon.** This category is a familiar starting point in conceptualizing the content of a language course—especially if one is teaching beginners. This area of language includes:

- The sound system (phonology) of the language. In syllabuses this is usually listed as **pronunciation.** This includes knowing how to produce the individual sounds of the language, to pronounce the unique combinations of sounds that form words, word stress, and sentence stress, rhythm, and intonation.
- The **grammar** of the language. This includes learning how words are classified and what their function is, (e.g., pronouns, prepositions), how words are ordered to form phrases and sentences, the verb tense system, and so on.
- The **lexicon** or **vocabulary** of the language. This includes learning a variety of content words (nouns, verbs, adjectives, adverbs), knowing how words are formed (e.g., compounding, derivation), how they are inflected (e.g., made into plurals,), and the meaning of prefixes and suffixes (e.g., *unfathomable*).

The above areas are traditionally grouped together because they make up the sentence level of a language and are concerned with *relatively* predictable systems. A syllabus organized around these elements of language is called a **structural syllabus** or a **formal syllabus**. These elements of language are familiar to anyone who has been a beginning language learner because they are the learner's lifeline.

As I wrote the first draft of this chapter, I was learning American Sign Language (ASL). I was a complete beginner, although I had spent time professionally and personally with Deaf educators. However, I had always communicated with them through interpreters. ASL, therefore, was new to me as a learner. As a beginner, I needed words (signs), I needed to know how to form them correctly (in ASL this includes hand shape, placement, motion, and facial expression), and I needed to know the order in which they went together to get my meaning across. Putting all three of those elements together required a great deal of practice and was overwhelming at times.

As soon as one considers language beyond the sentence level, one becomes concerned with interaction and communication between two or more people on the one hand, and with text or discourse on the other. We will look at communication between people first. Interactions between people are relatively unpredictable because one cannot predict how someone will interpret, much less respond to, a spoken or written message. The emphasis on communication opens up other ways to view the content of language learning.

Situations

Situations are the contexts in which one uses language. They typically include places where one transacts business, such as the supermarket, or the travel agency, or places where one interacts with others such as at a party. A syllabus built around situations is called a **situational syllabus.** Situations overlap with communicative functions in that the situational syllabus includes the type of transaction or interaction that will occur in the situation. For example, one requests information at the travel agency or socializes at a party. They also overlap with topics when there is a topic associated with the situation, such as food at the supermarket.

The text for my ASL class was a video which revolved around the life of a family of four, the *Bravo ASL! Curriculum* (1996). Some of the episodes were situation-based. For example, one episode took place at the breakfast table and another at the supermarket. In the supermarket episode we followed the family as they divided up items on a shopping list and shopped for various kinds of food.

Topics/Themes

Topics are what the language is used to talk or write about. They may be personal, such as family, food, hobbies; they may be professional and relate to employment practices or topics specific to the profession of the students; they may be sociocultural and relate to education, political systems, or cultural customs. Topics and themes are often used interchangeably. For me, the difference is that themes are broader relative to topics, although topics can be very broad. Another difference is that a theme may tie a group of topics together. A syllabus built around topics is called a **topical** syllabus. A syllabus built around themes is called a **thematic** syllabus. Topics and themes provide a good backbone or organizing principle for a syllabus because it is easy to weave elements from other areas around the topics or themes.

There was a topical component to my ASL course. In the first episode of the video that provided the course text, we learned about families and vocabulary associated with families. In another episode, we learned the vocabulary for food in the context of a trip to the supermarket. In another episode the topic was the house and we learned vocabulary associated with furniture and rooms in the house.

Communicative Functions

The purposes for which one uses language are called language **functions;** (Wilkins 1976.) They include functions such as persuading, expressing preference, and apologizing. In my experience, functions have been expanded to mean any kind of transaction or interaction such as "buying something," "asking for directions," "making small talk," and so on. Functions were initially paired with **notions,** in constructing a syllabus (Van Ek 1986). Notions include concepts such as quantity, distance, smell, and texture. In terms of syllabus types, the **functional syllabus** can be the organizing principle for a course; however, because functions need to be contextualized, they are often paired with situations. Additionally, some functions, such as apologizing, are not as amenable to a rich lesson as others such as expressing preferences. As Iris Broudy pointed out earlier in her narrative about developing a course, functional syllabuses often end up revolving around decontextualized inventories which are not particularly meaningful for the students. Notions tend to be abstract in conceptualization, so teachers often find it easier to make notions concrete in the form of topics. For example, the notion of quantity is learned within the topic of shopping, the notion of distance in the topic of transportation.

See page 40.

Functions were a component of the syllabus in my ASL class. For example, in the video episode "At the breakfast table" we learned functions related to meal etiquette, such as requesting (that someone pass food), and asking about and expressing preference (for orange juice over grapefruit juice).

Competencies

Competencies unite situations, linguistic skills, and functions. A competency attempts to specify and teach the language and behavior needed to perform in a given situation, for example, how to perform in a job interview, how to open a bank account. Competencies are an attractive way to conceptualize content because the elements can be specified and their achievement can be measured. They are problematic, because, as I pointed out above, in most human interactions we cannot predict the path the interaction will take or the language used to get there and so, for a given competency, the language and behavior the student learns and is tested on may not be what she or he encounters or needs once outside of the classroom. **Competency-based syllabuses** are particularly popular in contexts where the sponsor or funder wants to see measurable results.

My ASL class was not competency-based. A competency-based syllabus trains the students to perform in target language situations in the dominant culture.

Tasks

Tasks have been defined in a number of ways. A simple definition is "interactions whose purpose is to get something done." Tasks entered the field of ESL and EFL teaching as a reaction to teaching that focused on predetermined content from the categories listed above—grammar, vocabulary, functions, and so on. Tasks were seen as a way to promote classroom learning that focused on the *processes* of using language rather than language *products,* and on meaning as opposed to form (Nunan 1988). The assumption is that one develops language competence *through* action and interaction, not *as a result of* the interaction

See Markee (1997), pages 93–94, for a review of definitions.

(Breen 1989). How a task is accomplished involves negotiation on the part of the students. Additionally, the selection of the tasks themselves can be negotiated between teacher and students. Depending on one's students, tasks can be for work purposes, such as designing a brochure, for academic purposes, such as researching and writing an article, and for daily life, such as planning a trip. They can be an end in themselves as well as a means through which students perform functions, practice skills, and discuss topics. Some tasks approximate those performed in the real world, some are performed in the real world, and some are specific to the classroom. Information gap activities, in which student/group A has information needed by student/group B and vice versa, are a kind of task specific to the classroom.

One challenge with this area of conceptualizing what one will teach is that it encompasses such a broad range of activities, and that many tasks involve a series of smaller tasks. A syllabus which is built around tasks is called a **task-based syllabus.** A task-based syllabus is in the family of **process syllabuses.** A process syllabus in its "strong" form is one in which there is no predetermined content or outcomes for the course. The content is negotiated between teacher and students depending on the way students perceive their needs (Breen 1989.) I have not included a process syllabus as a category of conceptualizing content because I feel that such an approach depends on a teacher being able to mobilize what he or she understands about the other categories of content in the service of the choices negotiated with the students. In terms of conceptualizing content, task-based syllabuses and participatory syllabuses (described below) are types of process syllabuses.

In my ASL class, we did not reach the point of accomplishing specific tasks. Rather our interactions with each other focused on rehearsing the scripts of the video episodes we watched. An example of a task would be to plan a meal and decide together what we would buy at the supermarket, thus giving us the opportunity to use all the signs we had at our disposal in a purposeful way.

Content

Content is subject matter other than language itself. Courses in which students learn another subject (content) such as history or math or computer science through the L2 are organized around a **content-based** syllabus. The priority placed on the content relative to the L2 may vary. There are different models, depending on this relationship which range from greatest emphasis on the language to greatest emphasis on the content. (See Brinton, Snow and Wesche 1989 or Snow, Met and Genesee 1989.)

We did not learn particular content in my ASL class. To be content-based, the video we watched would have taught us math or history, for example, using ASL as the medium of instruction.

Four skills: Speaking, Listening, Reading, Writing

The four skills are the channels or modes for using and understanding the language. They are sometimes called the macro skills of language. Conceptualizing language as discourse—stretches of sentences connected for a purpose either in speaking or writing—means moving beyond language at the sentence level, and beyond inventories of functions and learned dialogues. Learning the four skills involves understanding how different text types serve different purposes, and how texts are organized, so that one can understand them—through listening or reading—and produce them—through speaking or writing. It involves learning the subskills that enable one to be proficient in each skill.

> Speaking subskills include knowing how to negotiate turn-taking and producing fluent stretches of discourse.
>
> Listening subskills include listening for gist, for tone, for invitations to take a turn.
>
> Reading subskills include predicting content, understanding the main idea, interpreting the text.
>
> Writing subskills include using appropriate rhetorical structure, adjusting writing for a given audience, editing one's writing.

When one (or more) of the four skills is the organizing principle for a syllabus it means that the emphasis is on learning the skill itself, as distinct from using the skill for another purpose, for example, to reinforce grammar or to practice functions. A syllabus organized around one or more of the four skills is called a **skills-based syllabus.**

In ASL the channel is visual rather than auditory. Literacy in ASL is called "signacy" (Nover 1997). We focused more on the linguistic level of getting our meaning across. If the teacher had used a skills-based syllabus, we would have focused on producing longer stretches of sentences in a coherent fashion, learning how to get and maintain turns, watching fluent signers communicate and trying to determine the gist of their messages, for example.

Genre

Language at the discourse level can also be viewed in terms of **genre,** communicative events or "whole" texts which accomplish certain purposes within a social context. Texts can range from an academic paper or presentation, to a supermarket flyer or phone message, to individual traffic signs. This approach to syllabus design draws on the systemic functional model of language (Halliday 1994) which sees language as a resource for making meaning and texts as the vehicle language users construct to make meaning. Those texts, in turn, are shaped by the social context in which they are used and by the interpersonal relationships among participants.

A course organized around genre or text would involve learners in understanding and analyzing texts on a number of levels including the lexico-grammatical level, the discourse level, and the sociocultural level; it would also involve them in producing texts (Feez 1998).

It is interesting to think about genre in ASL because most genre work has been with written texts. ASL is a visual/spatial language and does not yet have a written form. I have participated in one genre in ASL, the academic lecture. I attended lectures by Steve Nover, whose research is about the way language policies have affected the Deaf and their acquisition of language. I understood the lectures through voice interpretation. The lectures were similar to academic lectures in English, but different in subtle ways. Nover's lectures were built around a series of overheads that were highly visual in that they included lots of diagrams and images, although they also contained a great deal of print. The overheads were all horizontal, rather than vertical. Nover would leave time to read each visual prior to resuming the lecture, since understanding his lecture required watching him sign. His lecture wove together statistics and data with stories about the people responsible for the policies and with personal anecdotes. I subsequently had the opportunity to do an academic presentation for the same audience (through interpreters) and found it quite challenging to move into a visual/spatial mode.

*To summarize, the ways of conceptualizing content related to **language** include:*

Linguistic skills	Situations
Topics/themes	Communicative functions
Competencies	Tasks
Content	Speaking
Listening	Reading
Writing	Genre

Focus on Learning and the Learner

Affective Goals

Affective goals are concerned with the learners' attitudes toward themselves, learning, and the target language and culture. Affective goals include developing a positive and confident attitude toward oneself as a learner, learning to take risks and to learn from one's mistakes, and developing a positive attitude toward the target language and culture. It may also involve understanding one's attitude toward one's own language and culture.

In the first ASL class I was apprehensive about using sign language. When I tried to, I felt clumsy and inept. In our second ASL class, our instructor asked us to "turn off your voice." This put us into a kind of immersion and forced us to rely on different strategies to make sure we understood and got our meaning across. It made us less self-conscious about using sign language as a means of communication. While the instructor may not have had explicit affective goals, she was clearly aware of our affective needs.

Interpersonal Skills

Interpersonal skills involve how one interacts with others to promote learning. These are skills learners develop and use to interact with each other and with the teacher in the classroom. These skills are the basis for effective group work and cooperative learning. They include understanding and assuming different roles in a group and becoming an effective listener. One way this skill has been translated into a teaching goal is "Building a learning community." Another way is "Learning how to learn with others."

In my ASL class, the teacher did not emphasize interpersonal skills explicitly, although she helped us to learn each other's names (in sign) and asked us to work with each other in pairs and small groups. At times I was uncertain about how much initiative to take for fear of dominating the class. Because of my teaching background, I was acutely aware of the interpersonal dimension of the class.

Learning Strategies

For taxonomies of learning strategies, see Oxford (1990) and O'Malley and Chamot (1990).

Learning strategies focus explicitly on how one learns. They are the cognitive and metacognitive strategies we use to learn effectively and efficiently, such as monitoring our speech (self monitoring) or developing strategies for remembering new vocabulary. The aim behind developing learning strategies is two-fold. The first is to help students become aware of how they learn so that they can expand their repertoire of learning strategies and become effective learners in the classroom. The second is to help students develop ways to continue learning beyond the classroom. Thus, if a student learns to self-monitor or to use memory strategies in the classroom, the strategies can presumably be used outside of the classroom when using the target language. If, as part of your course, you design activities to teach students to be aware of and develop specific learning strategies, then strategies are one of the ways you conceptualize the content of your course.

In my ASL class, we did not address learning strategies explicitly. To focus on learning strategies, the teacher could have asked us to share the ways we tried to remember new signs, or the techniques we had developed to practice outside of class. This would have helped us become aware of our own and others' strategies. She could also have taught us strategies for practicing and remembering signs, sentence structure, and so on.

Focus on Social Context

The three areas of social context below, sociolinguistic, sociocultural, and sociopolitical, have a great potential for overlap, and it is often difficult to distinguish one from the other. For example, the sociocultural expectations of men and women in a given culture may be reflected in sociolinguistic features such as how men address women and vice versa, or language used exclusively to describe one or the other. They may have sociopolitical implications depending on how the teacher and students view gender roles. Using the letter to the editor example from Chapter 3, learning about sociolinguistic features of a letter, such as appropriate salutation and closing, may overlap with a discussion about the cultural values implicit in such letters as well as the political implications of writing such a letter.

See pages 27–30.

Sociolinguistic Skills

Sociolinguistic skills involve choosing and using the appropriate language and extralinguistic behavior for the setting, the purpose, the role and relationship. These skills include knowing the level of politeness (register) to use, e.g., using more informal speech with peers or children, more formal speech with strangers; exhibiting appropriate extralinguistic behavior, e.g., how close to be and appropriate body language. They also involve using appropriate spoken or written formulaic phrases for certain situations. Sociolinguistic skills are context dependent and so are generally learned through and alongside situations, the four skills, or specific content.

In my ASL class, we learned functions such as giving and getting personal information, and vocabulary, such as that related to family. Additionally, we learned about what is sociolinguistically appropriate and inappropriate within Deaf culture. For example, it is appropriate to wave one's hand toward the Deaf person or to tap a Deaf person on the shoulder to get his or her attention.

Sociocultural Skills

Sociocultural skills involve understanding cultural aspects of identity, values, norms, and customs such as those underlying kinship relationships, expectations of men and women, or gift-giving. Such understanding enables us to interpret explicit and implicit messages and behave and speak in a culturally appropriate way. Sociocultural skills are rooted in intercultural understanding in the sense that one must understand one's own cultural identity, values, norms, and customs, in order to know how and how much one can adapt to the target culture.

Each episode of the video we watched in the ASL class was accompanied by worksheets. There was a true-false or multiple choice "pretest" to test one's knowledge of culture, grammar, and vocabulary. The first question on the pretest for episode one was a true-false question: "Deaf people actually have their own culture." This question served to alert learners that Deafness is a culture, not a handicap. Another worksheet dealt specifically with cultural aspects of ASL and was labeled "Cultural notes." The culture notes for episode one pointed out that Deaf people have their own distinct culture (hence the capital D), with its own set of shared customs and values, equal to other cultures, and, as in any language instruction, cultural information would be included when studying ASL.

Sociopolitical Skills

Sociopolitical skills involve learning to think critically and take action for effective change in order to participate effectively in one's community. These skills include learning how to navigate systems such as medical, school, and employment systems, to know one's rights and responsibilities within them, and to take action to make positive changes. Sociopolitical skills also involve learning to be critically aware of how both spoken and written language are used to help or hinder a given social group. This has been called "critical language awareness" (Fairclough 1992.) The sociopolitical focus is most evident in programs for adult learners in the United Kingdom, Australia, Canada, and the United States. The **participatory syllabus** (Auerbach 1992) is an example of a syllabus that emphasizes learning to effect changes in one's community and workplace.

In my ASL class, the instructor, who was taught to use her "voice" in her own schooling, chose to use only sign and asked us to use only sign. This was a sociopolitical decision on her part because the schooling of Deaf children in "oracy," the use of their vocal cords, is regarded by many Deaf people as a form of oppression since it has prevented them from developing ASL as their first language. In the video episode about the home, we learned about accessibility; for example, visual modifications such as flashing lights when the doorbell rings and how to use the TTY (voice relay) telephone. The worksheet that accompanied the unit asked us to consider a number of questions including the following ones: "Think about how it would be if you were Deaf. How would you gain access to educational opportunities, emergency medical care, movies and theater, social events, etc.?" "Who should pay these costs?"

To summarize, the ways of conceptualizing content related to **social context** include:

- sociolinguistic skills
- sociocultural skills
- sociopolitical skills

The chart below summarizes the possible ways to conceptualize content, with examples of each.

Figure 4.4: Conceptualizing Content According to Language, Learner, and Social Context

Focus on Language

Linguistic Skills	*Situations*
pronunciation, grammar, vocabulary e.g., intonation, verb tenses, prefixes and suffixes	the contexts in which language is used e.g., at the supermarket, at a party
Topics/Themes	*Communicative Functions*
what the language is used to talk about e.g., family relations, the environment	what the language is used for e.g., expressing preferences, asking for directions
Competencies	*Tasks*
language and behavior to perform tasks e.g., opening a bank account, applying for a job	what you accomplish with the language e.g., planning a trip, designing a brochure
Content	*Speaking*
subject matter other than language e.g., science, architecture	oral skills e.g., turn-taking, producing fluent stretches of discourse
Listening	*Reading*
aural comprehension skills e.g., listening for gist, for tone, for invitations to take a turn	understanding written texts and learning reading subskills e.g., predicting content, understanding the main idea, interpreting the text
Writing	*Genre*
producing written texts and learning writing subskills e.g., using appropriate rhetorical structure, adjusting writing for a given audience, editing one's writing	spoken and written texts that accomplish a purpose within a social context e.g., analyzing a text in terms of its purpose and how it achieves the purpose within the social context; producing texts

Focus on Learning and the Learner

Affective Goals	*Interpersonal Skills*	*Learning Strategies*
attitudes toward learning, language, and culture e.g., developing confidence, learning from one's mistakes	how one interacts with others to promote learning e.g., learning to work effectively in groups	how one learns e.g., self-monitoring, memory techniques

Focus on Social Context

Sociolinguistic Skills	*Sociocultural Skills*	*Sociopolitical Skills*
choosing and using appropriate language e.g., levels of politeness, body language	understanding cultural norms and their relation to one's own e.g., expectations of men and women, gift-giving	learning to critique and take action for effective change e.g., navigating systems, critical interpretation of text

Figure 4.4 is meant to be a stimulus for ways to conceptualize the content of your course. It is *not* a map of everything you should include in your course. It is meant to give you choices. Nor is it the "last word" on possible categories. There may be categories that are not included, which you should feel free to add. For example, when I presented this chart to colleagues in South Africa, one of them proposed adding "thinking skills" to the chart, since that is an important aspect of how he conceptualizes the content of what he teaches. You might use different words to describe the categories and I invite you to annotate the chart with your own ideas.

I would like to return to a point I made earlier in the chapter. The categories above overlap with each other in useful ways. For example, in a writing class, students may learn writing skills such as how to edit a paper, they may learn strategies for transferring the writing skills outside of class such as how to ask people for feedback on their writing, they may learn vocabulary and grammatical structures, and they may learn about sociolinguistic features of a given text. To use another example, a genre approach integrates grammatical, lexical, sociolinguistic, and discourse features in analyzing texts. The overlap is positive in the sense that there is a limited amount of time in the classroom and one therefore wants to use the time as efficiently as possible. Learning how to have a given writing activity effectively accomplish a variety of purposes is a result of finding an organizing principle that can help to integrate the various strands of one's course.

The purpose of the next two investigations is to help you see ways in which some of the elements in the chart in Figure 4.4 have been integrated. The first one involves researching textbooks. The second one involves analyzing a course you taught or in which you were a learner.

4.3a *Find two different textbooks for ESL/EFL. Look through their tables of contents. How does each author conceptualize content? Which of the categories in Figure 4.4 are included? What is the organizing principle (or principles) that integrates the other elements?*

For more information about the organizing principles of a course, see Chapter 7.

4.3b *Think of a specific language course in which you were a learner or which you taught. Which aspects of the chart in Figure 4.4 did the course focus on? Which aspect or aspects were the organizing principles for the course?*

How Does One Go About Conceptualizing Content for a Course?

Figure 4.4 outlines 18 areas and additional sub-areas to consider. Clearly one has to make choices. Nevertheless, it may seem daunting at first, as John Kongsvik attests in his reflection at the beginning of the chapter on his initial attempt to conceptualize the content of his course.

4.4 *Iris Broudy made choices about what to include in her syllabus. Review her mind map in Figure 4.2 on page 41. Which areas outlined in Figure 4.4 are included in Iris's mind map?*

The "product" Iris generated was a mind map—actually, she generated a series of mind maps, of which Figure 4.2 is the last one. Other ways to capture the content of a course are grids and flow charts. Below you will investigate two grids. The remainder of the chapter will focus on mind maps and flow charts.

4.5 *As you look at the following grids, answer these questions:*

1. How did this teacher conceptualize the content of her course? What did she think it was important for her students to learn? Refer to the chart in Figure 4.4
2. What do you like about the way she conceptualized content?
3. What don't you like about it?

Figure 4.5 is Anne LeWarne's syllabus for a four week academic ESL course for adolescents offered during the summer at a private high school in the United States, St. Johnsbury Academy. Figure 4.6 is a section of Claire Winhold's syllabus for a five week beginning English course for adult professionals in a university in China. The context is described in some detail.

Figure 4.5: Course Design for St. Johnsbury Academy's Summer Program

Subject Area	*Activities*	*Skills**	*Sub-Skills*	*Goals*
Mainstream classes (United States history text that they'll use in history course)	taking lecture notes, discussions, reading texts, research papers, TOEFL prep (various)	wr/th s/l/th r/wr r/wr	paraphrasing, selecting main points, asking questions, supporting ideas with examples, skimming, scanning, using a dictionary, bubble diagrams	to prepare students for academic challenges of the mainstream classroom
Comparing cultures	Making a speech, interviewing people, collecting data from observation, keeping a dialogue journal, discussion, brainstorming, public speaking, show-n-tell	s/l wr/l	speech format, using examples, asking questions, paraphrasing, reported speech, synthesizing info, comparing cultures, looking at self/assumptions, using supporting details, organizing in "logical order"	to familiarize students with the culture in which they'll be living (self-awareness)
Living in the United States: dealing with homesickness, homestays, making friends, stress management	Dear Abby letter, brainstorm issues, write and perform role plays, dialogue journals, letter writing	r/wr wr/s l	grammar—modals, self expression, poetry, literature, coping techniques	to help students to deal with living in the United States
Students' interests: music, movies and videos, summer activities	song clozes, watching movies, making movies, summer activities, guides to St. J	l/s r/wr	pronunciation, suprasegmentals, tense aspect, observation, comprehension, grammar, idioms	to have fun—because it's summer!!

* wr=writing, s=speaking, l=listening, r=reading, th=thinking

Figure 4.6: Beginning English for Adult Professionals in a University in China

The class will meet for 2 hours, two times a week, over a period of 5 months. I was told that the emphasis should be on oral proficiency. Some of the students hope to immigrate to the United States, while others need English in order to interact with foreigners at their jobs. The students have studied English for years in school and have a good grasp of grammar, but they are unable to speak it. The course will have a functional/cultural focus, and it will consist of learning modules, each with a topical theme. The culmination of each module will consist of a classroom visit by native English speakers, when the students will have an opportunity to try out what they have learned of the English language and culture.

Overall goal: Students will be able to interact confidently and successfully, at a survival level, with native speakers of English.

	Topics/ Functions	*Culture*	*Language Skills*	*Affective Element*
Goals	Learn functions necessary for survival.	Examine the concept of culture and aspects of Chinese and American culture which relate to the functions.	Improve language skills necessary for oral proficiency at a survival level.	Increase confidence and motivation in speaking English.
Objectives By the end of the course the students should know . . .	*Personal and Family Identification* 1.greetings/ introductions/ leave-takings 2.how to ask for and give simple biographical information 3.how to give telephone numbers and addresses *Numbers, Time, Weather* 4.how to read and understand the calendar 5.how to tell time 6.how to talk about weather	1.the American conventional verbal and non-verbal behavior for each of the different functions Example: how Americans perform courtesy requirements 2.some American extra-linguistics 3.about American families 4.about American values of time 5.what Americans say as conversation openers 6.types of American food 7.how to read an American menu	1.how to correctly use grammatical structures in the functions 2.vocabulary related to the topics 3.which language style and degree of formality is appropriate in a given context 4.how to write a peer dialog journal 5.phonemes in English 6.how to write a short letter (to the American visitors)	1.that errors are positive and vital in the learning process 2.what one other classmate thinks and feels about Americans and about learning English (through dialog journal) 3.that risk-taking is important in language learning

Topics/ Functions	Culture	Language Skills	Affective Element
Social Interactions 7.how to thank, invite, accept and reject invitations 8.how to indicate a lack of comprehension 9.how to request politely 10.how to offer and ask for help 11.how to express likes and dislikes *Food and Shopping* 12.names of foods 13.how to order in a restaurant 14.how to give directions for a recipe *Daily Activities/ Sports* 15.how to talk about routines and interests	8.how to order in an American restaurant 9.about shopping in the United States		

Grids are useful as a way of laying out the content in an accessible, graphic form. However, it is difficult to show the relationship among the various elements of the syllabus. Moreover, working in grid form, at least initially, can be constraining. For a more dynamic image of a syllabus, mind maps are useful tools. A mind map is a non-linear way of representing the content itself, as well as factors affecting the content. A mind map enables one to see the course as a whole, the component parts, and the multiple relationships among the parts. I am indebted to Carmen Blyth, who first introduced me to mind maps as she sat in one of my courses and, instead of taking notes in the more traditional way, sketched out a series of mind maps as a way to keep track of her thoughts about what we were studying. She later wrote about her experience developing an English for Academic Purposes course using mind maps as a way of capturing the entire process (Blyth 1996). Another teacher, Rosa Silva, coined the term "messy-neat" to describe a mind map because it captured the non-linear (messy) way in which she perceived the course in an organized (neat) fashion. Generally, one goes through successive versions of a mind map as one refines one's thinking about the course. Mind maps may also be a first step prior to drawing up a chart or course sequence. Below we will look at some mind maps and some of the thinking that went into them. Following that, you will be asked to draw up your own mind maps.

4.6 *As you read what the teachers below say about their mind maps and study the accompanying mind maps, ask yourself,*

1. How did this teacher conceptualize the content of her course? What did she think it was important for her students to learn? Refer to the chart in Figure 4.3.

2. What do I like about the way she conceptualized content? What don't I like about it? Why?

Denise Maksail-Fine is a high school Spanish teacher in rural upstate New York. She describes the process of conceptualizing the content for her course for high school students in a third year Spanish class. She is redesigning the course after having taught it for three years.

Denise Maksail-Fine

> My initial thought on conceptualizing my course content was, "Oh, this is a piece of cake! Decide on the topic for the unit, then outline the related vocabulary, grammar structures, and possible activities." After all, I could do that in my sleep if need be. Then I remembered that the reason I was doing this was to force myself to make a marked departure from the way in which I had taught this course in the past. Otherwise, this was going to be a big waste of time and energy.
>
> After that healthy dose of realism, I backtracked to the three year period during which I had taught this course and thought about what it was that I did not wish to include in the redesign. I was able to pinpoint two related aspects: heavy reliance upon a textbook and a grammar-driven curriculum. The reason I had relied on a textbook so heavily in the past was because, as an itinerant teacher, with six different daily course preparations in two different locales, I simply did not have the time, nor the energy to design the curriculum in a way that I felt would be most effective.
>
> I wanted to do away with relying so heavily on the text for a few different reasons. It has the benefit of being organized topically, provides a wealth of lexical items and is very thorough in its treatment of grammar; however, it is primarily a grammar-based text. Through using the text in the past, my students have developed a

good understanding of how the Spanish language works, but I felt that they still needed more practice actually communicating in the language. I also felt that it would probably take just as much time and effort to adequately adapt the text to my students' needs as it would to redesign the course without using the text as the principal tool. It is my hope that future students will continue to use it as a reference tool.

Instead of doing a chart or a categorical listing of content, I chose to do more of a mind map, or visual representation, of the Spanish 3 content, in order to force myself to do things differently than I ordinarily might.

For my first mind map, I focused on everything that I might need to know or explain to someone unfamiliar with my curriculum. By including all relevant aspects, I also felt that it would assist me in becoming more comfortable with what I wanted my students to do and where I perceived the course to be heading.

Figure 4.7: Denise Maksail-Fine's First Mind Map for High School Spanish 3

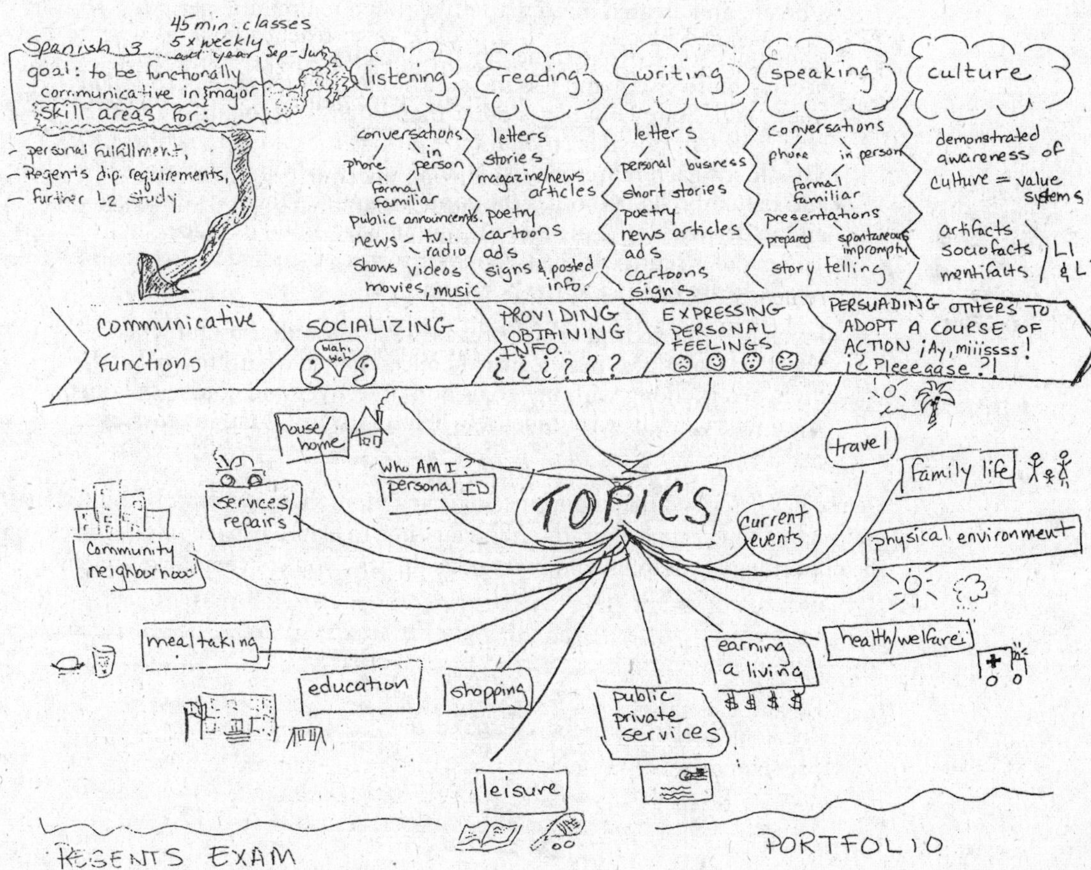

I started with the overall goal that led to my listing possible reasons why students might take the course to begin with. Then I added the major skill areas: listening, reading, writing, speaking, and culture. Under each major skill area, I listed the mediums through which I envisioned my students utilizing the skill. Then I added the communicative functions (socializing, providing and obtaining information, expressing personal feelings, persuading others to adopt a course of action) that the Board of Regents recommends students should be able to demonstrate using the skill areas. Next, I added the fifteen topic areas within which students are required to be communicatively functional. Finally, I added the two major forms of student assessment: the New York State Regents Comprehensive Examination in Spanish and a portfolio.

The resulting visual representation was, quite frankly, an absolute mess, yet the process of putting it all down on paper really helped me to comprehend the scope of what I was trying to do.

The second visual that follows is the final visual representation that resulted from the process and mess described above. After devising the first mind map, I left it for a while to rattle around in my subconscious. Approximately two weeks later, I sat down during a break, and created mind map #2 within a ten minute period.

It includes some of the same key components as #1; it simply became more visual and less messy. The sun includes the NYS LOTE (New York State Languages other than English) standards, and the rays represent possible student motivations for taking the course. The clouds each represent a skill area, the raindrops topic areas, and the umbrella embodies the communicative functions through and under which the process of communication takes place. The puddles represent the two major forms of student assessment: The Regents Exam and the portfolio.

I included this second visual because I have found it useful when trying to explain to people how I conceptualize what I teach. . . . I discussed it, along with my goals and objectives and course syllabus, at an interview. It was immensely helpful in conveying my message.

Denise has described the importance of doing more than one draft of a mind map and leaving time between drafts. Allowing time to elapse between drafts gives you the opportunity to rethink and reorganize the way you conceptualize content.

Figure 4.8: **Denise Maksail-Fine's Second Mind Map for High School Spanish 3**

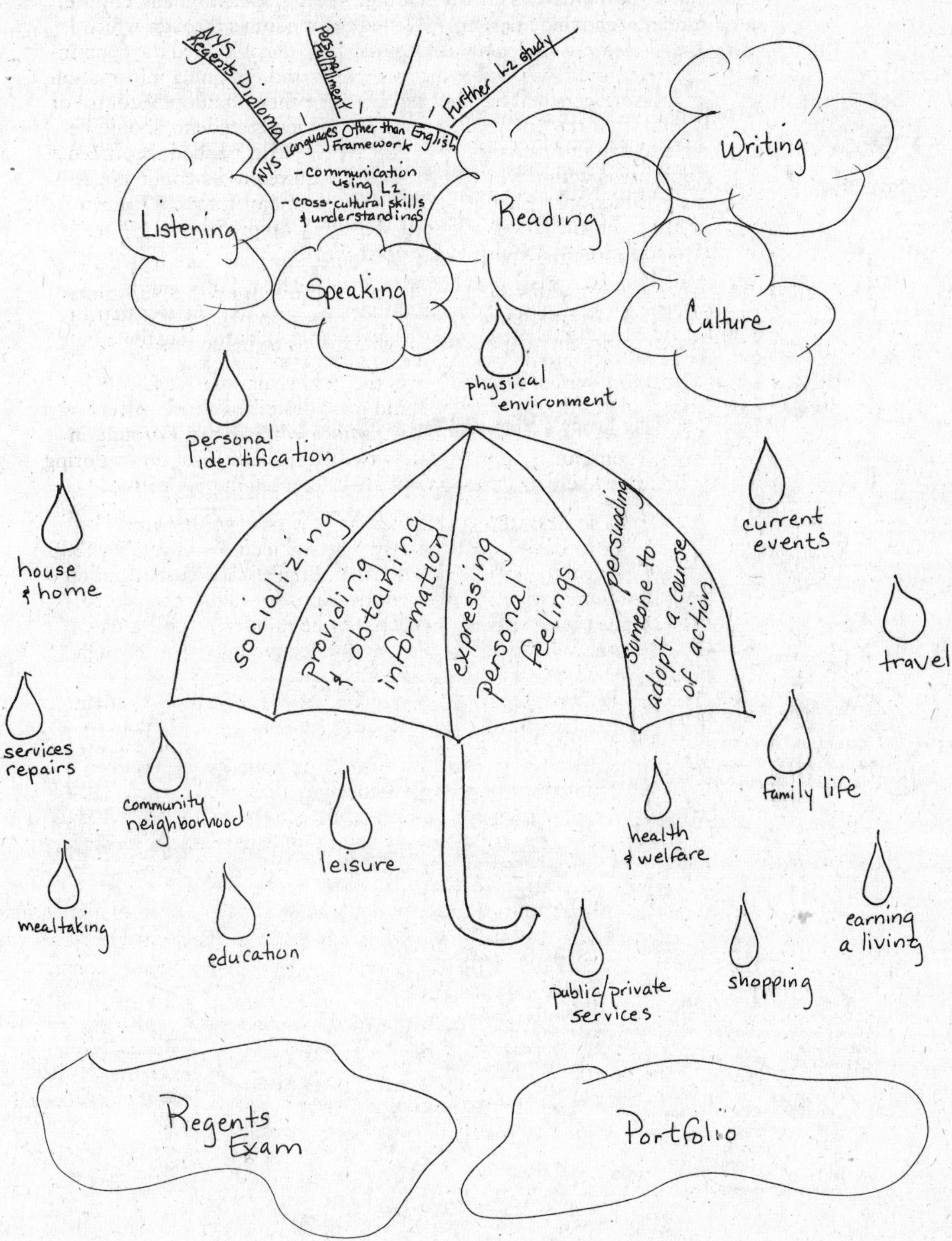

The following map is for a course which integrates the four macro skills of reading, writing, speaking, and listening, using the newspaper as the "text" for the course. The course is an 8 week course for high intermediate to advanced level students studying in an Intensive English Program. Toby Brody, the teacher who designed the course, writes about her mind map:

Toby Brody

> The mind map helped me to solidify the direction of the course, i.e., what the syllabus would look like, how I would define my syllabus. I began to see patterns emerge and from the patterns I could see that what I had was a task- and skills-based focus with a structural component to it. By looking at the pattern, I know that there will eventually be some items deleted, while others will be added. . . .
>
> The notion of the "newspaper" as something that can involve all four skills may be somewhat strange as, at first, I thought of it as a vehicle for teaching reading and that's all. So I like the fact that I could envision the newspaper as a versatile medium, one that could be used for limitless tasks covering all four skill areas.

Figure 4.9: Toby Brody's Mind Map for a 4 Skills Course Using the Newspaper

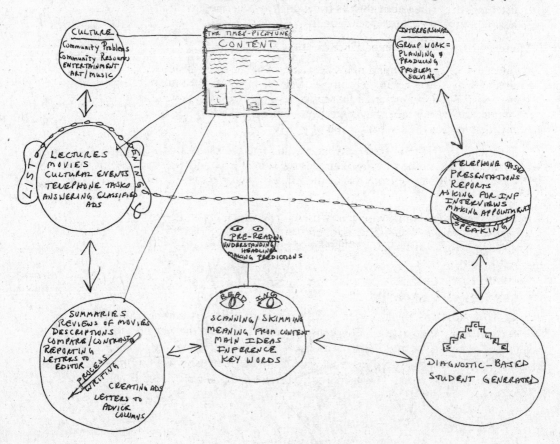

Toby Brody's map, like Denise Maksail-Fine's, uses icons and images to capture some of the elements of her course. The next mind map (Figure 4.10) is different. It uses bubbles and a conceptual framework of knowledge, awareness, skills, and attitude as the way to organize it. It is for a course taught by Mônica Camargo, a teacher at a language institute in São Paulo, Brazil. She wants to add a literature component to an existing course with a prescribed syllabus and required textbook. She realizes that she can't simply plunge in and teach literature "for its own sake," but that there are steps the class needs to go through first. She writes:

For more about this conceptual framework see pages 83–84.

Mônica Camargo

> One of the most important preliminary steps, according to one of the students involved in this project, is to read, to understand, to interpret, to establish a pleasant relationship with the text. In other words, people need some time and practice to get used to reading for thought, not only for information. Based on some talks with students and on my previous experiments with literary texts in EFL classes, I decided to choose texts which would be good samples of different moments of the literature of English speaking countries, and that could be used as integrated parts of the language classes—as pre-activities for listening tasks, as follow-ups to speaking, listening, or writing activities, as triggering tasks before a writing lesson, and as topics for discussion.

Mônica writes about her experience creating the mind map.

> I decided to work on mind maps because it was the most difficult thing for me to do before getting used to it. It was very hard for me to put down on paper all those bubbles and arrows for a very simple reason: my thoughts make sense, but when I try to visualize my ideas it looks like a basket full of kittens.
>
> The maps help me understand what is going on. The sensation I had when I looked at the finished map was the same I experienced when I saw a figure emerge from one of the Magic Eye posters for the first time: amazing!
>
> I have learned to work with a very useful tool which makes my plans much more organized and therefore simpler in terms of choosing the main stream and then inserting all the extras I can (and have to.)

Constructing a Mind Map

Each of the mind maps we have seen is different, not only because of the difference in the course being taught, but because of the difference in the way the individual teacher conceives and portrays it. The first step in drawing a mind map involves brainstorming everything you want to include in the course in map form, rather than list form. This is like the "discovery draft" in writing. It will be edited later.

Figure 4.10: Mônica Camargo's Mind Map

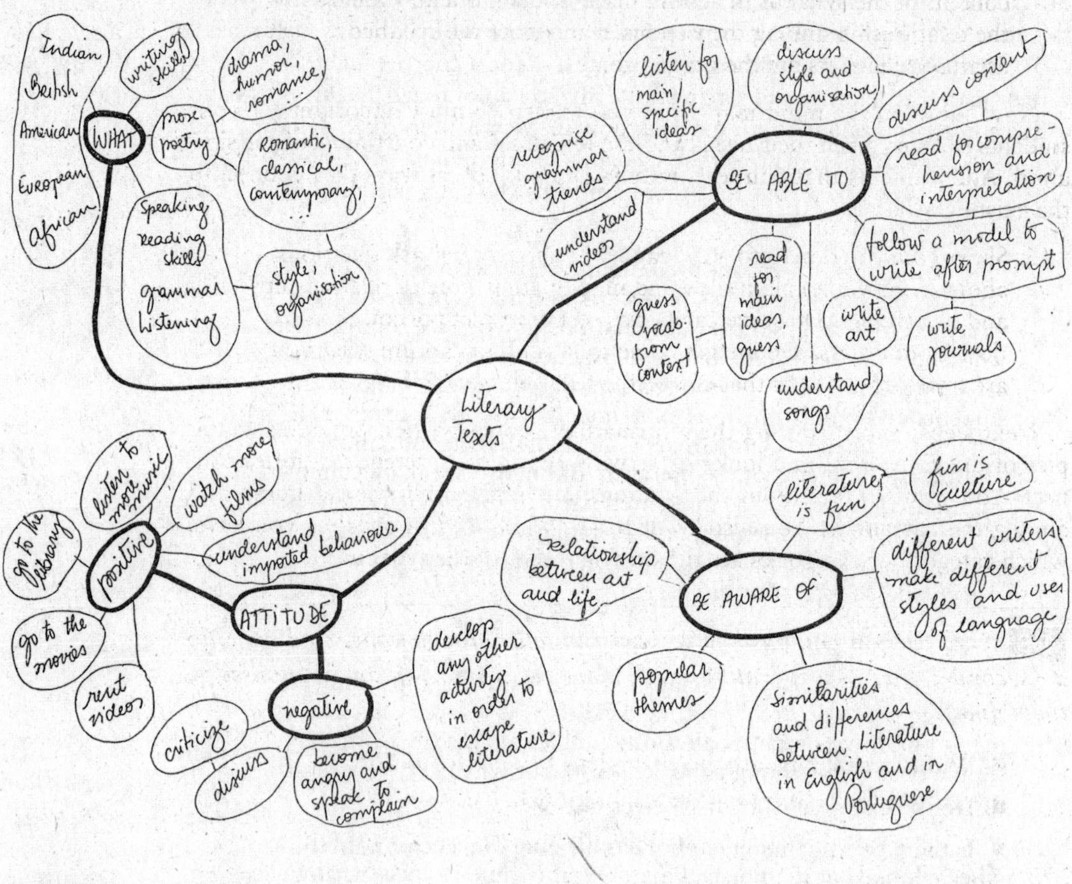

Literary Texts

WHAT
Indian
British
American
European
African
writing skills
prose
poetry
drama, humor, romance, ...
Romantic, classical, contemporary, ...
Speaking
Reading skills
grammar
listening
style, organization

BE ABLE TO
listen for main/specific ideas
discuss style and organization
discuss content
read for comprehension and interpretation
follow a model to write after prompt
recognise grammar trends
understand videos
read for main ideas, guess
guess vocab. from context
understand songs
write art
write journals

BE AWARE OF
literature is fun
fun is culture
relationship between art and life
different writers make different styles and uses of language
popular themes
similarities and differences between Literature in English and in Portuguese

ATTITUDE
positive
listen to more music
watch more films
understand imported behaviour
go to the library
go to the movies
rent videos
negative
develop any other activity in order to escape literature
criticize
discuss
become angry and speak to complain

4.7 *As described above, a mind map is a non-linear way of representing the content itself, as well as factors affecting the content. A mind map enables you to see the course as a whole, the component parts, and the multiple relationships among the parts. This is equally true for a course you are designing from scratch as for a course with a prescribed syllabus. Do step 1a if you are designing a course from scratch. Do step 1b if you are working with a prescribed syllabus or text.*

1a. Take out a sheet of paper and do a first map of how you conceptualize your course. Ask yourself, *What do I feel is most important for my students to learn given their needs and the resources and constraints of my situation?* Use words, phrases, and images to capture the areas you feel are important, as well as any questions that arise. Feel free to draw circles around them, use arrows, question marks. Use more than one sheet, if everything doesn't fit. The purpose of this first version of the mind map is to get out all the elements you feel you need to consider in planning what will go into your course.

1b. Study the prescribed syllabus or text carefully. Then capture the content of the syllabus in a mind map. The mind map should show the relationship among the various elements of the syllabus as well as which elements are the driving forces.

Now show on the mind map what you feel to be most important for your students to learn given their needs and the resources and constraints of the situation. Add elements that you feel are missing and look at ways they connect to the existing syllabus.

2. Show your mind map to a colleague. Let him or her ask questions about it. As you explain the mind map, make a note of relationships and hierarchies. Do some categories seem more important than or flow from others? Do images come to mind that capture what you are trying to show or that connect various elements?

Next steps involve sorting the information into categories, providing examples of the categories, and looking for ways in which different categories connect. You want to figure out the **relationships** both within the categories and among the categories. You also want to see what kind of syllabus you have, which category or categories are the driving forces of the syllabus.

4.8 *After each of you has had a chance to talk through your mind map, do a "second draft" incorporating ideas from the discussion and responses to these questions:*

- Within a category, are the examples of equal importance?
- Do the examples sort themselves into sub-categories?
- Is there overlap among categories that suggests some kind of streamlining?
- Are there categories that are the driving force or organizing principle, out of which other categories flow?
- Do **images** come to mind that help to capture the nature and relationship of the elements of the map?

It is important to achieve a balance between getting everything out and not getting bogged down in too much detail. If you find yourself getting stuck, move on to something else.

Because they capture one's ideas in a dynamic, non-linear way, mind maps, especially in initial drafts, may not be immediately accessible to others, unless the author explains what is meant. Taking time to talk through your mind map with a colleague will help you to clarify and refine your ideas, to get ideas from your colleague, as well as give your colleague food for thought about his or her own course. Even if you are using a textbook or working from a prescribed syllabus, mind mapping is a useful process for understanding the relationship among the elements of the syllabus, articulating your concerns and priorities, and exploring how both connect to the students in the particular context of your course.

4.9 *Compare the grids in Figures 4.5 and 4.6 with the mind maps in Figures 4.8, 4.9, and 4.10. How is a mind map different from a grid? What is the advantage of one over the other?*

Flow Charts

Another way to conceptualize and represent the content is through a flow chart. Below we will follow Chris Conley's process of conceptualizing the content for a course for adult immigrants in the United States, whose goals for studying English ranged from wanting to learn English for a better job to wanting to take the citizenship test. Chris has decided that he wants to use a participatory approach. In this approach teacher and students work together to identify problematic issues in the students' lives and then determine appropriate responses or solutions. He describes the process in the form of journal entries. I have taken excerpts from each entry.

4.10 *As you read through Chris's journal entries and look at his flow charts, ask yourself what you like about them, what you don't like about them and why.*

Chris Conley

Journal entry 1 excerpt

I find myself in a dilemma. On the one hand the participatory approach "doesn't involve a pre-determined curriculum, itemization of skills, set structures, materials, texts or outcomes" (Auerbach and McGrail 1991, p. 100). If this is so, how can I design a curriculum that uses this approach before meeting my students? This idea runs contrary to the traditional concept and process of curriculum development. On the other hand, this "doesn't mean, however, that a teacher goes into the classroom empty handed." (op. cit.) If this is so, what do I bring with me? What can I create before I meet the students and the class begins?

Journal entry 2 excerpt

In my mind, the overall goals of my students at the institute, my perceived needs for my students, and the goals of the approach seemed to mesh and to fit together like pieces of a puzzle. So my visualization of my context and the reasons for choosing the participatory approach to teaching and learning came together naturally.

Journal Entry 3 excerpts

So what is it that I can have in my hand when I walk into my participatory style class? Well, I think that it isn't so much in the hand as it is in the mind. . . . I feel that I have an idea of why I am choosing to initiate and implement such a syllabus in this context. I need now to conceptualize the process of the approach. In my interpretation of the participatory approach, process means the content of the course. How do I see the content play out in the process? Where does language fit in? And culture? What about the 4 skills of reading, writing, listening, and speaking?. . .

Figure 4.11: Chris Conley's Flow Chart #1

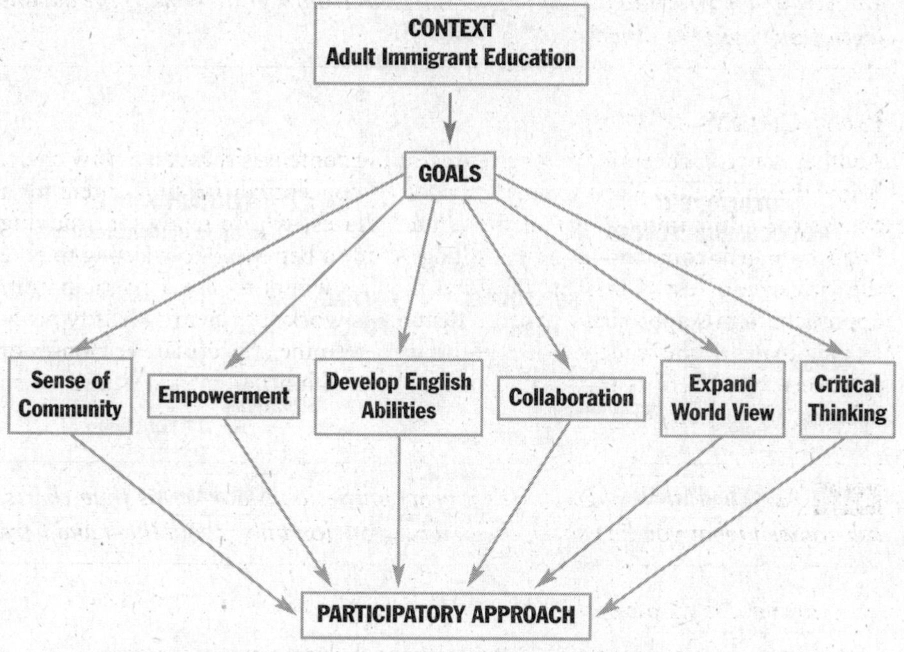

In my conceptualization of the content and process of the participatory approach, I feel that there are 4 forces at work. The first is the driving force of the approach. This is the process that teachers and students go through in order to create the content. I need to come back to this later as this is the cycle and sequencing of how the class and curriculum will play out on a thematic, cyclical basis. Secondly, . . . there is a sub-force of culture. Language and culture are inseparable and when there is one, the other is present. So in my course, culture will be addressed and presented along with the language of a given theme. A third level of forces seem to me to underlie or recur throughout the cycle of a theme. These forces are the 4 skills of the English language, grammar studies, vocabulary, and pronunciation. These forces can be used and reused as new themes are presented. The final level is a group that can be called upon at the request of the students. They represent a tertiary force and include functions, topics, situations, and various competencies.

My content must also be immediate, authentic and real. It must meet the immediate needs of the students. What do students need to learn today in order to function and live in this community? The content must come from authentic sources. What are the issues that my students face? Themes and issues must be real in that they are not made up and that they relate to the students' needs. I don't want to teach about something that has little or nothing to do with their reality. If I can achieve immediacy, authenticity and real content, I can engage my students in meaningful learning.

Figure 4.12: **Chris Conley's Flow Chart #2**

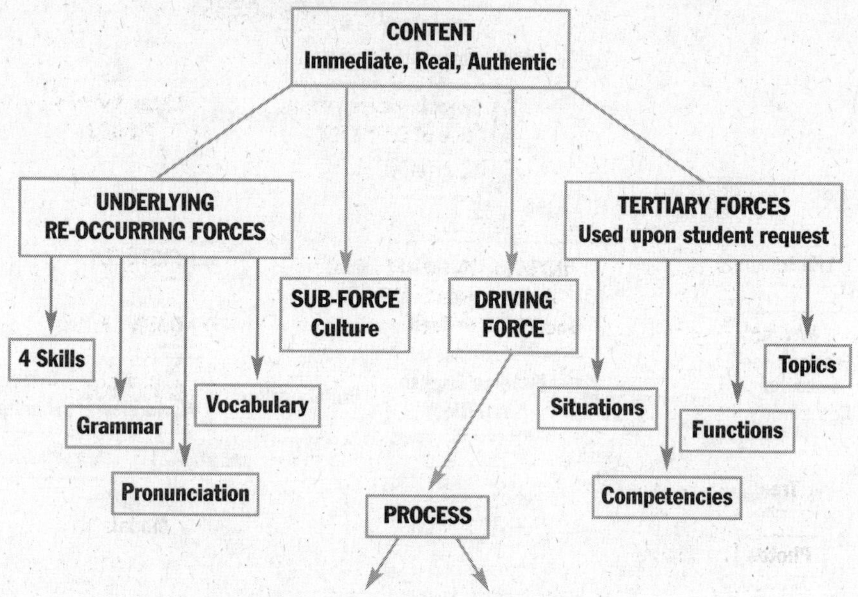

Journal entry 4 (excerpt)

I want to talk about the driving force, the process, that I wrote about in the last entry. As I said before, the participatory approach doesn't lend itself to a predetermined curriculum or set of skills. It is a cycle or series of steps to follow once a theme or an issue has been discovered. This becomes the content of the course. I, as the teacher, have to listen to what immediate, real issues my students are facing and are dealing with at the present moment and then build content around those issues. At first, I have to play a central role in finding the issues and building materials around them, but as the students feel more comfortable in the class, they can take on a larger role in finding issues and developing materials. In order to find issue and themes, I have to listen to my students in class and at break, or I may build lessons called catalysts (Wallerstein 1983) in order to find themes.

Chris Conley describes a lesson on pages 161–163.

The important question that arises in my mind is how do I present the catalyst activities? What forces do I use? Do I teach from a reading text? From a listening exercise? As a grammar exercise? My feeling is that I now have the freedom to use any means possible in presenting an activity and in listening for an issue. I can use grammar, listening, reading, writing, and/or a function as my means of presentation. I see this part of my curriculum as an integration of any and all the ways a teacher may present a lesson. It is up to the imagination and experience of the teacher to be creative and to achieve the goal of finding an issue.

Figure 4.13: Chris Conley's Flow Chart #3

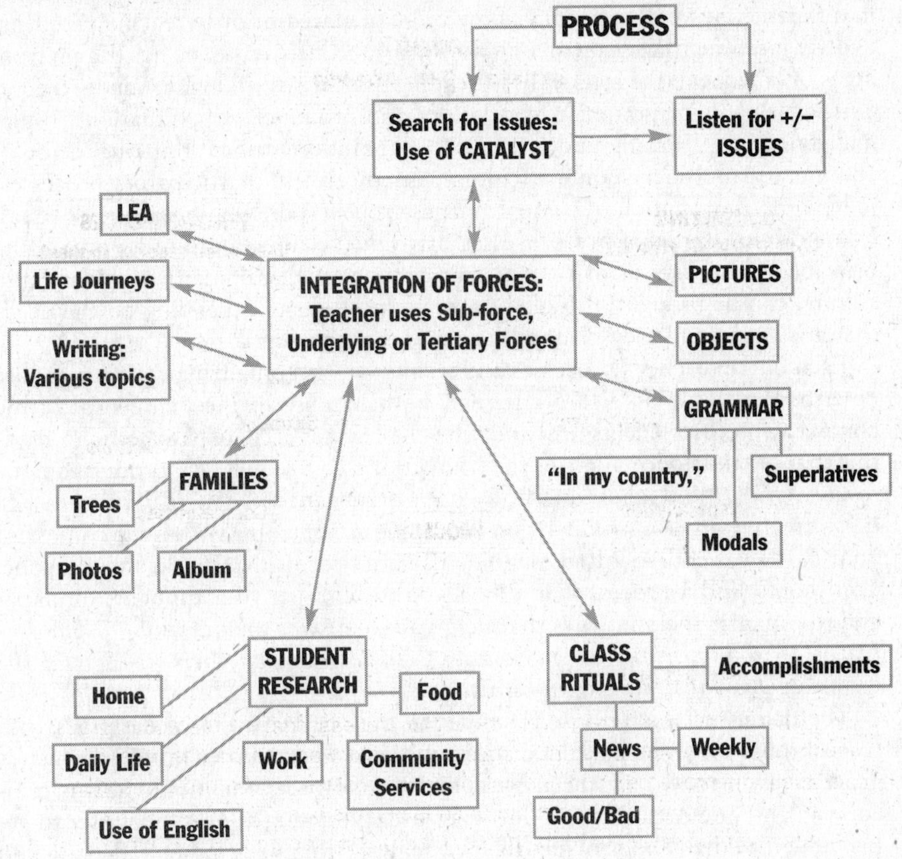

Journal entry 5 excerpt

There is another driving force that is more important than using and presenting catalyst activities and that is listening for real issues and themes that the students are facing in their immediate life. This part of the process of learning through participatory pedagogy represents a cycle of steps that the students and teacher go through in addressing the issues and themes. It is a sequence of events that I can conceptualize and hold in the back of my mind when an issue is raised. I, as the teacher, can guide the students through the steps of the cycle and offer them choices of direction upon which they can decide the content and path of the course. This cycle or sequence is one notion that I can visualize and bring with me to a teaching situation and prepare to deal with before ever meeting the students.

Chris Conley describes the cycle on pages 143–144.

Chris Conley's narrative and diagrams give a sense of how he tried to resolve the dilemma that he, John Kongsvik, and Iris Broudy have each articulated in different ways in this chapter: how to be prepared prior to teaching students and yet meet their needs on an ongoing basis. In Chris's case, he has drawn from areas of language, (the four skills of reading, writing, speaking, listening; the linguistic elements of grammar, vocabulary and pronunciation, situations, topics and functions), learning and learners (collaboration, critical thinking, sense of community) and social context (culture, empowerment, participatory processes) in his conceptualization of content. The areas he has drawn on are not all equally important. Participatory processes drive the syllabus and are its organizing principle. Other aspects of content such as functions, grammar, vocabulary, and culture, can be brought into play to serve the students depending on the needs that arise as he and they identify the issues that concern them.

Each of the teacher's processes and results in conceptualizing content that are described in this chapter are different, both because of the uniqueness of the context, who the students are, and who the teacher is. Each teacher who reads this chapter and conceptualizes the content of a course will also produce unique results. Grids, mind maps, and flow charts are meant to be tools in this process. It is a creative process in which you determine the outcome within the context of your particular course. Mind mapping is not a process that works for everyone. You should find a process that allows you to both get your thoughts on paper and to organize them in ways that help you to answer the question *"What do I feel is most important for my students to learn given their needs and the resources and constraints of my situation?"*

The duality of this process is similar to the one Peter Elbow describes with respect to writing. He makes a distinction between first order thinking which is generative, creative, and uncensored, and second order thinking which is critical, vigilant, and organized (1986.) First order thinking allows the writer to get his thoughts down and provides the raw material that he can then reflect on and organize via second order thinking. The dual processes allow the writer to produce a piece of polished work. The "polished work" for course design doesn't necessarily show up at this stage but in later stages of setting goals, organizing the course and developing materials. However, there is still a certain amount of editing and organizing in conceptualizing content. The process you use should allow you to be both generative and creative, so that you can then be critical, vigilant, and organized. The process is likely to be a back and forth between the two types of thinking before a product emerges that provides a practical foundation for further work on your course.

Suggested Readings

One of my favorite resources for conceptualizing content is *Threshold Level English* (1986) by Jan van Ek because of its useful lists of situations, notions, functions, grammar points, and topics. Sadly, it is out of print; however, it may be available in libraries. Chapter 3, "Language Teaching Objectives," in H. H. Stern's book *Issues and Options in Language Teaching* (1992) provides a thoughtful map of the territory of language learning and makes a compelling case for including the affective component. To learn more about task-based syllabuses, see *Tasks in a Pedagogical Context: Integrating Theory and Practice* edited by Graham Crookes and Susan Gass (1993). This book contains several useful articles on aspects of task-based curricula including how to design and sequence tasks and how to integrate them into one's teaching. To learn more about the four skills of speaking, listening, reading, and writing, from a genre perspective, *Text-based Syllabus Design* by Susan Feez (1998) is specifically about designing courses around texts and is written in a clear and accessible format. To learn more about the four skills of speaking, listening, reading, and writing, from a skills perspective, Alice Omaggio Hadley's book, *Teaching Language in Context* (1993), provides good background but is also dense and hard to wade through. To learn about the participatory approach, see *Making Meaning, Making Change: Participatory Curriculum Development for Adult ESL Literacy* (1992) by Elsa Auerbach.

For an example of mind mapping an entire course (from goals and objectives to materials), see "Designing an EAP Course for Post-Graduate Students in Ecuador" (1996) by Carmen Blyth.

5

FORMULATING GOALS AND OBJECTIVES

5.1 *Make a list of questions you have about goals and objectives. Use the list as a guide as you read the chapter.*

In a teacher training workshop I conducted recently I began by having each participant talk to another person and find out a few things they had in common. As I circulated to listen in on some of the conversations I came across two teachers who had found something they didn't have in common: their views on goals and objectives. One teacher quite vehemently stated that you couldn't teach without your objectives clearly spelled out, otherwise you wouldn't know what you wanted the students to learn. The other teacher, equally emphatically, said that objectives were a hindrance because everything was decided beforehand and students were forced to follow a path that might not be right for them. I suggested that they were both right. Their viewpoints represented what I see as one of the contradictions or paradoxes of teaching: it helps to have a clear idea of the territory to be covered—clear objectives—at the same time that it is important to follow the learners' lead as they move through the territory.

In principle, goals and objectives are a good thing. The question *How can you design a course if you don't know where you want your students to come out?* seems to be a good argument for setting goals. In practice, goals and objectives are one of the hardest aspects of course design for the teachers I have worked with, including myself. Why is this so? I think the reason lies in the nature of teaching and of teachers' lives. Studies on teachers' planning processes in the 1970s and early 80s showed that teachers are primarily focused on the "concretes" of the classroom: what they will teach, how they will teach it, the students in the classroom (Clark and Peterson 1986.) Aspects of planning which were not immediately tied to the here and now of the classroom, such as goals and objectives or how the class fit into the curriculum as a whole, were not in the foreground of their thinking. This doesn't mean that teachers don't have goals and objectives but rather that these are implicit in what they do rather than explicitly stated, or that they are a later part in the planning process. In my own planning, I tend to think in terms of content—the general areas of what I want to teach or students to learn—and to think about how to integrate those in the classroom. However, when I finally sit down to write goals and objectives, I am forced to be explicit about what I want students to get out of the course. Being explicit then keeps me accountable in the sense that the materials I develop and what I choose to teach need to fit with the goals and objectives. The goals and objectives also provide a map of what I need to assess.

One problem with goals and objectives is that what happens in the classroom is to a greater or lesser extent unpredictable, while goals seem fixed. Denise Lawson, whose beliefs about teaching an advanced writing course we saw in Chapter 3, puts it this way:

Denise Lawson

> Looking back over the process of designing this course, I realize that determining goals and objectives presented a real stumbling block for me. Although the idea of determining goals and objectives as a starting point made sense, I was reluctant to put mine on paper; it felt limiting, like a Tupperware container into which my course would have to fit.

Denise captures the tension between the organic nature of teaching and the way in which goals seem to constrain it, to force it into a "Tupperware container." I don't think that's a reason not to have goals. Goals provide guidelines and should be flexible enough to change, if they are not appropriate. There are two bigger obstacles to formulating goals and objectives. One is lack of time. Generally, the very full working days of teachers do not provide the planning time needed to formulate goals and objectives for their courses. The other is that people don't know how to formulate them. This chapter is meant to help you formulate goals and objectives for your course in a way that makes sense to you. In the chapter we will explore what goals and objectives are and the relationship between them as well as a variety of ways to formulate and articulate them.

A Tupperware container is a plastic container used to store food.

If you haven't had experience with formulating goals and objectives, you will probably go through a few drafts or need to put the first draft aside and come back to it once you have worked on other aspects of your course. The goals themselves or the wording may change. You will write them differently if you plan to give them to your students or if they provide a working document for you. You will be clearest about them after you have finished teaching the course! However, once you have learned the "discipline" of writing goals and objectives you will find that they will help you make decisions so that you can shape a coherent and satisfying course. Dylan Bate, a teacher who designed a course for university students in China, expresses this view in this way:

Dylan Bate

> Teaching is making choices. There are many worthy and precious things that can be done in the second language classroom, but they can't all be done. Choices must be made, and the only appropriate arbitrator in these decisions are the goals and purposes defined by the teacher for the specific course in its specific context. Once I realized this, the other parts of the puzzle either became irrelevant or quickly fell into place.

5.2 *What has been your experience with formulating goals and objectives? Do you feel more like Dylan Bate? More like Denise Lawson? Why?*

Frameworks

What Are Goals and Objectives and What Is Their Relationship?

Goals

Goals are a way of putting into words the main purposes and intended outcomes of your course. If we use the analogy of a journey, the destination is the goal; the journey is the course. The **objectives** are the different points you pass through on the journey to the destination. In most cases, the destination is composed of multiple goals which the course helps to weave together. Sometimes, teacher and students reach unexpected places. When you do veer "off course," it may be because you need to adjust your course for a more suitable destination for your students and so you must redefine and refine your goals. On the other hand, goals can help you stay on course, both as you design the course and as you teach it.

Stating your goals helps to bring into focus your visions and priorities for the course. They are general statements, but they are not vague. For example, the goal "Students will improve their writing" is vague. In contrast, "By the end of the course students will have become more aware of their writing in general and be able to identify the specific areas in which improvement is needed" while general, is not vague. It also suggests that there will be other goals which give more information about the ways in which students will improve their writing.

A goal states an aim that the course will explicitly address in some way. If, for example, one of the goals of a course is to help students develop learning strategies or interpersonal skills, then class time will be explicitly devoted to that goal. Because class time is limited, and the number of goals is not, choice is important. While you may be able to think of many laudable goals, they should address what can be realistically achieved within the constraints and resources of your course, i.e., who the students are, their level, the amount of time available, the materials available. They should be achievable within the time frame of the course with that group of students (see Figure 5.1).

See Chapter 2, page 16.

At the same time, goals are future oriented. In his book on curriculum design, J. D. Brown proposes that goals are "what the students should be able to do when they leave the program." (1995, p. 71). The following is an example of a goal from a writing course using computers which illustrates this point: "By the end of the course students will have developed the ability to use the computer for a variety of purposes." Finally, goals are the benchmarks of success for a course. The course can be deemed successful and effective if the goals have been reached. I suggest applying this "formula" to your goals: If we accomplish X goals, will the course be successful? This last question foreshadows the relationship between goals and assessment, which I will discuss later in the chapter.

Figure 5.1: **Making Choices about Goals**

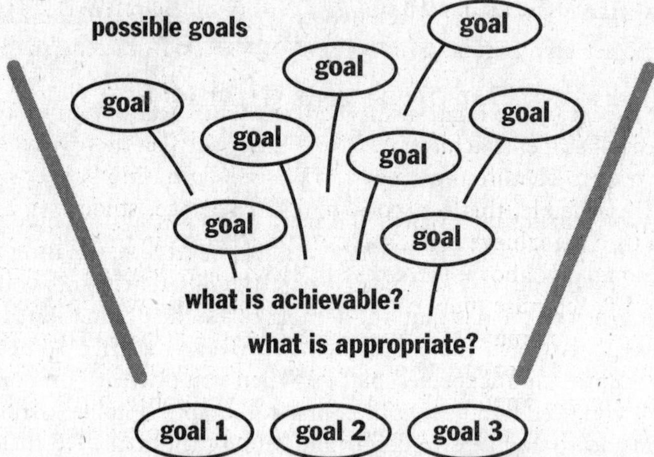

Objectives

Objectives are statements about how the goals will be achieved. Through objectives, a goal is broken down into learnable and teachable units. By achieving the objectives, the goal will be reached. For this reason, the objective must relate to the goal. For example, in a first pass at formulating goals for his course, one teacher stated one goal as, "Students will be able to interact comfortably with each other in English." One of the objectives he listed under that goal was for students to learn to tell stories. There is nothing wrong with students learning to tell stories, but telling stories generally does not require interaction, and so for this teacher's goal, learning to tell stories was not the most appropriate objective. The teacher asked himself, "Will achieving this objective help to reach the goal?" When he determined that the answer was no, he eliminated that objective and sought other, more appropriate objectives.

The following analogy was used by two teachers in an EFL reading class, Carolyn Layzer and Judy Sharkey, to help their students understand goals, objectives and strategies.

> I told the students that a friend wanted to lose 10 pounds that she had gained over the winter. I wrote, "I want to lose 10 pounds" on the left side of the board. Then I asked the students for some advice on how to achieve her goal. I wrote their responses on the right side of the board. Some of their advice was very general, for example, "exercise" and "don't eat junk food." I told them my friend's schedule was very busy and asked what kind of exercise she could do given her time constraints. This led to some more specific suggestions, for example, "She should always take the stairs instead of the elevator." Students could see that the more specific the advice, the easier it would be to follow it.

Showing how the suggestions could cause the effect of losing weight illustrates the relationship between goals and objectives: If I work out at the gym and stop eating junk food, then I am likely to achieve my goal of losing 10 pounds. My first objective is to set up a regular gym routine; My second objective is to stop eating junk food.

Thus another aspect of the relationship between goals and objectives is that of cause and effect. If students achieve A, B, C objectives, then they will reach Y goal. Figure 5.2 tries to capture the cause and effect relationship between goals and objectives. In principle, this is a good idea. In practice, students may not achieve the goal or may achieve other goals the teacher hadn't intended. Using the losing weight analogy above, the workout at the gym may improve muscle tone and density, and because muscle weighs more than fat, weight loss due to the reduction in junk food may be minimized. However, the person may end up feeling more energetic and not care about the weight loss anymore! On the other hand, if the goal remains important and is not achieved through the means or objectives described above, then the objectives may need to be examined and changed or refined so that the goal can be reached.

Figure 5.2: Cause and Effect Relationship between Goals and Objectives

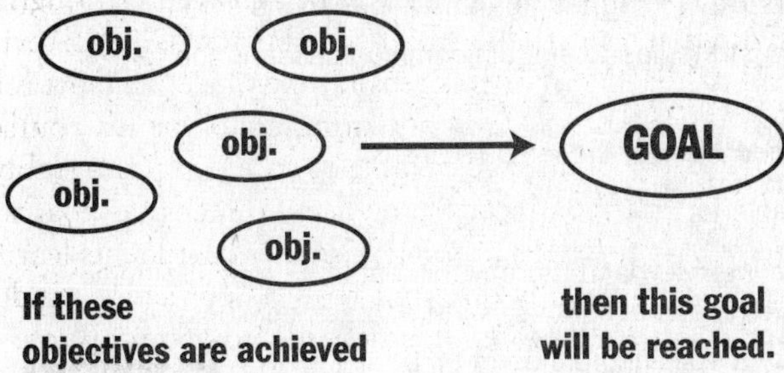

Objectives are in a hierarchical relationship to goals. Goals are more general and objectives more specific. Brown (1995) points out that one of the main differences between goals and objectives is their level of specificity. For every goal, there will be several objectives to help achieve it, as depicted in Figure 5.3. Goals are more long term, objectives more short term. To return to the weight loss analogy above, losing weight could be an objective if there is a larger goal, for example to improve one's overall health. Some teachers have found it helpful to have three layers of goals and objectives. The important point is that each layer is more and more specific.

Figure 5.3: For Every General Goal There Are Multiple Specific Objectives

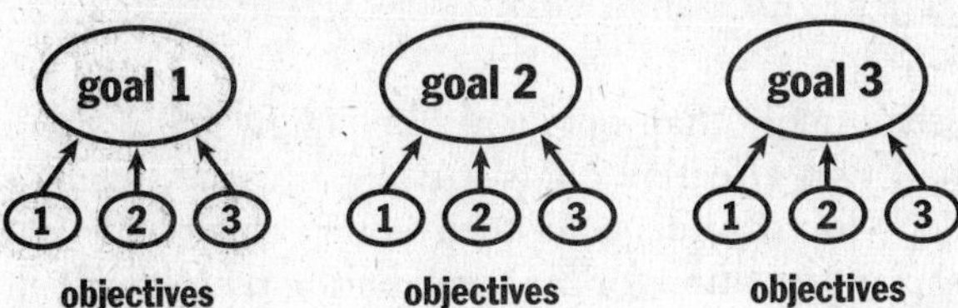

The Australian Language Levels guidelines have four layers for their goals and objectives. The goals, which provide direction for the teaching and learning, are written from the teacher's perspective. They are divided into broad goals, which are the general aims of the course, and specific goals, which break down the broad goals and make them more tangible. Objectives spell out what the students will actually learn or be able to do by the end of the course. General objectives spell out holistic results and specific objectives spell out particular knowledge or skills the students will acquire (Vale, Scarino, McKay 1996). The relationship among these four layers is depicted in the chart in Figure 5.4 below for a syllabus module on "Self and others" at the senior secondary level.

Figure 5.4: A Four-Part Scheme of Goals and Objectives From the Australian Language Levels

*One of five **broad goals** is "learning-how-to-learn":*

Learners will take a growing responsibility for the management of their own learning, so that they learn how to learn, and how to learn a language

*The **specific goals** are to enable learners to develop the:*

- cognitive processing skills to understand and express values, attitudes, and feelings; process information; think and respond creatively
- communication strategies to sustain communication in the target language.

*Some **general objectives** for these goals are:*

Learners will be able to:

- take part in an interview and thereby talk about self, family, home; make suggestions, ask questions; state and ask opinions;
- keep a diary for a specified period of time

*Some of the **specific objectives** for the general objectives are:*

Learners will be able to:

- generate questions
- state and ask opinions
- record information

5.3 *Study the relationship between the different levels of objectives and goals in Figure 5.4. Can you see how the specific objectives will help to achieve the general objectives? How the general objectives will help to achieve the specific goals? How the specific goals will help to achieve the broad goals?*

One objective may serve more than one goal; see Figure 5.5. For example, Denise Lawson had two affective goals for her advanced composition course: "Students will develop confidence in their ability to write in English." "Students will develop an appreciation for the contribution their knowledge and experience (and that of their peers) make to the learning process." These goals are served by the same objectives. Among them are: "Students will be able to document their strengths as writers, highlighting areas in which they can serve as 'teachers' to other students." "Students will be able to use assessment forms to evaluate their own and their peers' writing." "Students will be able to articulate how they can use feedback from their peers to improve their writing."

See Appendix 5-3, page 244, for Denise Lawson's complete set of goals and objectives.

Figure 5.5: One Objective Can Serve More than One Goal

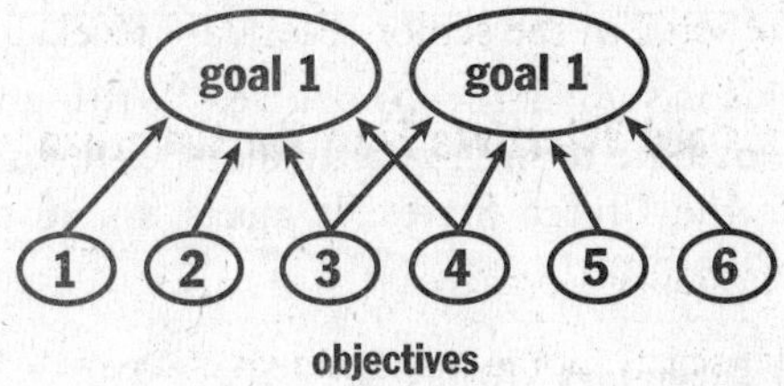

5.4 *Use the diagrams in figures 5.1, 5.2, 5.3 and 5.5 as a basis for summarizing the information about goals and objectives and the relationship between them.*

Formulating goals and objectives helps to build a clear vision of what you will teach. Because a goal is something toward which you will explicitly teach, stating goals helps to define priorities and to make choices. Clear goals help to make teaching purposeful because what you do in class is related to your overall purpose. Goals and objectives provide a basis for making choices about what to teach and how. Objectives serve as a bridge between needs and goals. Stating goals and objectives is a way of holding yourself accountable throughout the course. Goals are not a "wish list." For example, if one of your goals is for students to be able to identify areas of improvement in their writing, then you will need to design ways for students to evaluate their writing as well as ways to assess their effectiveness in identifying those areas they need to improve. Finally, a clear set of goals and objectives can provide the basis for your assessment plan.

What Are Ways to Formulate and Articulate Goals and Objectives?

Examples of goals

The goals and objectives you will read about below were written by the teachers for themselves to serve as a planning tool for their courses. When you write your own goals, you should keep in mind the audience for the goals. If it is your students, you will need to consider whether the language you use is accessible to them. Even if you alone are the audience for the goals and objectives, you should try to make them transparent enough for someone else to understand. Unpack the language to simplify and clarify it and also to find out if what you thought was one goal or objective is actually more than one.

5.5 *Study the two sets of goals for two writing courses below.*

1. What do you like about each set? What don't you like about each one? Why?
2. What do the goals tell you about each teacher's course? About their beliefs?
3. What are similarities and differences in the way the goals are stated?

The goals below are David Thomson's goals for his course, "Writing using computers." The course is for intermediate to high intermediate level students in an Intensive English program in the United States. It meets for 30 hours over 4 weeks.

David Thomson

See Appendix 5-1, page 239, for David Thomson's complete set of goals and objectives.

ACTFL is an acronym for American Council of Teachers of Foreign Languages.

Figure 5.6: Goals for a "Writing Using Computers" Course

Awareness

Goal 1. By the end of the course, students will have become more aware of their writing in general and be able to identify the specific areas in which improvement is needed.

Teacher

Goal 2. Throughout this course, the teacher will clearly communicate to students what his standards are for successful completion of tasks.

Goal 3. By the end of the course, the teacher will have developed a greater understanding of student needs and will make adjustments to ensure these needs can be met the next time he teaches the course.

Attitude

Goal 4. By the end of the course, students will have developed a positive attitude toward writing.

Skills

Goal 5. By the end of the course, students will have developed the ability to use the computer for a variety of purposes.

Goal 6. By the end of the course, students will improve their writing to the next level of the ACTFL Proficiency Guidelines Writing scale.

Knowledge

Goal 7. By the end of the course students will be able to understand the elements of and what constitutes "good writing"

Goal 8. By the end of the course, students will be able to understand the appropriateness of using computers for different writing and research purposes.

The following goals are for Denise Lawson's 10 week, 40 hour, Advanced Composition course in a university extension program in the United States.

Figure 5.7: Goals for an Advanced Composition Course

I. Proficiency

Students will develop effective writing skills transferable to any context.

II. Cognitive

Students will gain an awareness of the influence of sociocultural issues on their writing.

III. Affective

- Students will develop confidence in their ability to write in English.
- Students will develop an appreciation for the contribution their knowledge and experience (and that of their peers) makes to the learning process.

IV. Transfer

Students will gain an understanding of how they can continue to improve their writing skills.

Denise Lawson

See page 32 for her statement of beliefs.

David and Denise have organized their goals in different ways. David has used a framework which he calls "A TASK," which is derived from the KASA (knowledge, awareness, skill, attitude) framework, and Denise uses Stern's 1992 framework of cognitive goals, proficiency goals, affective goals, and transfer goals. I will explain those frameworks in more detail below. For some teachers, frameworks are helpful as a way of organizing their goals. For other teachers, the categories they have used to conceptualize content, for example, functional, topical, grammatical, tasks, reading, writing, affective, etc., provide the categories for the goals. Denise Maksail-Fine conceptualized the content for her high school Spanish course in the categories of speaking, listening, reading, writing, cross-cultural skills, and cooperative learning skills. These categories provide the basis for her goals below.

See page 83 for the KASA framework and pages 84–85 for Stern's framework.

See her mind map in Chapter 4, page 61.

5.6 *Study the goals for the Spanish 3 course below.*

1. What do you like about them? What don't you like about them? Why?
2. What do the goals tell you about the teacher's course? About her beliefs?
3. Compare them with the two sets of goals above. What are similarities and differences in the way the goals are stated?

These are Denise Maksail-Fine's goals for her year long high school Spanish 3 class:

Denise Maksail-Fine

See Appendix 5-2, page 242, for Denise Maksail-Fine's complete set of goals and objectives.

Figure 5.8: Goals for Spanish 3

Goal 1: Students will be able to utilize the skills of listening and speaking for the purposes of: socializing, providing and obtaining information, expressing personal feelings and opinions, persuading others to adopt a course of action, in the targeted topic* areas, by: (her objectives for this goal follow).

Goal 2: Students will be able to utilize the skills of reading and writing for the purposes of socializing, providing and obtaining information, expressing personal feelings and opinions, persuading others to adopt a course of action, in the targeted topic* areas, by: (her objectives for this goal follow).

Goal 3: Students will develop cross-cultural skills and understandings of perceptions, gestures, folklore, and family and community dynamics by: (her objectives for this goal follow).

Goal 4: Students will develop skills that enable them to work together cooperatively by: (her objectives for this goal follow).

**The targeted topic areas are: personal identification, house/home, services/ repairs, family life, community and neighborhood, physical environment, mealtaking, health/welfare, education, earning a living, leisure, public and private services, shopping, travel, current events.*

Formulating goals

The first step is to list all the possible goals you could have for your particular course, based on your conceptualization of content, your beliefs, and/or your assessment of students' needs (see Chapter 6). The list may be ragged, it may not be clear what is truly a goal or how to state it, and there may be repetition and overlap. Next steps are to look for redundancies, and to identify priorities based on your beliefs and your context. What is most important to you? What are the expectations of the institution, the students? Because all of these factors come into play, your goals will go through several drafts as you consider different aspects of the course and as you try to make the way you express them clearer.

5.7 *Make an initial list of goals for your course. Keep in mind the image of a destination with multiple aspects or the formula "The course will be successful if . . ."*

Once you have a list or map of your goals, how do you organize them into a coherent plan? One way to organize your goals is to use the **categories you have used for conceptualizing content,** as Denise Maksail-Fine did for her Spanish course. (You may want to look again at her mind map in Chapter 4.) These categories might include communicative functions, topics, grammar, tasks, reading, writing, interpersonal skills, etc. For example, if your course integrates the four skills of speaking, listening, reading, and writing, then you can have four major goals, each one related to a skill.

Teachers have also found that different conceptual frameworks can help them to organize their goals. I have worked with two. The first one is called **KASA,** which is an acronym for **knowledge, awareness, skills,** and **attitude.** The second one comes from H. H. Stern (1992) and includes **cognitive** goals, **proficiency** goals, **affective** goals and **transfer** goals. I will also introduce a third framework developed by Genesee and Upshur (1996).

The KASA framework was developed by the faculty in the Department of Language Teacher Education at the School for International Training, where I have taught for the last 16 years, and is used as a basis for our MA program goals. **Knowledge** goals address what students will know and understand. These goals include knowledge about language and about culture and society. **Awareness** goals address what students need to be aware of when learning a language. These include areas of self-knowledge, understanding of how the language works, and understanding of others' use of language, for example, becoming aware of the strategies they use as learners, or the importance of extralinguistic factors in communication. **Skills** goals address what students can do with the language. This is perhaps the broadest area, encompassing the four skills of speaking, listening, reading, and writing, as well as the functions and tasks one accomplishes through language. **Attitude** goals are those that address the affective and values-based dimension of learning: students' feelings toward themselves, toward others, and toward the target language and culture. These goals include respect, self-confidence, and valuing community. I have found that objectives related to attitudes depend a lot on the teacher's attitude and what the teacher does. For example, if a goal is to develop a positive attitude toward writing in a second language, then the teacher herself needs to develop an attitude that values writing, both her own and her students'.

Here is how the KASA framework might work for a teacher who is learning how to formulate goals and objectives.

> **Knowledge:** I know that goals are X, that objectives are Y, that one can state them in this way.
>
> **Awareness:** I never realized how useful it is to set goals and objectives. Now I do.

Knowledge is not particularly useful without awareness. You can take a test about how to formulate goals and objectives, but if the "penny hasn't dropped" about their usefulness, then the knowledge is useless. Having awareness and knowledge about goals and objectives is not sufficient however; one must also develop the skill through practice and use.

> **Skills:** After many attempts and reflection on those attempts, I know how to write goals and objectives.
>
> **Attitude:** Although it can be frustrating, I feel that I will get better at doing this, and that goals and objectives are essential to developing a coherent course.
>
> **OR** I feel that goals and objectives are mechanistic and a waste of time.

Clearly, the attitude expressed in the last sentence will make it difficult to achieve any of the above, which is one reason that I feel that affective/attitudinal goals are worth having.

As we saw above, David Thomson used the KASA framework to formulate the goals for a writing course using computers, but he added another layer, goals for the teacher, and turned the acronym around to read: ATASK. He writes:

David Thomson

> I have listed the goals and objectives under the headings A TASK (A [Awareness], T [Teacher], A [Attitude], S [Skills], and K [Knowledge]. I have called it this because a "task" to me connotes something done on an ongoing and as-needed basis. Tasks are done regularly and routinely and require modification and adaptation to fit the needs of the situation. I want my goals and objectives to have that same dynamic and flexible sense.
>
> Just having finished a teacher-training program has given me a new perspective on my role in the classroom. I want to, more appropriately need to, be accountable for my teaching, my actions, and my relationships with my students. Having goals and objectives written down (not in stone, of course) is one way for me to hold myself accountable and keep me focused on my responsibilities during the course.

David notes at the end of his list of goals and objectives:

David's goals and objectives can be found in Appendix 5-1 on page 239.

> These are the goals and objectives for the course. I still am not certain if the "knowledge" goals are appropriately labeled and belong under that heading, but that is a semantic issue I can attend to later. For now I feel they are broad enough to cover the areas I feel are the core to the course. I would feel comfortable starting off this class with them, especially knowing that they do not have to be "etched in stone."

David makes three points that are important to keep in mind. First, goals and objectives should reflect not only what you want your students to accomplish in the course, but also your beliefs. David has chosen to explicitly include goals related to his teaching because of his belief that he needs to be accountable for what he does. Your beliefs will be expressed differently; for example, you may feel that beliefs about teaching are implicit in other goals. Second, the purpose of goals is to give you a clear sense of what the course is about and where you are headed. How they are worded is something you can work on over time. Third, they are not "etched in stone" and can be changed if they do not work or can be modified to fit the reality of your course.

Stern (1992) has a similar framework for setting goals. He proposes the following categories:

> **Proficiency:** these include what students will be able to do with the language (e.g., mastery of skills, ability to carry out functions).

Cognitive: these goals include explicit knowledge, information, and conceptual learning about language (e.g., grammar and other systematic aspects of communication) and about culture (e.g., about rules of conduct, norms, values).

Affective: these include achieving positive attitudes toward the target language and culture as well as to one's own learning of them.

Transfer: these include learning how what one does or learns in the classroom can be transferred outside of the classroom in order to continue learning.

Denise Lawson used Stern's framework to organize the goals for her composition course. She writes the following:

Denise Lawson

> [My] goals and objectives are a direct expression of my teaching principles. As I have already mentioned, I have found formulating goals and objectives to be the most difficult part of the curriculum design process. After experimenting with different formats (including categories based on Knowledge, Attitudes, Skills, and Awareness), I decided to use Stern (1992). This format makes sense to me because it addresses four areas I want to emphasize: proficiency, cultural knowledge, students' attitudes, and learning strategies. I determined one goal each for Stern's Proficiency, Cognitive, and Transfer categories, and two for the Affective category. Five broad goals are appropriate and achievable for a forty-hour course.

See Chapter 3, page 32, for a list of Denise's principles.

A fourth way to organize goals is described by Fred Genesee and John Upshur in their book *Classroom-based Evaluation in Second Language Classrooms* (1996). Their framework includes:

Language goals: language skills learners are expected to acquire in the classroom

Strategic goals: strategies learners use to learn the language

Socioaffective goals: changes in learners' attitudes or social behaviors that result from classroom instruction

Philosophical goals: changes in values, attitudes and beliefs of a more general nature

Method or process goals: the activities learners will engage in

In their book, Genesee and Upshur focus on language goals, because they are concerned with what can be evaluated by teachers. They suggest that each goal or objective should focus on only one skill or area (e.g., reading or writing, not both) because objectives applicable to one may not be applicable to another, and students may attain one but not the other.

I have described four approaches to organizing goals: using your categories for conceptualizing content, using the KASA framework, using the Stern framework, and using the Genesee and Upshur framework. You may also choose to develop your own framework, which could combine elements of the above, and add in ones that are not included.

The three frameworks above all include affective goals of some sort. Not all teachers feel it is appropriate to state affective goals, even though they may be implicit in their teaching. Kay Alcorn shares this view as she writes about her approach to writing goals:

Kay Alcorn

> When I envisioned goals and objectives they looked similar to what I had seen in course syllabi created by past and present professors that detailed what we would learn, not the actual affective means by which we would do so. I have never seen goals that state "The students will develop a sense of community through x, y, and z." Nor have I seen objectives that declare "The students will take risks by means of process writing." When future administrators require course outlines along with goals and objectives, it is my sense that they won't expect me to include my teaching philosophy. Hopefully, through the interviewing process and departmental lines of communication they will come to know my teaching beliefs so that I will not need to perpetually restate them for every new course I embark on.

5.8 *Go back to your initial list of goals from Investigation 5.7 and organize them according to the framework you are most drawn to of the four suggested above: your categories for conceptualizing content, the KASA framework, the Stern framework, the Genesee and Upshur framework. You may also combine the aspects of each framework that appeal to you.*

Formulating Objectives

A classic work on formulating objectives is Robert Mager's 1962 book on performance objectives, written when behaviorism and stimulus-response theories of learning were still in vogue. Mager suggests that for an objective to be useful, it should contain three components: performance, condition, and criterion. Performance describes what the learners will be able to do, condition describes the circumstances in which the learners are able to something, and criterion, the degree to which they are able to do something. To these three components, Brown (1995) adds subject, who will be able to do something, and measure, "how the performance will be observed or tested." (p.89) For example, look at this objective from Brown and the five components below it.

> *Students at the Guangzhou English Language Center will be able to write missing elements on the appropriate lines in a graph, chart, or diagram from information provided in a 600-word 11th grade reading level general science passage.*
>
> **Subject:** students at the GELC
>
> **Performance:** write missing elements . . . in a graph, chart, or diagram from information provided in a . . . passage."

Conditions: on the appropriate lines . . . 600 word 11th grade reading level general science passage

Measure: to write the correct words (observable part of the objective)

Criterion: the criterion is 100%, all the missing elements

Figure 5.9: Brown's Components of Performance Objectives, Adapted from Mager

Subject: who will achieve the objective

Performance: what the subject will be able to do

Conditions: the way in which the subject will be able to perform

Measure: the way the performance will be observed or measured

Criterion: how well the subject will be able to perform

The above approach to objectives is both useful and problematic. I find it useful for a number of reasons. First, it proposes that objectives should communicate clearly what you want your students to achieve and it outlines how to make them clear. Second, the subject is stated in terms of those who will achieve the objective, in the case of a course, the students. Teachers often fall into the trap of writing objectives from the point of view of what *they* will do, not what their student will learn. Another value, as Brown points out, is that the more specific one can be, the more useful and comprehensible the objectives will be to others.

Third, the performance is stated in terms of something the students will be able to do. This is useful because it looks at learning as active, participatory, and outcome based. It heads off vagueness and lack of clarity. Brown provides an excellent list of performance verbs on page 88, drawn from Mager and adapted from Gronlund (1985). Mager contrasts vague verbs like "know," "appreciate," "understand," with precise verbs like "construct," "identify," "contrast."

I find the element of performance problematic because not all learning is observable, and much of what happens in learning is unpredictable. As Ron White points out in his excellent analysis of behavioral objectives, "If education is viewed as a voyage of discovery, the pre-specification of outcomes inherent in behavioral objectives may be seen as conflicting with the essential speculative nature of the education process." (1988, p. 30) He goes on to quote Skilbeck (p. 32):

> The implausibility of predicting detailed performances (when there can be unexpected outcomes) and the inherent freedom of the learner in an educative process are not reasons for supposing that we cannot or must not try to specify performance objectives. We can agree that students' performances (a) cannot or should not be pre-specified in detail and (b) are a part but not the whole of what we mean by education, but why should either of these considerations be inconsistent with stating objectives as the directions in which we are trying to guide student learnings?

Toward this end, Mager's list of verbs is helpful in focusing our thinking about areas of learning that are not measurable. For example, instead of saying "Students will appreciate the difference between their culture and the target culture," one can say "Students will be able to identify two differences between their culture and the target culture and explain how they feel about them."

In describing "criterion," one states the "quality or level of performance that will be considered acceptable" (Brown 1995, p. 23). This is useful because it helps to set standards and to hold oneself and one's students accountable. I find the criterion component the most problematic, however, for a number of reasons. It may be impractical for a teacher planning a course to take the time to figure out the degree of specificity for each objective, it may "box him in" prior to having met the students, and it may be unrealistic. One teacher who was designing a course for hotel employees formulated an objective in this way: "Students will be able to greet guests to the hotel with the correct use of time of day (good morning/afternoon/evening) and correctly respond to standard greetings ("How are you?" "Nice day" etc.) three times out of four." The teacher was trying to include a criterion by stating three times out of four; however, for the students this would be problematic because, even though they may reach the standard, they may fail at their jobs. What the students need is not to be able to get it right three times out of four, but to know what to do the fourth time when they don't get it right. An additional objective might be "Students will be able to use a variety of strategies for repairing breakdowns in communication."

5.9 *Choose one of the goals you wrote in Investigation 5.7 and write an objective for it in which you try to use the five components from the Performance objectives described in Figure 5.9. What was easy to write? What was difficult to write? Why?*

Iris Broudy writes about her experience trying to use Brown's framework as she formulates the objectives for her intermediate conversation course in Mexico.

Iris Broudy

See Chapter 4 for Broudy's insights in conceptualizing the content of her course.

> The issue of specificity has been rather problematic in writing objectives. Brown (1995) says that objectives should include not only performance (the students will be able to ...) but also conditions and criteria. In other words, I may have an objective that says that students will be able to use the hypothetical conditional, but under what circumstances? Written quiz? Controlled speaking? Free use? And by what standards? All the time? 90 percent? 50 percent?
>
> Brown helped me to focus on what is reasonable to cover in a twelve-week course and what degree of competence I might expect. Being specific about how performance will be measured forces the teacher to really pay attention to what is going on in class and to consider whether she is "teaching to the objectives." However, such specificity during the initial conceptualization of objectives may not be possible, or even appropriate. In fact, "too close a specificity can lead to suffocation of initiative and interest." (Yalden 1987, p. 105) Yes! It can suffocate the teacher, too. I felt locked in, writing such

> objectives as "Students will be able to give advice or warnings using appropriate modal forms with 80 percent accuracy in cloze exercises." How can I possibly determine such details before the course begins? I would just be guessing at criteria and conditions, pulling numbers out of the air.

My own view is that measure and criterion are probably more important when designing an assessment plan, once you have met the students and spent time teaching them. In other words, you might be much more specific about measure and criterion in designing a test or setting up an assessment task like a role play or written task, because you can tailor it to your students. Because objectives may be based on what you perceive to be the needs of the students, they are subject to change once you have actually met them. Additionally, you may want (and be able) to negotiate objectives with your students, in which case, having objectives too clearly specified in advance may make it difficult for you to give them up. Nevertheless, a clear set of objectives, even without the kind of detail in Figure 5.9, can be immensely helpful in designing an assessment plan since they provide a chart of what is to be learned and therefore a basis for what can be assessed.

Iris Broudy illustrates some of these points:

> Moreover, in establishing criteria, I see an important distinction between passive knowledge (getting it right on the exam) and true acquisition (producing a form consistently in free use). Toward which proficiency should the objectives be geared? Should there be a separate objective for each? And how do I take into account the fact that individual learners will be in different places in their interlanguage? Learning does not suddenly jump from point A to point Z, and that reality further complicates the task of establishing criteria when setting objectives.
>
> The main point here, I think, is that if my teaching is to be student-centered, if my course is to be fluid and flexible, then the goals and objectives must reflect that.

Denise Maksail-Fine, whose goals we saw on page 82, successfully used the way she conceptualized content as the framework for her goals and elements of the Mager/Brown formula as the framework for her objectives for her year-long high school Spanish 3 course. She writes:

Denise Maksail-Fine

> When it came to writing the goals and objectives for this course, I began by thoroughly reviewing the goals of each standard and their corresponding indicators as listed under Checkpoint B of the New York State LOTE (Languages other than English) Standards for Modern Languages. According to the standards, "Checkpoint B corresponds to the level of performance that all students should demonstrate in order to obtain a high school diploma." (page v).
>
> My first step was to adapt the goals listed under each standard so as to use them as some of the goals that form the basis of the Spanish 3 course. Then, I adapted the performance indicators for use as objectives for each goal where appropriate and practical.

My measure for what was appropriate and practical was twofold: a) whether or not I could realistically provide students with the resources and context essential for supporting them in working toward achieving that objective; b) given the constraints (temporal, linguistic, financial, etc.) of my context, whether or not I would be capable of measuring said objective. For example, I ended up omitting the wording "on the telephone" from objective 1.1 because I felt that I would not only be unable to measure students' comprehension in this way, but I could not, within regularly scheduled class time, provide students with opportunities for interaction using the telephone medium.

My next step was to reflect on ways in which my own approach to teaching had begun to shift and to formulate some of those changes into goals and objectives as well. Much of this change of thinking is reflected in Goals 3 and 4 and their accompanying objectives. For example, as reflected in Goal 4, I really want students to work much more cooperatively with each other than I have required them in the past. I felt strongly enough about this requirement to explicitly address it within the framework of the course. The objectives listed under Goal 4 illustrate my vision of what it means for students to work together cooperatively.

I faced a few different internal struggles as I compiled and refined the goals and objectives for this course. One of the first conflicts I faced was taking New York State's goals and objectives for my students and somehow investing something of myself in them in order to make them my own. I felt that without ownership of them, they were pretty much useless to me. This is because I have found that unless I am invested in something and I value it, I have a difficult time effectively teaching it.

I was able to derive some personal investment from the state's goals and objectives by modifying them to outline more clearly what I perceived as appropriate and practical for my students. This process of refinement also assisted me in reconciling my second internal conflict, which centered on whether or not the state's goals and objectives were realistic and appropriate given my teaching context.

See Denise Maksail-Fine's mind map in Chapter 4, page 61.

Another conflict I faced focused on how much to include in the goals and objectives (I wanted to include EVERYTHING) and to what degree of specificity. This has been an ongoing struggle throughout this entire curriculum design process. Being a perfectionist, I did not want to leave anything out, nor did I want to be too vague. Given the fact that this course spans an entire academic year (i.e., forty weeks), I really had to work to feel comfortable with leaving the minute details to the unit and lesson planning levels. As a final comment, I think that it is important to note that by working through the aforementioned struggles, I emerged and remain satisfied with the resulting course goals and objectives.

Below are the two New York State standards for Languages other than English (LOTE) and Denise's first goal and objectives. Her complete list of goals and objectives can be found in Appendix 5-2 on page 242.

Figure 5.10: The First Goal and Objectives for Spanish 3

NYS LOTE Standard 1: Students will be able to use a language other than English for communication.

NYS LOTE Standard 2: Students will develop cross-cultural skills and understandings.

Goal 1: Students will be able to utilize the skills of listening and speaking for the purposes of: socializing, providing and obtaining information, expressing personal feelings and opinions, persuading others to adopt a course of action, in the targeted topic areas, by:*

Objectives**
Students will be able to:

1.1. comprehend messages and short conversations when listening to peers, familiar adults, and providers of public services in face-to-face interactions

1.2 understand the main idea and some discrete information in television and radio or live presentations

1.3 initiate and sustain conversations, face-to-face, with native speakers or fluent individuals

1.4 select vocabulary appropriate to a range of topics, employing simple and complex sentences in present, past, or future time frames, and expressing details and nuances by using appropriate modifiers

1.5 exhibit spontaneity in their interactions, particularly when the topic is familiar, but often relying on familiar utterances.

targeted topic areas: personal identification, house/home, services/repairs, family life, community and neighborhood, physical environment, mealtaking, health/welfare, education, earning a living, leisure, public and private services, shopping, travel, current events.

***criterion: student-produced written work and spoken utterances must be of the level that they can be understood by a native speaker of the L2, who speaks no English, but is used to dealing with non-native L2 speakers and writers.*

5.10 *Take one of Maksail-Fine's objectives and analyze it according to the framework in Figure 5.9 on performance objectives. Which components are included? Which are not included? Do you feel that the objectives are clear as they stand? Would you modify them in any way? Why? What do you like about Maksail-Fine's approach to goals and objectives? What don't you like? Why?*

Another way to formulate objectives is to use a framework developed by Saphier and Gower (1987). Saphier and Gower's cumulative framework includes **coverage, activity, involvement, mastery,** and **generic** thinking objectives. **Coverage objectives** describe the material (textbook units, topics, curriculum items) to be covered in the course. They point out that, unfortunately, that is the way in which many teachers (and administrators) view a given course: it "covers" the material in Book 2, or the items on the curriculum list, irrespective of whether the students actually learn the material. **Activity objectives** describe what the students will do with the material. For example, fill out a worksheet or answer comprehension questions about a reading. **Involvement objectives** describe how the students will become engaged in working with the material. For example, make up their own comprehension questions about a reading and give to peers to answer. **Mastery objectives** (also called learning objectives) describe what the students will be able to do as a result of a given class or activity. For example, to use and describe two different reading strategies. **Generic thinking objectives** (which I also call critical thinking objectives) describe the meta-cognitive problem-solving skills the students will acquire. For example, to explain how they decide which reading strategies are appropriate for which texts.

Figure 5.11: Saphier and Gower's Cumulative Framework for Objectives

coverage: the material that will be covered in the unit, lesson

activity: what students will do in a unit, lesson

involvement: how students will become engaged in what they do in the unit, lesson

mastery: what students will be able to do as a result of the unit, lesson

generic thinking: how students will be able to problem solve or critique in the unit, lesson

Denise Lawson used the Stern categories for her goals and the Saphier and Gower framework for her objectives for her advanced composition course. She writes:

Denise Lawson

> The objectives are listed under the categories: Activity, Involvement, Mastery, and Critical Thinking. An additional category, "Coverage" suggested by Saphier and Gower, was not appropriate for my purposes here because it relates to material covered, such as chapters in a textbook. In place of a textbook I have prepared a diverse list of materials (including literature, films, and songs) that will be selected as writing prompts by the students; as a result, I do not have specific "Coverage" objectives.

Below are her first goal and the objectives. For the complete set of goals and objectives, consult Appendix 5-3 on page 244.

Figure 5.12: First Goal and Objectives for an Advanced Composition Course

I. Proficiency

Students will develop effective writing skills transferable to any context.

Activity

- Students will use a five-step process writing model to write three paragraphs: descriptive, personal narrative (memory), and expository; two essays; and a group research paper.

The five steps in the process: brainstorm, draft, revise, edit, publish.

- Students will use assessment forms to evaluate their own and their peers' writing.
- Students will annotate their reading and maintain reading logs.

Involvement

- Students will develop criteria for a well-written paragraph, essay, and short research paper.
- Students will work with peers to generate ideas, get feedback, and to write a research paper.

Mastery

- Students will be able to use the process writing model.
- Students will be able to assess writing (their own and others') based on criteria for good writing.

Critical thinking

- Students will be able to determine and articulate characteristics of a well-written paragraph, essay, and short research paper

---

Investigations

5.11 *What do you like about Denise Lawson's approach to goals and objectives? What don't you like? How would you adapt the approach? Why? What are the similarities and differences between Denise Lawson's and Denise Maksail-Fine's way of stating objectives?*

I'd like to conclude with both encouragement and caveats. Goals and objectives are not cast in cement. The image of cement alone conjures up something fixed and immovable, which are not good qualities of goals and objectives. They are an informed guess at what you hope to accomplish given what you know about your context, your students' needs, your beliefs about how people learn, and your experience with the particular content. As you teach the course, you will have the opportunity to test the goals and objectives and to modify and adapt them accordingly. Therefore, goals and objectives should be dynamic and flexible. If you are developing ones for a new course, they will probably become clearest once the course is over and you can look back at what you and your students were and were not able to do. You should be as complete in describing goals and objectives as you can, however, because they can provide a guide for the materials and assessment tools you develop. When I read over a teacher's goals and objectives, I have a clear idea of what the course is about, what the students will learn, and what is important to the teacher about what and how they will learn.

Below is a summary of guidelines to consider when formulating goals and objectives:

1. Goals should be general, but not vague.
2. Goals should be transparent. Don't use jargon.
3. A course is successful and effective if the goals have been reached. Try this "formula" for your goals: if we accomplish [goal], will the course be successful?
4. Goals should be realistic. They shouldn't be what you want to achieve, but what you can achieve. They should be achievable within the time frame of the course with that group of students.
5. Goals should be relatively simple. Unpack them and make them into more than one goal, if necessary.
6. Goals should be about something the course will explicitly address in some way. In other words, you will spend class time to achieve that goal.
7. Objectives should be more specific than goals. They are in a hierarchical relationship to goals.
8. Objectives should directly relate to the goals. Ask yourself: "Will achieving 'x' objective help to reach 'y' goal?"
9. Objectives and goals should be in a cause-effect relationship: "if objective, then goal."
10. Objectives should focus on what students will learn (e.g., students will be able to write a term paper) and/or processes associated with it (e.g., be able to make an outline), not simply on the activity (e.g., students will write a term paper).
11. Objectives are relatively short term. Goals are relatively long term.
12. There should be more objectives than goals. However, one objective may be related to more than one goal.
13. Don't try to pack too much into one objective. Limit each objective to a specific skill or language area.
14. The goals and objectives give a sense of the syllabus of the course. Objectives are like the building blocks of the syllabus.
15. A clear set of goals and objectives provides the basis for evaluation of the course (goals) and assessment of student learning (objectives).

16. Both goals and objectives should be stated in terms of the learner. You may, however, have specific, separate goals for yourself as a teacher.
17. Your course may have two or three layers of goals and objectives, each more specific, depending on the length and nature of your course. The point is for you to have a clear and purposeful vision of your course.

5.12 *Write up your goals and related objectives in a way that makes sense and is useful to you. After you have written them, consider how you could convey the information they contain in a memo or letter to your students.*

Suggested Readings

The literature on goals and objectives is not very teacher-friendly—goals and objectives are explained, but examples to illustrate them are sparse. The best and most comprehensive examples I've seen of how goals relate to objectives are in the Australian Language Level (ALL) Guidelines, which were developed for primary and secondary school teachers in Australia. *Pocket ALL* (1996) is a guide to how the guidelines can be used as a basis for developing a course and provides examples of goals and objectives within syllabus modules and "units of work" within those modules.

For more on performance-based objectives, see Brown's chapter on goals and objectives in his book, *The Elements of Language Curriculum* (1995). He presents the pros and cons of those types of objectives, although he clearly favors them. He also provides examples of goals and objectives developed for a program in China and a program in Hawaii.

Designing A Seventh-Grade Social Studies Course for ESL Students at an International School by Pat Fisher (1996) describes how she successfully grapples with the process of putting together goals and objectives for her course.

6

Assessing Needs

6.1 *In your experiences as a learner, have you ever been invited to express your learning needs? If no, why not? If yes, what was your reaction? What was the result?*

Jeri Manning's experience with needs assessment, which she describes below, is in many ways typical of teachers who are exploring how to work with it in systematic ways. Her description serves as a point of departure for the chapter, because she raises interesting issues about the hows, whats, and whens of needs assessment. She describes her experience during her teaching practicum.

Needs assessment is also called needs analysis.

Jeri Manning

> Prior to doing my MA, I had done needs assessment only on an informal level. My needs assessment was done through my own observations, and by asking students for oral input on what they would like to do in class. Because I taught the same students for a year or more, we had a level of trust that allowed them to give me honest feedback.
>
> In my MA courses, I learned more about needs assessment. During my internship at an intensive English program in Boston, I decided to try doing a couple of written needs assessments with my students. I observed my mentor's class during the month of January and taught my own class in February. One of the needs assessments that I adopted was one that my mentor had used. The curriculum for each level has so many items in it that no teacher could cover it all in one month. I gave the students a copy of the curriculum and asked them to mark the points they were most interested in learning. Then I tallied the answers, to give me a guideline of students' interests and perceived needs. One concern that I had, however, was that students would be overwhelmed by all the information on the sheet. However, this did not seem to be the case. I also did formal needs assessments that dealt with students' learning styles and knowledge of grammar.
>
> The needs assessments did give me useful information about my students, which helped me to shape the curriculum as the month progressed. There are points that I would change, however. First, I think it was a mistake to give three written forms of needs assessment in the first two days. It felt like too much paper coming at the students at once. In fact, I had one more needs assessment that I decided not to use. I felt torn, however, because students were only there for one month, and I wanted to be as responsive to them as

possible. If I had the course to do over, I would space the needs assessments out, relax, and rely on my observation skills more.

Another change that I would make would be to integrate needs assessment into the lesson plan, so that it becomes an integral part of the lesson, rather than an interruption in the flow. By doing that, I would hope that in addition to making the class flow smoothly, students would feel more willing to give honest feedback, especially given that a month is not a lot of time for students to learn that you really do want their *honest* feedback. Essentially, I want to develop needs assessments that will be an effective use of class time for students and give me the information I need to structure an effective course.

6.2 *Write a short description of your experience with needs assessment as a teacher. What have you assessed? Did you get the information you wanted? What did you do with the information? Was your experience similar to Jeri Manning's? Then consider the course you are designing, redesigning, or adapting as you read through this book (See Chapter 1, Investigation 1.4). What questions do you have about needs assessment with respect to the course? Use the questions to guide you as you read the chapter.*

Jeri Manning's narrative touches on four important areas that we will explore in this chapter. The first is the **role** of needs assessment in the development of a course. The second is the **areas of learning** needs assessment addresses. The third is **when** one should do needs assessment The fourth is **how** teachers can do needs assessment in ways that students understand, that are a good use of students' and the teacher's time, and that give the teacher information that allows him or her to be responsive to students' needs.

The Role of Needs Assessment in the Development of a Course

Essentially, needs assessment is a systematic and ongoing process of gathering information about students' needs and preferences, interpreting the information, and then making course decisions based on the interpretation in order to meet the needs. It is an orientation toward the teaching learning process which views it as a dialogue between people: between the teacher and administrators, parents, other teachers; between the teacher and learners; among the learners. It is based on the belief that learning is not simply a matter of learners absorbing pre-selected knowledge the teacher gives them, but is a process in which learners—and others—can and should participate. It assumes that needs are multi-faceted and changeable. When needs assessment is used as an ongoing part of teaching, it helps the learners to reflect on their learning, to identify their needs, and to gain a sense of ownership and control of their learning. It establishes learning as a dialogue between the teacher and the learners and among the learners.

Derica Griffiths expresses such a view of her needs assessment questionnaire for high school ESL students in a content-based history class:

> . . . I use this [questionnaire] to convey to the students that I do care about them as individuals, and they do have a role and voice in the class. I feel the questionnaire is my first attempt to facilitate them in the expression of their voice. This is important to me as a teacher because I feel that a class is a community and as such, should be inclusive of all voices and opinions.

Derica Griffiths

Seeing needs assessment as a form of dialogue is not the way I originally understood it. My first encounter with needs assessment as a formal undertaking was reading through Munby's 1978 book, *Communicative Syllabus Design*, in which he outlined numerous and detailed specifications for determining learners' needs. I was teaching English in Japan at the time, primarily to Japanese employees of a US-Japanese joint venture company. As a language teacher, I wondered how I would ever be able to get so much information, and if I could, what I would do with it. The lists and level of detail scared me off. In fact, had I known then what I know now about needs assessment, I believe I could have designed and taught a more focused and responsive course. Some years later, when I was writing the *East West* series, my co-author, David Rein, and I found the needs assessment inventories developed by the Council of Europe (Van Ek 1986) for planning language programs to be an extremely useful tool in conceptualizing and organizing the content of the series.

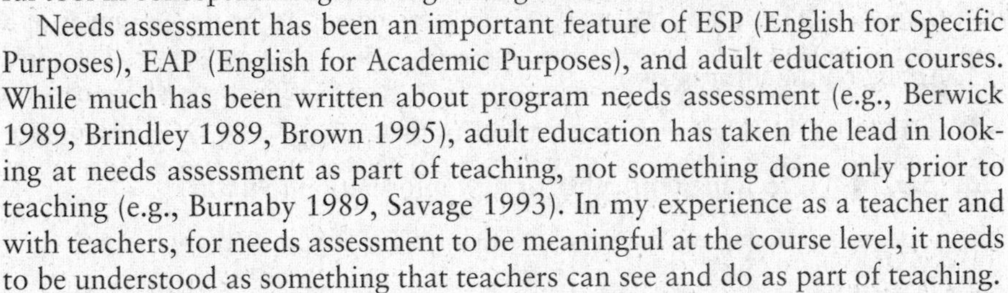

Needs assessment has been an important feature of ESP (English for Specific Purposes), EAP (English for Academic Purposes), and adult education courses. While much has been written about program needs assessment (e.g., Berwick 1989, Brindley 1989, Brown 1995), adult education has taken the lead in looking at needs assessment as part of teaching, not something done only prior to teaching (e.g., Burnaby 1989, Savage 1993). In my experience as a teacher and with teachers, for needs assessment to be meaningful at the course level, it needs to be understood as something that teachers can see and do as part of teaching.

I remember a conversation with a teacher from Honduras to whom I had given a copy of David Nunan's *Designing Tasks for the Communicative Classroom* (1989). She came to my office in a state of panic. She used her hands to describe her feeling that the ground was shifting under her feet and she could no longer maintain her balance. The book suggested that she invite learners to give input into the design of activities, and she didn't see how this was possible or even a good idea. She mainly taught pre-teens and teenagers, so she had a point. But the conversation was really about a shift in her perception of the role of the learners and the teacher in the classroom. I think that needs assessment, as I have described it above, is one place in the development of a course in which a teacher must examine how she or he views the roles and power dynamic in the classroom.

The teacher is not the only person who has views about the roles and power dynamic in the classroom or the needs of the learners. The students themselves will have expectations that may *not* include being asked to express their needs or to be partners in decision making. In fact, they may see it as clearly the teacher's role to make decisions about what to teach. If partnership and dialogue are at the root of one's view of needs assessment, then it must be done in such a way that students feel skillful in participating and see the value of it, both while doing it and in the results. Likewise, teachers need to learn how to feel skillful in conducting and responding to needs assessment.

What can happen in the classroom is also affected and determined by the institution the class is a part of, and by other stakeholders, such as parents and funders, depending on the setting. Needs assessment can be as much about reconciling different views as about finding out what the needs are. Berwick, for example, makes a distinction between "felt needs," those the learners have, and "perceived needs," the way the needs are viewed by the teacher, the institution and other stakeholders (1989, p. 55). Even when needs assessment only involves the teacher and learners it is still a complex undertaking because different learners within the same class usually have somewhat different needs.

The Process of Needs Assessment

The process of needs assessment involves a set of decisions, actions, and reflections, that are cyclical in nature:

1. Deciding what information to gather and why
2. Deciding the best way to gather it: when, how and from whom
3. Gathering the information
3. Interpreting the information
4. Acting on the information
5. Evaluating the effect and effectiveness of the action
6. (back to 1) Deciding on further or new information to gather

This process can be viewed as a cycle as depicted in Figure 6.1.

Figure 6.1: The Needs Assessment Cycle

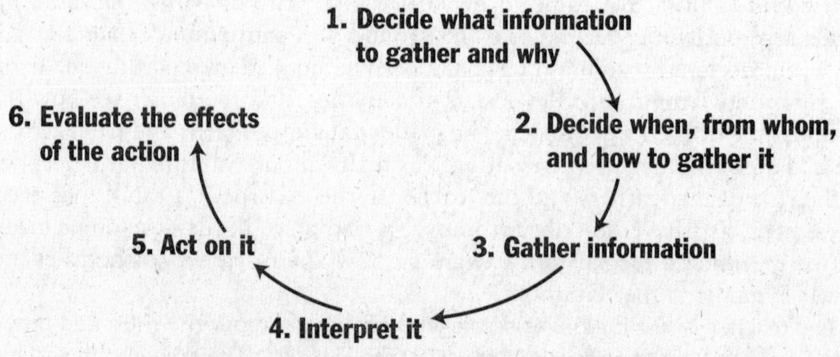

The view of needs assessment as a process of gathering information and interpreting it is very close to Kathi Bailey's definition of assessment in her book in this series, *Learning About Language Assessment* (1998, p.2). She writes, "The main purpose of language assessment is to help us gain the information we need about our students' abilities and to do so in a manner that is appropriate, consistent, and conducive to learning." Needs assessment and language assessment overlap when needs assessment is concerned with assessment of language ability, as in assessing proficiency at the start of a course, or when diagnosing language needs as part of ongoing needs assessment. Needs assessment also overlaps with course evaluation when it gathers information about how the way the course has been designed and is being conducted is or is not meeting the needs of the students so that unmet needs can be addressed. In Chapter 10, we will focus on designing an overall assessment plan for the course, which includes needs assessment, assessment of learning, and course evaluation.

What Areas of Learning Does Needs Assessment Address?

In the cycle in Figure 6.1, the first step is deciding what information to gather. When designing and teaching a course to meet students' needs, we assume that there is a gap to be bridged between a current state and a desired one, or progress to be made toward a desired goal, or a change to be made. The purpose of the course is to bridge the gap or some part of it, to help students make progress or to effect the desired change. For a course to meet learners' needs it is necessary to gather information about both the current state of the learners, where they stand in terms of language ability, learning preferences, and the desired goals or change, and where they would like to be or what they want to achieve, change, and so on. The cycle in Figure 6.1 can be repeated throughout the course at various times, depending on what you—and the learners—want to know. Figure 6.2 below shows the relationship between the purpose of a course and the purpose of needs assessment.

Figure 6.2: Basic Purpose of Needs Assessment

Purpose of course:

learners' abilities, attitudes, preferences before course ------- **to make progress toward** ------→ **desired abilities /change outcome**

Purpose of needs assessment:

to gather information about ← → **to gather information about**

in order to make decisions about what will be taught, how it will be taught, and how it will be evaluated.

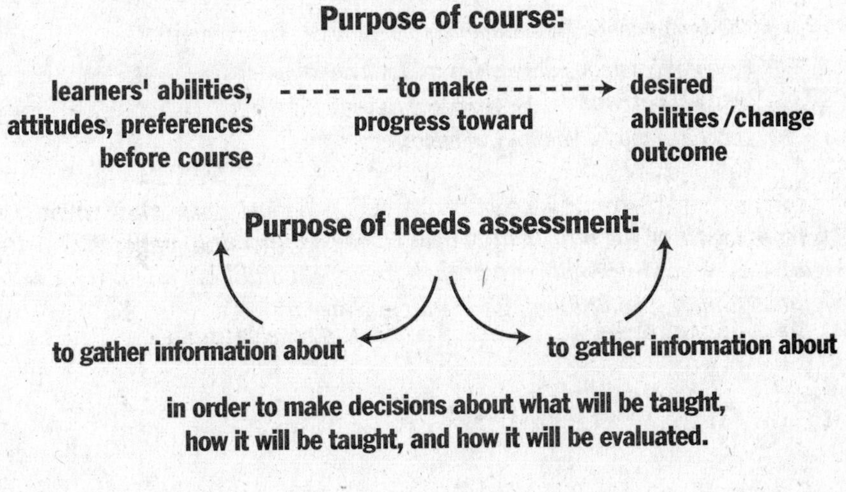

6.3 *What information could you gather about your learners prior to or at the beginning of the course? What information could you gather about the desired learning or improvement the course is supposed to bring about? Who can you gather the information from?*

The list below (Figure 6.3) outlines information that can be gathered for the left side of the chart in Figure 6.2, learners' abilities, attitudes, and preferences now; and the right side of the chart, desired abilities and/or change. Numbers 1 through 6 are a list of what learners bring to a course or program. Numbers 7 through 10 are a list of where they would like to be or what they want to make progress toward. As the course progresses, the information about the "present" will change as the learners make progress toward the "future." Information can be gathered about how the course is or is not meeting the needs negotiated, both in what is being taught and how it is being taught. Needs related to the "future" may also change as the course progresses.

Figure 6.3: Types of Information that Can Be Gathered when Assessing Needs

We can gather information about:

The present:

1. *Who the learners are*
2. *The learners' level of language proficiency*
3. *The learners' level of intercultural competence*
4. *Their interests*
5. *Their learning preferences*
6. *Their attitudes*

The future:

7. *The learners' [or others involved] goals and expectations*
8. *The target contexts: situations, roles, topics, and content*
9. *Types of communicative skills they will need and tasks they will perform.*
10. *Language modalities they will use*

6.4 *Before reading the information below, take a moment to look over the list in Figure 6.3. What information will each item yield and how might it be helpful in understanding and planning for students' needs?*

After reading about each type of information, make a preliminary list of the information you feel you would like to gather for the course you are designing.

Frameworks

Information about the present

1. Who the learners are

What is their age, gender, educational background, profession, nationality? Is it a multicultural or single culture group? What languages do they speak?

This information can help provide the background for the remaining questions; for example, we will ask for or interpret information differently if the students are children or adults, literate in their first language or not, of mixed nationality or of one nationality.

2. The learners' level of language proficiency

What is their level of proficiency in each of the four skills in the target language—speaking, listening, reading, writing? With respect to grammar, vocabulary, pronunciation, functional skills? Are they literate in their own language?

This information can help to make choices about the kinds of texts to use, which skills to develop, which elements of grammar to emphasize and so on.

3. The learners' level of intercultural competence

What is their experience in the target or in other cultures? What is their level of understanding and skills with respect to sociocultural and sociolinguistic aspects of the target language and differences with their own language?

This information can help to make choices about the kind of material to use, and the sociolinguistic and sociocultural skills to develop and emphasize.

4. Their interests

What topics or issues are they interested in? What kinds of personal and professional experience do they bring?

This information can help teachers to gear the course toward students' experience and interests. In the absence of specific target needs (see #8 and #9 below), it can help teachers design the course around topics that will engage the learners.

5. Their learning preferences

How do the learners expect to be taught and tested? How do they prefer to learn? How well do they work in groups? What role do they expect the teacher to take? What roles do they expect to take?

This information can help teachers to know whether the learners will be comfortable with certain kinds of activities, or will need to be taught how to do them; for example, how to work cooperatively with each other. It will help to know how to set up activities, or what kinds of bridges will need to be built between students' expectations of how they should learn and the teacher's approach and beliefs.

6. Their attitudes

What is their attitude toward themselves as learners? What is their attitude toward the target language and culture?

This information can help teachers to know whether the learners feel confident about using the target language, are comfortable with making mistakes, feel positive about being in the classroom.

Information about what the learners need to learn, want to change

7. The learners' [or others' involved] goals and expectations

Why are they taking the course? What are their goals? What do they expect to learn?

This information can help to shape goals and also to alert learners to what is realistic within the constraints of the course.

8. The target contexts: situations, roles, topics, and content

In what situations will they use English beyond the classroom? Who will they use English with? What topics will they need to be able to communicate about or what content will they need to know? For example, if they are university students, will they be in lectures, seminars, dormitories? If they are business people, with whom will they transact business and about what? If they are immigrants, where and with whom will they use the target language?

9. Types of communicative skills they need and tasks they will perform

For what purposes are they using the language? Will they need to understand and give directions? Will they need to give and get information on the telephone? Will they be listening to lectures? Will they need to persuade clients? Will they be talking to their children's teachers?

10. Language modalities they will use

Do they need to speak, read, listen, and/or write in the target language?

The areas outlined above will yield both **objective information** about the students and **subjective information** (Brindley 1989, Nunan 1988). Objective information includes facts about who the learners are, their language ability, and what they need the language for. Subjective information includes attitudes and expectations the learners have with respect to what and how they will learn. Subjective information is important because if you don't take it into account, the objective information may be useless. For example, if your learners are expecting you to stand at the front of the class and answer their questions, and you put them in small groups and ask them to find their own answers, they may feel very uncomfortable in your classroom and unable or unwilling to learn in that way—at least initially—regardless of how appropriate the content is. Or, if your students have expectations that they will make a vast improvement in a short period of time, and your course has more modest goals, you will need to help them reach more realistic expectations.

6.5 *In the list of kinds of information that can be gathered outlined in Figure 6.3, which numbers will yield information about objective needs and which about subjective needs? How might each type of information help you?*

You will not necessarily be able to get all the information listed above. In an EFL setting there are often no clear-cut needs for using English outside of the classroom for a given group of students, and so the teacher cannot base the course on needs that don't exist. In that case, I feel it is crucial to find out about their interests and backgrounds and to build the syllabus around that information, so that they will be engaged. When I was first in Japan, I taught a group of housewives for whom the study of English was a hobby. They did not have plans to use English outside of the room in which we met. I tried to assess their proficiency so that I could gear the lesson to their level, and find out what their interests were so that they would have something to talk about. The situation was quite different when, recently, I taught a group of adult immigrants in my town. We readily came up with a list of immediate target contexts and communicative needs for their English: how to use the bank, how to interact in a parent-teacher conference, how to talk on the telephone, how to read the store flyers with information about sales, how to engage in small talk on the bus to class.

Another distinction I have found useful is between **target needs**—what students need to learn and for what purposes, and **learning needs**—how they expect to learn, what motivates them as learners (Hutchinson and Waters 1986). These areas need to be in harmony so that the ways the students are asked to learn keep them sufficiently engaged so that they can learn what it is they are supposed to learn. This is as true in an ESL setting as in an EFL setting. In the class of adult immigrants I mentioned above, they told me that they wanted to learn about how the English language was structured. My initial reaction was that they were basing this need on their previous schooling, which had emphasized learning the rules of grammar, and that more work on those rules would not help them improve their actual output, their spoken and written English, which I perceived as their primary need. They viewed their target needs as structure-based. I viewed their target needs as task-, skills- and participation-based—practice with using the telephone or understanding how to participate in a parent-teacher conference. However, the same grammatical errors kept recurring. I started having them reflect on examples of the language they generated to derive their own rules. For the first time, the way the language worked made sense to them. I realized the key was to figure out what their learning needs were (to understand how the language "works"), so that they could meet their target needs.

The list in Figure 6.3 is designed to help teachers see the choices they have in determining which information to gather. You cannot assess everything all at once—trying to do so provides too much data and can be overwhelming for the students and for the teacher—and so it is important to make choices about what to assess.

Some Factors that Can Guide Your Choices

The purpose of the course. It is important to gather information that is relevant to the purpose(s) of the course. An assessment of students' writing skills would not be a priority in a course whose purpose was to improve their oral skills. If you know that students don't have immediate needs for the L2 outside of the classroom, as was the case with the Japanese housewives I taught, then assessing the target contexts could be confusing to them. One teacher, Kay Alcorn, describes how she changed the focus of her needs assessment because she realized it would not give her information pertinent to the course she was teaching. Her course was for Mexican students studying English for the tourism industry. In her original needs assessment she had listed such questions as "What past experience has taught you an important life lesson? What did it teach you?" "Describe your favorite place. What do you do there? How does it make you feel?" and "Who do you admire? Why? Would you like to be more like this person?"

She writes:

Kay Alcorn

> The questions that I formulated were intended to be on a handout which students could draw from all semester and answer in their dialogue journal. I intended to introduce it approximately 3 weeks into the semester once students were comfortable communicating with me. After much reflection I realized that what I was after was self serving and really had no relation to teaching English for the tourism industry. I realized I needed to find ways to know my students better through other means that were much more pertinent to the subject matter and goals for the course.

Your beliefs. For example, if you believe that language is learned through interaction, then you will probably want to assess students' learning styles and attitudes in order to know how skilled or disposed they are to working in groups.

Information you already have about the students. For example, students may have already provided a writing sample for a placement test or you may already have information about the target contexts and communicative skills they will need. In such cases, you don't need to reinvent the wheel unless you need more specific information about the type of writing they can do or about the types of writing they need to learn.

Finally, you should only gather information that **you know you can use.** I have seen teachers get excited about the idea that needs assessment can help them learn about their students' needs and tailor the course to those needs. They then try to get too much information in too short a time and are overwhelmed with the data and unsure of what to do with it. For that reason, it makes sense to choose only a few types of information initially and to learn how to use it effectively so that your students see the value in it. This will help you to build the trust that Jeri Manning mentions at the beginning of the chapter.

Below, we will look at two different needs assessment plans, one for a writing course and one for an adult education course. Each teacher made different choices about what to assess based on who the students were, the type of course, and her or his beliefs. The first is Denise Lawson's needs assessment plan for her advanced composition class at a university extension program in the United States.

6.6 *Which of the ten areas in Figure 6.3 did Denise choose to focus on? What appeals to you about Denise's needs assessment plan? What doesn't appeal to you? Why?*

Figure 6.4: Denise Lawson's Needs Assessment Plan for Advanced Composition Course

Denise Lawson

See page 32 for a list of Denise's principles and page 244 for her goals and objectives.

1. Letter to students

I will introduce the importance of feedback in my introductory letter. (See the letter in Appendix 6-1 on page 247.)

2. Writing case history

As the homework assignment for the first day of class, students will write "case histories" of their experiences, writing in their native language and in English. This exercise raises students' awareness about the affective domain in regard to writing, and how their progress might be influenced by their attitudes and prior experiences. It establishes a baseline against which students can measure any changes in attitude throughout the course.

3. Personal goals and objectives

Students will set three to five goals for the course and track their progress in a daybook.

4. Questionnaires: initial, midterm, final

- Initial: In the first week, students will answer short survey questions about possible goals for the course to prepare them to write their own goals and objectives.
- Midterm: The midterm questionnaire prompts students to reflect on progress toward meeting their course goals.
- Final: Students assess their progress toward reaching their goals, and the usefulness of various aspects of the course (materials, activities, teacher feedback, etc.) in helping them reach them.

5. Anonymous feedback cards

In order to encourage students to respond honestly, it is important to include opportunities to provide anonymous feedback. Students unaccustomed to criticizing teachers may feel more comfortable commenting on unsigned cards. In my experience, asking students to answer a few questions on index cards is a quick, easy, and non-threatening way to check in with students on how the class is going.

6. In-class discussions

It is also important to have in-class discussions regarding students' responses to the course. It provides students the opportunity to hear their peers' views; in addition, the popcorn quality of dialogue may generate some new ideas.

7. Student-teacher conferences

As a student, I benefited enormously from teacher-student conferences and, as much as possible, would like to make them a part of my teaching as well. I plan to dedicate half of two midterm classes to one-on-one conferences during class, with the emphasis on students' progress toward their goals. I would offer an optional follow-up conference shortly before the end of the course.

Denise has devised a plan that spans the course, not just the beginning of the course, so that she can fine-tune and adjust the course as she teaches it. In this way, it is part of her overall assessment plan. The student goal setting is an important part of the course. In effect, students are individually defining their needs by setting the goals for their writing. Having students set goals is one way for them to define their needs. One problem is that students may never have done this before and will not know how to do it. Chris Conley, whose needs assessment plan follows, told me that when he introduced a goal-setting exercise the first time he taught an adult education class, the students didn't know what "goal" meant. Even when he explained its meaning, they were not sure how they could answer it. For this reason, students need to be given support and guidance in how to set goals.

See Chapter 10 about designing an assessment plan.

See Gorsuch (1991) "Helping Students Create Their Own Learning Goals."

Denise will also need to let students know whether the goals the students have set are realistic within the context of the course. An important aspect of needs assessment is what you do with expectations that you know cannot be met because they are unrealistic, because there are too many, because there is not enough time in the course, or because the course is focused on something different. Teachers have three choices in responding to students' expressions of expectations or needs. One is to act on them. Another is not to act on them, but to let students know why. (If you do not explain why you are not acting on them, students will assume you are ignoring what they have said and will not see the value in letting you know their expectations.) A third is to think about how to include them in your course at a later date. Again, it is important to let students know that you are planning to act on the information at a later time. Each response treats the input as valuable and part of an ongoing dialogue with the students.

The second needs assessment plan is one Chris Conley designed for his adult education course for immigrants in the United States. The students are from a variety of countries and are at an intermediate level of proficiency in English.

6.7 *Which of the ten areas in Figure 6.3 did Chris choose to focus on? What appeals to you about Chris's needs assessment plan? What doesn't appeal to you? Why?*

Figure 6.5: Chris Conley's Needs Assessment Plan for Adult Education Class

Chris Conley

1. "Find someone who . . ."

In this activity students develop questions to ask each other and find people in the class who answer "yes" to the questions. This activity can assess students' linguistic abilities re forming questions, asking and answering them orally, and also assess their pronunciation. I can learn something about their learning styles in how they work in pairs to create questions, how they feel about creating their own questions, and how comfortable they are mingling with the whole class to find people to answer the questions. (See Appendix 6-2 on page 249) for the activity.)

2. Letter of Explanation

This letter explains what we will be doing in the course, my initial expectations, student/teacher roles, and a description of the approach. (See Appendix 6-3 on page 250 for the letter.)

See Chris's flow charts on pages 67–69.

3. Mind-mapping

I give a word that is somewhat loaded like "class," "teacher," "student," "home," "food," "America," and have them do a group mind map around the word. I can assess students' capacity to generate words, their vocabulary, and the freedom or lack of freedom they feel in speaking out in class. I can also turn this mind-map into a discussion or writing exercise in order to assess spoken or written abilities.

4. Paragraph about self

The students and I write a paragraph about ourselves to share with the class.

5. Participatory cycle

The cycle is a form of ongoing needs assessment because it is based on students' needs. The teacher listens for issues the students face, an issue is addressed, teacher and student negotiate their language needs with respect to the issue as well as how to resolve it (or not) through action of some kind.

See pages 143–144 for an explanation of the cycle.

6.8 *Look over the initial list you made in Investigation 6.4. Given the purpose of the course you are designing, your beliefs about what is important, what you already know about your students, and what you feel you will be able to act on, modify the list to reflect the information you wish to gather.*

The information described in the categories in Figure 6.3 can be gathered within the context of the classroom, but is also affected by the larger framework of the institution and community in which the course is being taught. As pointed out earlier, needs assessment is a process of reconciling competing needs and views of what should be taught and how. Students within a class may have different needs, the teacher's view of what needs to be learned and how may not match the students' expectations, the institution's view of what needs to be learned may be at odds with the teacher's. Reconciling these views necessitates finding out what they are, as well as finding ways to communicate and bridge differences.

Sarah Benesch (1996) has challenged the assumption that when assessing target needs for EAP or ESP courses, the context in which English will be used is a given. Such a view presumes that the point of needs assessment is to get information about the context so that one can prepare the student for it. She advocates what she calls "Critical Needs Analysis." She illustrates critical needs analysis with an example from her teaching. She taught an adjunct ESL course for students taking a university psychology course. Rather than accept the way the psychology course was conducted as a given, she analyzed the limitations of the target situation, and identified three: The course was held in a huge lecture hall and students felt unable to interrupt the lecturer in order to ask questions or seek clarification. The amount of material covered was unmanageable for the students. The tests were multiple choice. Benesch contacted the professor and was able to bring about two changes. He agreed to answer written questions, which students prepared collaboratively after a lecture, at the beginning of the following lecture. He also visited their ESL class to discuss their questions in a more informal setting conducive to real dialogue.

The participatory process that Chris Conley outlines also assumes that students should not necessarily accept the status quo of the target situation but work together to figure out ways to make it work for them.

6.9 *Who are the stakeholders in your course? Who, other than the students, can or should you consult with respect to your students' needs? Do you anticipate areas of conflict? How can they be resolved?*

When Should One Do Needs Assessment?

There are three time frames for gathering information: **pre-course, initial,** and **ongoing.** They are complementary, not exclusive.

Pre-course needs assessment takes place prior to the start of the course and can inform decisions about content, goals and objectives, activities, and choice of materials. Generally, assessment activities that determine placement are done at the program level so that students can be placed in the right course at the right level. Pre-course needs assessment activities may be diagnostic and help to pinpoint specific areas of strengths and weaknesses and thus help to determine what needs to be addressed in a given course. They may gather information about learners' target needs and thus help determine the content of the course, which language items, skills, etc. will be taught; as well as which materials and texts should be used. They may gather information about students' learning needs and thus help determine what kinds of activities will be used. Teachers who are able to gather information prior to teaching a course can use it to plan the course so that it is responsive to students' needs right from the first day of class. In many cases, however, teachers do not meet their students prior to teaching them, and so must rely on initial and ongoing needs assessment to allow them to be responsive to their learners' needs.

Initial needs assessment takes place during the initial stage of a course, the first few sessions, the first week or weeks, depending on the time frame of the course. The kinds of information gathered prior to teaching a course can also be gathered during the first few class sessions.

Ongoing needs assessment takes place throughout the course. One advantage of ongoing needs assessment is that it is grounded in shared experiences and thus can be focused on changing the course as it progresses. It helps to determine whether what is being taught, how it is being taught, and how it is being evaluated, are effective for the students. You may need to change or adjust the content, the materials, and the objectives, depending on what you find out in ongoing needs assessment. Students are asked to reflect on something they have done, and to base their assessment and suggestions on these concrete experiences. For example, questions about how students learn may be easier to answer once they have a variety of learning experiences to reflect on. In order for ongoing assessment to work, however, it must be geared toward those aspects of teaching you can change. An advantage of both initial and ongoing needs assessment is that they are done once the class has started and so you can do both a **direct** needs assessment, in which the focus of the activity is on gathering specific information, or an **indirect** needs assessment, in which a "regular" teaching activity is given a needs analysis focus. Or you can do an **informal** needs assessment, in which you simply observe—but carefully and conscientiously—the students.

6.10 *Is it feasible for you to gather pre-course information? Using your list from Investigation 6.8 do a mind map of the types of information you can envision getting in pre-course, initial and ongoing needs assessment .*

Ways of Doing Needs Assessment

At the beginning of the chapter I raised the following question about the "how" of needs assessment: How can teachers do needs assessment in ways that students understand, that are a good use of students' and the teacher's time, and that give teachers information that allows them to be responsive to students' needs? John Kongsvik describes his dilemmas with these questions in his experience with initial needs assessment for a course for beginners at the University of Queretaro in Mexico:

John Kongsvik

> Before teaching at the University of Queretaro, I planned the initial needs assessment I would use at the beginning of the course. I knew the length of the course was short, 30 hours, and wanted to get as much information about each participant as quickly as I could. I decided to split the assessment into three sections: a written questionnaire, an oral interview, and a class activity.
>
> My primary purpose in using the questionnaire was to get some background information on each of the students. I questioned whether to write it in English or both English and Spanish. I opted for the former, concluding that the students could help one another if needed.
>
> I also asked them to write as much as they could in English about the following: What did you do today? What are you going to do this weekend? I explained this process to the entire student body and then began interviewing students one by one.
>
> I knew that I could not spend a large amount of time speaking to each student and decided that three minutes would be ample. I used a grid to record the results of the interview. After all the interviews were completed, we began the final activity.

We performed an activity using introductions that had them work individually as well as in groups. This, I thought, would give me an idea of both the proficiency level of each student as well as the group dynamics. The class ended just as we finished, and as the students walked out the door, I reflected on what had happened.

The questionnaires, I noted, were of little value. Most of the questions had not been answered and the ones that were, offered one or two word responses. Even though I saw students explaining the task to others, the information sought was absent. Should it have been in Spanish and English? After all, with the exception of two short answer questions, I was interested in getting background information on them. Should I have explained it better or gone over it with them, making that into a lesson in and of itself? What kind of feelings did I evoke by shoving a questionnaire in each student's face the second they entered the classroom? Furthermore, my oral interviews had been constantly interrupted by new arrivals and questions from confused students.

The second part of the assessment was particularly fruitful. Within a minute, I was able to get a feel for each individual's level. Unfortunately, it was difficult to record specifics about each person, and, after sixteen interviews, I could scarcely remember all that I wanted. I realized I should have recorded it on video or audio. It would have served as a better assessment tool and could have been used to check progress throughout the course. I'm not sure how that would have affected student performance, but I'm sure I could have explained its purpose well enough to assuage negative feelings.

The final part was perhaps the most successful. With an even greater ease, I could discern who had no or little English and who had had prior instruction. I also could see how each participant interacted in small and large group settings. It was also the most satisfying and comfortable activity we did that day. It made me think of how I could use this type of assessment tool to get a better idea of what the students wanted and needed.

The statement, a teacher is most prepared to teach a class after it has been taught, is equally valid for needs assessment. Were I to do it again, I would structure it differently. For one thing, I think I was trying to get too much information too fast. I was more concerned with the end product than the process, which affected the benefits of the assessment.

It would have been better to initially focus on the students' oral proficiency and their comfort level in group activities. I also felt the need to have everyone (including myself) introduce themselves. This would also have given me information on who they are as people, for example, what they like to do, how they see themselves. Even without a lot of language, using visual posters could be the language vehicle. A written assignment could be given in class or for homework such as, "Write a letter to me in English or Spanish telling me why you want to learn English." I could devote the following day to discerning individual learning styles. I could also use that day to learn what they want to learn. By the third day, we would be comfortable enough with one another to video (or audio) tape an activity for long and short term assessment.

6.11 *What did John learn about how to get information in ways the students could understand, that would be a good use of class time, and that would be useful to him in analyzing their needs?*

John Kongsvik has captured some of the benefits and pitfalls of initial needs assessment. First, the information gathered can help to shape the course right from the start to meet learners' needs. Second, initial needs assessment activities signal to the learners the teacher's intention to engage them in dialogue and decisions about their learning. However, initial needs assessment activities may not necessarily give one the information desired. As John Kongsvik's experience illustrates, the learners may not be sure how to respond to the questions, either because they don't understand them, don't have the language to respond, haven't thought about them, or don't want to offend the teacher. For these reasons, it is important not to give up after the first try. Being responsible for thinking about one's needs and how to meet them is a skill that may take the learners time to develop. Figuring out how to do needs assessment effectively is a skill that may take time for the teacher to develop.

In Investigations 6.8 and 6.10 you explored the what and the when of needs assessment: the kind of information you would like to get, and when the best time is to get it. Below we will look at the how: ways to get the information. We have already seen a range of activities in the examples given above. More ideas follow. The first five are discrete activities that you could also use on a regular, ongoing basis. The next five are meant to be used in a regular, ongoing way, in order to be successful.

Most of the activities are designed to gather more than one type of information. Some of the activities have a direct needs assessment focus, while others gather the information indirectly. Some are regular teaching activities, which are given a needs assessment focus because the teacher is using them as an opportunity to gather information by observing students. Some of the activities are meant to be combined.

In deciding which ones to use, think about what is feasible within your context. Some of them you will have to adapt. For example, if you have a class of fifty students, you will probably not have the time to interpret fifty questionnaires each with ten questions. It may make more sense to divide the class into groups of five, with each group reporting a summary of the group's answers.

When designing a needs assessment activity, consider the six questions in Figure 6.5 below:

Figure 6.5: A Framework for Designing Needs Assessment Activities

1. What information does it gather?
2. Who is involved and why?
3. What skills are necessary to carry it out? Is preparation needed? In other words, are the students familiar with this type of activity or do they have to be taught how to do it?
4. Is the activity feasible given the level and number of your students? How could you adapt it?
5. Is the activity focused only on gathering information which you will analyze or does it also ask students to
   - identify problems and solutions?
   - identify priorities?
6. How will the teacher and learners use this information?

6.12 *Use the questions above to analyze the needs assessment activities that follow.*

Needs assessment activities that can be used once or on a regular basis.

1. Questionnaires

Questionnaires are an obvious choice for needs assessment, but not always the most effective, depending on when they are given and how well the learners understand the kind of information that is sought. The advantage of questionnaires is that you can tailor the questions for your particular group. The disadvantages are that teachers sometimes go overboard with questions, students are not sure what the "right answer" is, or they don't have the language to answer them. For example, in an effort to find out what kinds of learning activities students prefer, if "role plays" are on the list, and the students have never heard of a role play, the teacher will not get the information he seeks. For this reason I suggest that questionnaires about ways of learning be given after the students have experienced different ways of working in the class so that their answers are grounded in experience.

Cyndy Thatcher-Fettig gave the following questionnaire to her students in the Intensive English Program (IEP) at Cornell University. The questionnaire was filled out individually by students, handed in to her, and then used as a basis for an individual interview, described below.

Figure 6.6: Cyndy Thatcher-Fettig's Needs Assessment Questionnaire

Cyndy Thatcher-Fettig

I General Questions

1. Name _______
2. Address in Ithaca _______
3. Phone number in Ithaca _______
4. Nationality _______
5. Other foreign language learning experience _______
6. Have you been to the U.S. before? Why? How long? When?_______
7. Purpose for taking this course: _______
8. In what setting will you need English? _______
9. Length of stay (from now): _______
10. Future goals: _______

II English Language Study Questions:

1. Have you taken an English conversation course before? If yes, where and for how long? _______
2. What specific points of the English language do you want to improve?

   a. speaking skills (conversation, discussion, presentations, _______)

   b. listening skills (TV, radio, lectures, service people, _______)

   c. reading skills (newspaper, magazine, textbooks, books, _______)

   d. writing skills (papers, professional letters, stories, _______)

   e. practical situations (greetings, telephone, restaurant, _______)

   f. grammatical skills _______

   g. idiomatic expressions _______

   h. other (please explain) _______
3. Present TOEFL score: _______ needed TOEFL score: _______
4. Comments _______

6.13 *What do you find useful about Cyndy's questionnaire? Why? What don't you find useful? Why? How might you adapt it to your context?*

---

2. Interviews

Interviews can take different forms: the teacher interviewing the student(s), or the students interviewing each other, or the students interviewing the teacher. Cyndy Thatcher-Fettig followed up her questionnaire above, for use in her IEP speaking/listening class, with a series of interviews or conferences with individual students.

Cyndy Thatcher-Fettig

First Week Conferences

The first week of school I set up student conferences. I like to individually speak with each student and get a better feel for their English proficiency level in speaking and listening. The manner is casual, friendly, and I try to make them feel as comfortable as possible. I go over the information sheet [above] they handed in to me on the first day of class and we talk about the information they wrote in more detail. I like to ask them about their housing situation to make sure that they have a place to stay and that they are settled. I also get more information on what they were doing before coming to our program so that I am better able to understand what kind of acculturation stage they may be going through. I make sure that they feel they are placed properly in my class as well as other classes, and I assure them that they should feel free to come to me if they have any problems. I also explain that we will have this type of student conference a few times during the semester.

Before they leave, I hand the students a learning style survey for them to do in preparation for our second conference (see Appendix 6-4 on page 251). I also give them some questions to think about which include: "What kinds of activities do you like to do in class?" "What are you going to do to help yourself improve your speaking/listening ability in English outside of class?" "What are your expectations of me and of yourself this semester?" I am interested in getting to know their learning styles, preferences, and expectations. Gathering this kind of information from the start makes it easier to plan a student-centered course and shows the students exactly what I expect of them.

Round Two Conferences

I set up my second conferences around the beginning of the third week. We review the "learning style survey" and talk about their findings about their personal learning style. We also discuss the questions that I had given them in the first conference. In addition to getting information about their learning styles and attitudes about learning English, I use this second conference to try to get some kind of commitment—possibly in written form—from the students on the effort they are going to put forth in learning English inside *and* outside of class. . . . I believe in getting students to take on more responsibility for their own learning. Talking about ways to do that and getting a written commitment helps them realize how important it is for them to get out of the traditional "back seat" of learning. Conferences early on and throughout the semester help build that awareness.

6.14 *What appeals to you about the way Cyndy uses conferencing? Why? What doesn't appeal to you? Why not? How might you adapt this type of activity to your context?*

Another type of questionnaire/interview is one the students ask each other. "Find someone who" is an activity that teachers typically use as an ice-breaker or first day activity so that students can get to know each other. See Chris Conley's version in Appendix 6-2 on page 249.

When students interview each other, the teacher can observe their interaction. This is an important point about in-class, interactive needs assessment activities: you can glean information from both the content of the activity and the way the students do it.

3. Grids, charts, or lists.

One activity I have used is to have students interview each other and then fill in a class grid or chart with information about their partner's background, interests, profession, and so on. A grid can also be used to get other kinds of information such as students' target needs and learning preferences.

4. Writing activities

Writing activities can serve a variety of purposes for needs assessment. They can help to assess proficiency or diagnose strengths and weaknesses. They can also help to gather information about students' objective and subjective needs, depending on how the activity is focused. One teacher, Wagner Veillard, changed his initial writing assignment, in an ESL class in an international school in São Paulo, from the usual "What I did during my summer vacation" to one which gave him information about his students' expectations for the course:

Wagner Veillard

> Write a letter to a friend telling him or her that you have just started a new school year. Be sure to mention:
>
> a) your expectations regarding this year, this semester, or the first day of classes
> b) the classes you will be taking
> c) your reasons for taking this course (ESL Writing)
>
> You may include any other information if you wish, but be sure to address the three points mentioned above.
>
> Exchange letters. As you read, look for similarities and differences. In groups, come up with a list of reasons for taking this course.

Wagner comments:

> In the past, I would have asked my students to write about their vacation (essay.) A letter is more realistic. The task is more natural. I can assess writing ability and course expectations as well.

See Denise Lawson's writing activity on page 107 from her needs assessment plan for another example of how writing can be used.

5. Group discussions

Discussions can be used as a way for the group to address some of the areas related to needs. An advantage of discussions is that they allow students to hear different points of view and allow the teacher to watch how individual students participate. A disadvantage is that those who are reluctant to participate may not have their views heard.

My colleague, Paul LeVasseur, used this activity on the first day of class during the years he taught in an Intensive English Program:

> *Teacher and Student Responsibilities*
>
> Teacher and students: individually write out what you think are the responsibilities of the teacher and of the students.
>
> Make a list of responses on sheets of paper or on board, one for teacher responsibilities, one for students.
>
> Discuss responses and agreements and disagreements.

Sharon Rose-Roth designed the following activity for a group of high beginning level Mexican university students:

Sharon Rose-Roth

> I want to know what the attitude of my students is toward North American culture as well as how much they know about it.
>
> On the board, I have taped four sheets of paper. At the top, I have printed various nationalities: French, Japanese, North American, Mexican. During class, I invite students to use markers to write whatever short descriptions (can be one word) come to mind when they think of those specific nationalities.
>
> When everyone seems to have finished writing, I read the descriptions and ask any clarifying questions that might be needed. I then use this information [as a basis for a discussion] about culture and stereotypes. I also discuss with the class the concept of how other nationalities might describe Mexicans.

6. Ranking activities

An example of a ranking activity is to ask students to list where and for what purpose they use English outside of the classroom and to rank them from the most important to the least important.

Ongoing needs assessment activities

Ongoing needs assessment activities follow the basic needs assessment cycle: gather information about where the learners are and where they need to or would like to be, interpret that information, act on it and evaluate it. Ongoing needs assessment may take place through careful observation of the students as they learn; based on that observation, you can make decisions to adjust how to structure their learning. Such observation and adjustments are the foundation of good teaching because they require the learners to be engaged in learning in order for the teacher to have something to observe and assess. The type of ongoing needs assessment activities described below, however, explicitly ask learners to reflect on and assess their learning on a regular basis throughout the course.

For such activities to work, they must be focused on the students' learning and their perceptions of it or on issues they wish to address in the class.

1. Regular feedback sessions

Regular feedback sessions offer the opportunity for learners to reflect on the class up to that point and to express their views about what has been productive and what hasn't with respect to their needs as learners. One of the challenges of this type of assessment is to focus it on the learning so that learners do not perceive it as an evaluation of the teacher's performance. These feedback sessions are like an oral version of learning logs, which are described in #3 below, except that they are done with the whole class. Here is how Dylan Bate outlines his plan for doing such reviews with university students in China:

Dylan Bate

> First, I elicit from the students the activities we have done that week, going into enough detail so that everyone clearly recalls the activity and its procedure. I list these on the blackboard in chronological order. Next, I write up two or three questions for students to rate/assess them with. For example:
>
> 1. How valuable was this activity in helping you with _____? (e.g., pronunciation, listening)
> 2. What did we, or you, do that made it helpful?
> 3. What would you change next time?
>
> These could change to address certain specific issues/subjects depending on what the class has done that week or where I want to draw their attention, or they can be varied depending on how familiar/comfortable the class is with the feedback process: starting with concrete, specific questions initially, and moving toward more open ended questions as students become familiar with and skilled at giving feedback.
>
> Students' familiarity with giving feedback would be a factor in whether or not I launch into this with the class as a whole orally or follow a more roundabout route. For instance, since I expect that my Chinese students will not be familiar or comfortable with giving feedback, especially as individuals, I will probably start by having them discuss these questions in pairs, then small groups, and finally have them report to the whole class their findings. This way I may be able to depersonalize it sufficiently to get some good, informative feedback.

2. Dialogue journals

Students write regularly (e.g., weekly) in a journal which the teacher responds to. The journal content can be structured or unstructured. (See Peyton and Reed 1990.)

3. Learning logs or learning diaries

Learning logs are records kept by the students about what they are learning, where they feel they are making progress, and what they plan to do to continue making progress.

The following is excerpted from Collaborations, a series for adult immigrants developed by Huizenga and Weinstein-Shr (1994).

Language Learning Diary

A. This week I learned ________

B. This week I spoke English to ________

C. This week I read ________

D. My new words are ________

E. Next week I want to learn ________

F. Outside of the classroom, I would like to try ________

When using learning logs or diaries, it is important for students to have a clear focus for what they are to write about, at least initially. Once they are comfortable using them, students can take the initiative in deciding what to write about.

4. Portfolios

Portfolios are collections of students' work, selected according to certain criteria, to show progress and achievement. One approach to portfolios in a writing class will be described in Chapter 10. For more information about portfolios, see Bailey (1998).

5. Participatory processes

See Chris Conley's needs assessment plan and his approach to conceptualizing content at the end of Chapter 4.

In summary, designing a needs assessment plan for your course requires you to consider:

- The **kind of information** you want to get and what you hope to do with it. See the list in Figure 6.3. Don't try to assess everything. Problematize your situation: what is the most important information that you can handle and that will help you meet the challenges of designing or modifying the course?
- The **types of activities** you plan to use, whether they are appropriate for your students, and what kind of information they will give you. See the Framework in Figure 6.5. Consider activities that are already part of your repertoire. Remember that the first time you conduct a needs assessment activity you may not get the information you had intended to. You can modify or adapt it the next time.
- **When** you want to conduct the activities. Don't try to do too many at one time. Don't overwhelm your students with your need to find out about their needs!

6.15 *Draw up a needs assessment plan for the course you are designing. Refer to Denise Lawson's and Chris Conley's plans on pages 107 and 108 for examples..*

Suggested Readings

A lot has been written about needs assessment, also called needs analysis, most of it geared to students who will use English in academic or professional contexts. I like Hutchinson and Waters' introduction to needs assessment in their book, *English for Specific Purposes* (1987), Chapter 6, "Needs Analysis," in which they explain the difference between target needs and learning needs. Their examples are from ESP courses, and so the points they make about target needs are mostly relevant to ESL settings, but the points they make about learning needs are relevant to any type of course. J. D. Brown's chapter on needs analysis in *The Elements of Language Curriculum* (1995) provides a detailed overview of its purposes and ways to get information. As with the Hutchinson and Waters book, the examples are from programs designed for students who will use English in specific contexts, in this case, academic contexts.

Sarah Benesch's article, "Needs Analysis and Curriculum Development in EAP: An Example of a Critical Approach" (1996), provides a thoughtful challenge to assumptions that it is our students who must adapt to the target contexts and not the other way around. "Designing Workplace ESOL Courses for Chinese Healthcare Workers at a Boston Nursing Home" by Johan Uvin (1996) shows how taking a narrow, context-specific view of students' needs may backfire. I like the teacher- and student-friendly work done by Suzanne Grant and Catherine Shank in Arlington, Virginia, which my students alerted me to after attending one of their presentations at TESOL. Their article, "Discovering and Responding to Learner Needs: Module for ESL Teacher Training," is available through ERIC (1993). The short summary article, "Needs Assessment for Adult ESL Learners," by Kathleen Santopietro Weddel and Carol Van Duzer is also available from ERIC (1997). This summary provides a definition of needs assessment, examples of assessment activities that can be done as part of teaching, and a good reference list for Adult Education.

7

ORGANIZING THE COURSE

7.1 *In preparation for reading this chapter:*

1. Choose a language course you have taught recently or one in which you were a learner. Write a few descriptive comments about the course syllabus: what it focused on, how it was organized and sequenced, and why it was organized that way.
2. For the course you are designing, redesigning, or adapting as you use this book, make a list of the questions you have about organizing and sequencing it to use as a guide as you read through the chapter.

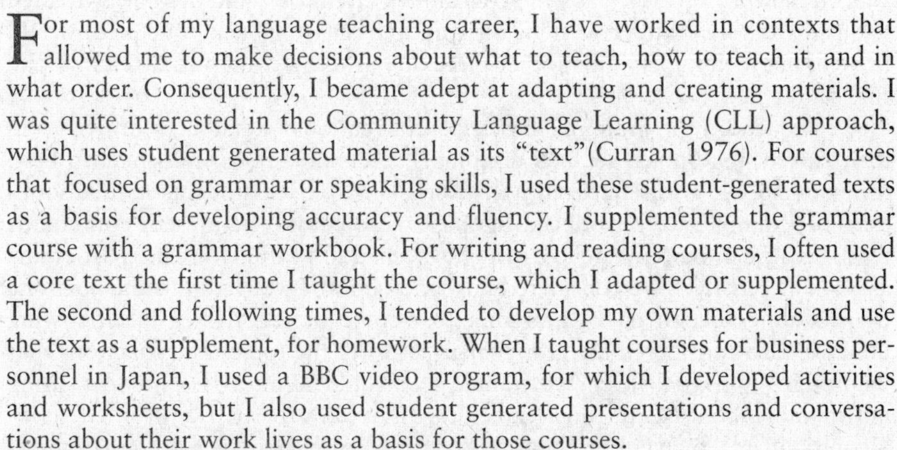

For most of my language teaching career, I have worked in contexts that allowed me to make decisions about what to teach, how to teach it, and in what order. Consequently, I became adept at adapting and creating materials. I was quite interested in the Community Language Learning (CLL) approach, which uses student generated material as its "text"(Curran 1976). For courses that focused on grammar or speaking skills, I used these student-generated texts as a basis for developing accuracy and fluency. I supplemented the grammar course with a grammar workbook. For writing and reading courses, I often used a core text the first time I taught the course, which I adapted or supplemented. The second and following times, I tended to develop my own materials and use the text as a supplement, for homework. When I taught courses for business personnel in Japan, I used a BBC video program, for which I developed activities and worksheets, but I also used student generated presentations and conversations about their work lives as a basis for those courses.

See Stevick (1998) for more about CLL.

I generally did not have a conception of each course as a whole. I did not know how to formulate goals and objectives but rather saw a course as a series of lessons, each one showing me what the students needed to work on, limited by what I could perceive. For example, in a grammar course, I would design activities to address the grammar points that arose from errors students made in the conversations they generated. I would then devise tests that assessed what we had covered. This approach worked in the grammar courses, but did not work as well in reading courses, for example, since I did not have a clear idea of what one needed to learn in order to become a fluent second language reader.

My formative experience in organizing and sequencing came when I embarked on co-authoring the adult basal series, *East West* (1988) with my colleague, David Rein. As originally conceived, *East West* was to have three levels, with the first level aimed at false beginners, the second at low intermediates, and the third at

See Chapter 9 for the way one teacher adapted Unit 1 of *East West Basics.*

high intermediates. I subsequently wrote a fourth, beginners' level with Alison Rice, *East West Basics* (1994). The publisher had specified that they wanted the series to have a grammatical core around which functions and topics would be woven. Each level was to include work on the four skills of reading, writing, speaking, and listening, but give prominence to listening and speaking. There was to be an episode of a suspenseful story at the end of each unit. Most of the writing would be assigned in the workbook. David and I felt that a cultural component and a pronunciation component were also important, so we added them to the list of specifications.

When we began work on the syllabus for *East West,* we wrote up inventories of grammar, functions, and topics on 3 by 5 cards. The inventories came from our own experience as teachers, David's in Mexico, Liberia, and the United States, mine in Japan, Taiwan, and the U.S. We were greatly helped by *Threshold Level English,* (Van Ek and Alexander 1986), one of several syllabus documents published by the Council of Europe as part of its efforts to develop a Europe-wide approach to teaching foreign languages to adults. It contains exhaustive lists of settings, functions, general and specific notions, topics, and forms. We also looked at the table of contents of all the current textbooks we could find. The process of narrowing down and then deciding the order of what was on our 3 by 5 cards was time-consuming, circuitous, and opaque. We often felt as if we were taking two steps forward and one step back. One piece would fit well, but then knock out another piece. It was like a giant puzzle with no picture on the box.

We sequenced the grammar based on conventional wisdom as drawn from then current textbooks, such as teaching "be" and personal information first, for example. We also sequenced it based on what we felt students needed soonest. For example, we introduced the past tense before the present continuous tense because in our experience, students needed to be able to relate past events as soon as possible. We considered how each unit might lead into the next one by providing vocabulary or grammar that could be recycled in the following unit. We also considered the grammar in terms of the topics and functions that would give it textual flesh. We wanted to include a culture component, using information about North American culture as a basis for analyzing and describing the students' own culture(s). It was not easy to decide which grammar points to cluster together, nor which topics were best suited to the grammar. Some of the overall sequencing made sense, some of it was, of necessity, arbitrary. We found that we could not gear the suspense story to the grammatical, topical, and functional content of each unit, and so treated it separately. (In fact, we only included a story in the false beginners' level.) Deciding how to structure each unit was a whole other matter.

I learned three lessons from my teaching and writing experiences, each one a theme running through this book. The first is that you have to make choices, because you can't do everything. The second is that there isn't one, right way to organize a course, although there are principles that can help provide order to the seeming chaos of possibilities. The third is that what you choose and how you organize it must make sense to you so that you have a basis for your decisions. In this chapter we will explore what it means to organize and sequence a course, how to decide on an appropriate organization and sequencing, and different ways to organize the course.

What Does It Mean to Organize a Course?

Organizing a course is deciding what the underlying systems will be that pull together the content and material in accordance with the goals and objectives and that give the course a shape and structure. Organizing a course occurs on different levels: the level of the **course as a whole;** the level of **subsets of the whole:** units, modules, or strands within the course; and then **individual lessons.** In this chapter we will focus on the first two levels: how to organize the course as a whole, and how to organize subsets of the whole. In Chapter 8 on adapting and developing materials we will again look at the second level, how to organize subsets of the whole, and at the third level, how to organize lessons. The product of organizing and sequencing a course is a syllabus. The syllabus may take a variety of forms, depending on how you plan to use it. Most syllabuses that are given to students contain a chronological list or chart of what the course will cover. If it is a document that only you will use, then it could also take the form of a map or a diagram. We will look at four different syllabuses and one syllabus unit in this chapter.

Organizing a course involves five overlapping processes: 1) determining the organizing principle(s) that drive(s) the course; 2) identifying units, modules, or strands based on the organizing principle(s); 3) sequencing the units; 4) determining the language and skills content of the units; 5) organizing the content within each unit. We will look at each of these aspects in this chapter. The processes do not follow a specific order; you may work on the content and organization of a unit or strand before deciding how to sequence the units over the course as a whole; you may also decide the sequence of the modules or units once the course is underway. The five processes or aspects are captured in a flow chart below:

Figure 7.1: Five Aspects of Organizing a Course

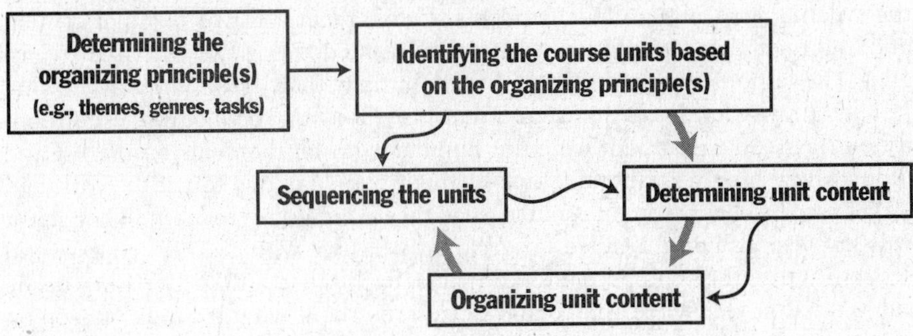

The terms "unit" and "module" give a sense of complete wholes within the larger course. The term "strand" applies to courses that are not organized around units, but around strands that are carried through the whole course. For example, Barbara Fujiwara (1996) describes a listening course she taught that was organized around three strands: a video series, specific work with learning strategies, and student projects. Approximately a third of each class was devoted to each strand. Within each strand, there were units of work.

Why Organize a Course?

For some teachers the question *Why organize the course?* will seem inappropriate, even ludicrous. Of course you have to have some idea of the organization and sequencing of your course, or how will you know how the course fits together and is sequenced in such a way that students will learn? But for teachers who are considering some form of process syllabus in which they negotiate some or all of the syllabus with their students, this question is important to ask. This is the dilemma Chris Conley described in Chapter 4 as he explored ways to have his students participate in determining the content of the course. (See pages 66–69.)

See Chapter 4, page 47, re process syllabuses.

Having a negotiated syllabus does not mean that you walk into the course with no plan in mind. Here I agree with Stern when he says, "But an emphasis on learner autonomy does not absolve the curriculum designer of his responsibility to plan the options within which the learner will be encouraged to exercise his judgement. In short, careful and comprehensive curriculum planning is compatible with adaptability at the class level for both teachers and students. Therefore, the laudable intention to give freedom to the teacher and responsibility to the student must not serve as an excuse for not planning the curriculum." (1992, p. 45–46). I would like to make a case here for having some kind of organization in mind, because it is a way to bridge the goals and objectives with the actual lessons; because most students expect it; and because it provides the arena or "options" within which to make decisions together. I am not against negotiating a syllabus with students: on the contrary, I hope it is clear by now that I feel that for a course to be successful, there must be ongoing interaction with students. However, I believe that a negotiated syllabus works best when there is a conceptual "container" to support it.

When I first started teaching linguistics, I decided that I wanted to negotiate the syllabus with my graduate students. I gave them a list of possible content and told them that I would teach what they wanted and in the order they wanted it. The response was mild shock. I think initially there was some concern that I didn't know what I was doing, and that I was foisting some of my responsibility on them. Some of them were not familiar with all the items on the list and didn't know how to respond. Some of them were anxious to get to work and didn't want to spend time deciding what they were going to learn. They felt it was my responsibility. I ended up deciding what we would do the first several sessions. Once they had gotten to know me, each other, and the territory of the subject matter, they were able to make decisions about what to study. When you negotiate aspects of the syllabus with your students, make sure that they have the tools with which to negotiate. By the same token, if you have a syllabus prepared in advance, this does not mean that you cannot change it. We sometimes give too much power to written documents.

How Does One Decide on an Appropriate Organization?

The way you organize your course depends on a number of factors which include **the course content, your goals and objectives, your past experience, your students' needs, your beliefs and understandings, the method or text,** and **the context.**

The way you have conceptualized the **content** and defined the **goals and objectives** of the course provides the foundation for organizing the course. For example, courses that focus on writing skills are often organized around types of composition (e.g., narrative, argument). A course in which the four skills of reading, writing, speaking, and listening are integrated may be organized around themes; a content-based history course may be organized chronologically around historical periods or around historical themes. A task-based course may be organized around a series of cumulative tasks. See Chapter 4, Conceptualizing Content, for other examples of the content around which a syllabus can be organized.

The way that you conceptualize content and set goals and objectives depends on your teaching (and learning) **experience** in general, and of this kind of course in particular; what you **understand** about how people learn languages; and the **students' needs,** or what you know about their needs. For example, if your students are children, you may choose to organize your course around themes rather than linguistic skills. If your students are business personnel, you may choose to organize your course around the types of tasks they perform. Your experience allows you to build on what you have found effective in the past.

Your **beliefs** about how learners learn also play an important role. For example, beliefs about the importance of learner autonomy may lead you to organize your course around learner projects. Beliefs about the role of learner's experience may lead you to organize your course around learners' stories (Wrigley and Guth 1992).

If you adopt a particular approach or method, you may organize the course around certain material or procedures. For example, the Community Language Learning Approach uses student generated material as the core "text" for the course (Rardin and Tranel 1988). An **existing syllabus** or **textbook** may provide the organizational structure for a course. It may be possible to reshape the syllabus, depending on the institutional givens.

The teaching **context** also plays a crucial role. If your course is part of an institutional curriculum, the course organization may, to some extent, be predetermined. Your decisions about organization may occur more at the unit and lesson level than at the course level. Time is also an important contextual factor. For example, the amount of time for the course, how often the course meets, and over what period will help to determine the number and length of your teaching units or modules, or how many strands you can follow. If there is an examination schedule, you will need to organize the course to meet the exam requirements.

What Are Different Ways to Organize and Sequence a Course?

Organizing the course

As I pointed out earlier in the chapter, there is no one way or "best way" to organize a course. You may organize a course one way the first time you teach it and reorganize it because of what you learned about what worked and what didn't the next time you teach it. I personally like to experiment with the way I organize and sequence my courses. For example, the pedagogical grammar course I teach includes three modules: phonology, lexicon, and an introduction to transformational grammar. I have taught it in that order, which is typical: moving from units of sound, to units of meaning, to the sentence level. However, I have also taught it beginning with lexicon, then phonology, then grammar, because the work with lexicon provides the language items on which to base the phonology work. And, earlier in my career, I taught phonology last, because I was intimidated by the subject myself and wanted the students to know and trust me so that I wouldn't be nervous when teaching it to them!

I have found that in the long run, changes I make to the order or systems don't make a huge difference in the experiences of the students, as long as I have thought out my reasons for making the changes. Part of this is due to the nonlinear and organic way in which we learn (Larsen-Freeman 1997). Part is due to the flexibility of the human spirit. Part is due to the fact that the students don't know that I did it a different way before. This doesn't mean that the changes always work! It also doesn't mean that there aren't principles for organizing a course, or that I didn't have reasons for making the changes I did.

Example syllabuses

Below we will look at two syllabuses for two very different contexts, a high school Spanish course and an ESP course for scientists.

7.2 *Study the following two syllabuses and answer the questions:*

1. On what basis did each teacher organize her course:
   What was the organizing principle or focus for each unit?

   On what basis are units sequenced?
2. What do you like about the way the teacher organized her course? Why? What don't you like? Why not?
3. Why are they so different?

The first syllabus is for Denise Maksail-Fine's high school Spanish 3 course. The course is a year long (36 weeks), so only the first twelve weeks are included in Figure 7.2. (The complete syllabus is in Appendix 7-1 on pages 252–255.)

Figure 7.2: The First Twelve Weeks of Denise Maksail-Fine's Year-long (36 week) Syllabus for her Spanish 3 Course

Spanish 3

Week 1: ***Personal Identification*** (Sept) Biographical Data Introductions, Greetings, Leave-taking, Common Courtesy Review: Present tense verbs	Week 2: ***Personal Identification*** (Sept) Physical Characteristics Psychological Characteristics Review: Present tense verbs
Week 3: ***Family Life*** (Sept) Family Members Family Activities *Cultural Awareness:* *Día de Independencia (Mexico)* Review: Noun-adjective agreement, articles	Week 4: ***Family Life*** (Sept) Roles and Responsibilities *Cultural Awareness:* *Hispanic vs. USA Families* Review: Noun-adjective agreement, articles
Week 5: ***House and Home*** (Oct) Types of Lodging Review: Prepositions	Week 6: ***House and Home*** (Oct) Rooms, Furnishings, Appliances Review: Prepositions
Week 7: ***House and Home*** Routine Household Chores *Cultural Awareness:* *Día de la Raza* Review: Imperative	Week 8: ***Services and Repairs*** Repairs and Household Goods Review: Imperative
Week 9: ***Community and Neighborhood*** Local Stores, Facilities Recreational Opportunities *Cultural Awareness:* *Día de los Muertos* Review: Imperative	Week 10: ***Private and Public Services*** Communications: Telephone, Mail, E-Mail Review: Imperative
Week 11: ***Private and Public Services*** (Nov) Government Agencies: Post Office, Customs, Police, Embassies Review: Imperative	Week 12: ***Private and Public Services*** Finances: Banks, Currency Exchange

The second syllabus was developed by Brooke Palmer for an ESP course for scientists. The course is 12 weeks long and meets twice a week for a total of 48 hours.

Figure 7.3: Brooke Palmer's Syllabus for an ESP Course for Professionals in the Sciences

Week 1: Introduction to ESP; Presentation Skills Workshop

Week 2: Amplified definitions

Week 3: Description of a mechanism

Week 4: Description of a process

Week 5: Classification

Week 6: Abstract writing

Week 7: Research reports

Week 8: Research reports

Week 9: Peer editing of research reports

Week 10: "Mini conference"—Presentations of research reports

Week 11: "Mini conference"—Presentations and peer evaluations

Week 12: Self evaluations and video evaluations of presentations

See Chapter 4, pages 59–61, for her mind maps and rationale, and Appendix 5-2, page 242, for Denise Maksail-Fine's goals and objectives.
See Chapter 8, pages 165–166, for a complete unit.

How are the courses above organized? Denise Maksail Fine's Spanish course is organized around topics. Thus topics are the organizing principle of the course. Each topic is the focus of a unit that lasts two to three weeks. Within each unit, students learn about aspects of the topic. For example, in the second unit, Family Life, which is two weeks long, students learn to talk and write about family members, family activities, and family roles and responsibilities. As we know from her reflections in Chapter 4, Denise had to struggle not to have grammar be the organizing principle for her course. In this syllabus, grammar takes a supporting role, and is introduced in relation to the topic. Another element is culture, which is also linked to the particular topic. In the unit on Family Life, students explore similarities and differences between families in the United States and families in Mexico and Spanish-speaking countries in South America. Other elements will be included in each unit, such as work on the four skills of reading, writing, speaking, and listening, which we know from Denise's goals and objectives; however, these are not specified in the syllabus. They will be specified at the materials development level, which we will see in Chapter 8.

In Brooke Palmer's course, the organizing principle is not topics, but texts, specifically scientific texts, which she calls "technical writing products." These include amplified definitions, describing a mechanism, describing a process, and so on. The main focus is on being able to write each of those kinds of text. The course culminates in a "mini conference" in which the students present their final paper, a research report, to each other. The six types of text are the basis for the course units which span twelve weeks. The first week and the last three weeks address presentation skills. Speaking, reading, and listening are also included as part of the units, although that is not apparent from the syllabus list above. We will hear from Brooke about why she organized her course that way later in the chapter.

See pages 139–140.

These two syllabuses provide us with examples of three of the processes of organizing a course outlined in Figure 7.1: determining the organizing principle, which in turn provides the basis for the syllabus units or modules, which in turn are sequenced in a certain way. The topics in the Spanish course are sequenced so that they follow a progression from the individual to the home to the community and beyond. The ESP course follows a progression from simpler writing texts/tasks to more complex writing texts/tasks, each building on the preceding one. The fourth and fifth aspects of organizing a course, unit content and organization, are not evident, or only partially evident, in their syllabus documents.

We will look at two more syllabuses below which provide information about all five aspects of organizing a course, including the content and organization of individual units.

7.3 *Study the following two syllabuses.*

1. On what basis did each teacher organize her course:
   - What was the organizing principle or focus for each unit?
   - Within a unit, what are the language learning components? For example, vocabulary, grammar, four skills, communicative skills, cultural skills, etc.
   - Within a unit, how are the language learning components organized?
2. What do you like about the way the teacher organized her course? Why? What don't you like? Why not?
3. What are the similarities and differences between them?

The first syllabus is Toby Brody's, for an eight-week course for high-intermediate to advanced level pre-university students from different cultures. The course takes place in an intensive English program in the United States, and meets for 2 hours daily. It uses the local newspaper as the core text for the course.

Toby has called it an integrated skills course because it integrates work on the four skills of speaking, listening, reading, and writing. She chose the newspaper as the text for her course for several reasons. Newspapers are a genre that students are familiar with, since newspapers exist in every culture. Newspapers report current events and reactions to the events as they occur and so are a means to connect students to the larger world. The newspaper also reports on sports, the arts, business, and local news and the community. Newspapers are cultural products and so provide insights into the target culture. She writes:

Toby Brody

> The adaptability of the newspaper to academics gives this material grounding as a versatile resource. When I began to consider the skills pre-university students would need to hone, tasks emerged which reflected the richness and variety contained in the newspaper. University-level courses, generally, challenge students' abilities in expository writing, summarizing, arguing a point, and researching

See Chapter 4, page 62, for Toby Brody's mind map for the content of her course.

provocative questions, for example. The newspaper is a huge stock of information placed into a user-friendly, accessible format and, as such is a practical resource for students to tap. I believe that every student can find something of interest to explore, given the multi-dimensional nature of the paper.

The first four weeks of the syllabus are shown below. The complete syllabus is in Appendix 7-2 on pages 256–257.

Figure 7.4: The First Four Weeks of Toby Brody's Syllabus for an Eight-week Integrated Skills Course Based On the Newspaper

Week 1	Week 3
Introduction: Newspaper scavenger hunt	
Focus: Summarizing	*Focus:* Objective reporting
Tasks: Scanning for 5 W's and H Questions Predicting main ideas from headlines Reading for main ideas Answering comprehension questions Listening for main ideas —Short News Report Oral and written summaries	*Tasks:* Reconstructing a strip story Following and reconstructing a developing story Reading first part of an article that "jumps" and creating an ending Sequencing a radio news report
Linguistic Focus: Forming questions	*Linguistic Focus:* Transitions and adverbial connectors
Culture Focus: Asking colloquial questions (e.g., What's up?)	*Culture Focus:* Formats of newspapers and radio broadcasts

Week 2	Week 4
Focus: Interviewing	*Focus:* Proposing Solutions
Tasks: Predicting main ideas from headlines Skimming and scanning Reading and role-playing an interview article Interviewing students with "interview cards" Writing feature story based on interview Interviewing a native speaker Reporting orally on interview with a native speaker	*Tasks:* Reading about and summarizing community problems Researching community problems Reporting on community problems and describing action to be taken Creating a visual to capture a problem and its solution Presenting a synopsis of the visual
Linguistic Focus: Review questions Student-generated structures	*Linguistic Focus:* Conditionals
Culture Focus: Interview a native speaker re a culture question	*Culture Focus:* Connecting community problems to local realities

The second syllabus was designed by Valarie Barnes for a four week holiday (or vacation) course for young adults. It takes place in the United States, although it was designed based on her experience with such courses in both Singapore and the United States. The students have classes in the morning and afternoon. Valarie knew from experience that these young people were not interested in devoting their holiday to the study of grammar or academic skills, so she designed the course so that students would need to actively use the language they had learned more formally at school. She also designed it to take advantage of their curiosity about the environment and to introduce them to an exploration of their own cultures in light of the target culture. The syllabus in Figure 7.5 shows the first three weeks. The complete syllabus is in Appendix 7-3 on pages 258–259.

Toby Brody has organized her course around what she calls "pre-university skills" or skills that the students will need to master in order to do well in university. Each skill is the focus of the unit and is labeled as such. The skills for the first four units are *summarizing, interviewing, objective reporting* and *proposing solutions*. Each unit is a week long. The supporting components she has labeled tasks, linguistic focus and culture focus. Within a unit, each sequence of tasks develops the language and skills needed to be able to master the focus skill. For example, the focus skill of week 2 is to be able to conduct an interview. Students learn to read an article based on an interview and then role-play the interview. They then interview fellow students using questions provided on interview cards and write a newspaper story based on the interview. Finally, they interview a native speaker about a cultural question and report to the class what they learned in the interview. The grammar focuses on reviewing questions that are used in interviews as well as grammar points the students choose. The cultural aspect is the basis for the interview of a native speaker. The eight week course culminates in the final week, when the students produce their own newspaper. As the course progresses, the tasks associated with the focus skill place more complex demands on the students' language and thinking abilities.

The organizing principle for Valarie Barnes' course is quite different from Toby's. Her course is organized around theme-related field trips. Each module is a week long and follows something of a predictable sequence or cycle of activities: prepare for the field trip, take the field trip, learn from the field trip. The preparation for the field trip weaves together work on the vocabulary and the communicative and cultural skills the students will need. During the field trip they each have language- and culture-based tasks to perform. For example, during the field trip to the shopping mall, their tasks include going into certain stores to find out whether they carry certain merchandise or give student discounts as well as interviewing shoppers about their views on the difference between shopping at the mall and shopping in downtown stores. After the field trip they reflect on their experiences, and consolidate their linguistic and cultural learning in a variety of formats, some regular such as journals and scrapbooks, some particular to the unit such as skits or collages. Each week, the field trip demands more linguistically of the students.

Figure 7.5: The First Three Weeks of Valarie Barnes' Syllabus for a Four-week Holiday Course for Young Adults

A Holiday Course

Monday	*Tuesday*	*Wednesday*	*Thursday*	*Friday*
Week One	**Theme: Shopping**			
■ Getting to know you ■ Program overview ■ Attitudes and opinions ■ Shops found downtown ■ Concentration game ■ Discussion ■ The interview ■ Downtown walkabout	■ Writing in journals ■ Walkabout follow-up ■ Song: "Big Yellow Taxi"	■ Field trip to the mall	■ Field trip follow-up ■ Discussion ■ Writing ■ Language lab ■ Panel discussion groups ■ Homework	■ Discussion groups ■ Feedback ■ Journals ■ Scrapbooks
Week Two	**Theme: Food**			
■ "This tastes ____" ■ Adjectives for foods ■ Identify the foods ■ Categories worksheet ■ "Do you like ____" ■ ABC game ■ Self-interview	■ Small group discussion ■ Interview an American ■ Discussion ■ Menus ■ Restaurant role play ■ Register ■ Vocabulary	■ Listening ■ Small group work ■ Practice ■ Error correction ■ Shops role play ■ Follow-up ■ American weights and measures ■ Language lab	■ Half-day field trip to a supermarket, a food cooperative, and a restaurant ■ Discussion ■ Synthesis activity	■ Skits ■ Feedback ■ Journals ■ Scrapbooks
Week Three	**Theme: Animals**			
■ Game ■ Brainstorming ■ Reading ■ Discussion ■ Interview preparation ■ Homework	■ Drawings ■ You become an animal ■ Process writing ■ "Talk Show" ■ Video the talk show ■ Journals	■ Field trip to the zoo	■ Field trip follow-up ■ Language lab ■ Synthesis activity ■ Homework	■ To the teacher's home ■ Murals/collages ■ Feedback ■ Journals ■ Scrapbooks

The four syllabuses you have investigated thus far in the chapter each have a different organizing principle: *topics, writing texts/tasks, academic skills,* and *theme-based field trips*. Organizing principles provide the basis for identifying units. In a course that is organized around topics, a different topic will be the subject of each unit. In a course organized around types of writing, a different type of writing is the basis of each unit. In a course organized around tasks or projects, a different project is the basis for each unit. A course may also be organized around two complementary organizing principles. For example, a writing course may choose a different type of writing and different topic for the writing for each unit. The content of a unit brings together the language and skills that will enable students to achieve the focus of the unit. For this reason, organizing principles must be capable of bringing together a variety of language and skills elements to support it in achieving the objectives. I discourage teachers from using grammar and functions as the organizing principle for their course because they are better viewed as supporting elements in achieving communicative and analytical skills than as an end in themselves. They do not readily allow for weaving together other elements in each unit but are better viewed as one of the threads in the fabric. Even if you have been asked to design a grammar course, I think it is still more productive to use topics or skills as the organizing principle. The investigation below asks you to consider possible organizing principles for your course.

7.4 *Consult the mind maps or charts you developed in Investigation 4.8 to conceptualize the content. Discuss the following questions with a colleague:*

1. Is there an organizing principle, one which brings together the other elements of content? (Some possible organizing principles are: topics, themes, types of writing, academic skills, genre, tasks, stories.)
2. What are some possible units in your course, derived from the organizing principle? (For example, in Brooke Palmer's syllabus, the organizing principle was types of scientific writing and the units were classification, description of a mechanism etc. In Denise Maksail-Fine's course, the organizing principle was topics and some of the units were family life, house and home, community, and neighborhood.)

In Investigation 7.4 you explored the first two aspects of organizing a course: determining the organizing principle and identifying units based on the organizing principle. In the next section, you will explore in more detail the third aspect, sequencing the units.

Sequencing

Sequencing involves deciding the order in which you will teach what. At the course level, sequencing involves deciding the order in which you will teach the units and, to some extent, the order within each unit. You may choose to determine the sequence of units and within units after the course has begun, depending on how much flexibility your context permits.

One of the main principles of sequencing in putting a course together is based on the common sense principle of **building.** In other words, **step A prepares in some way (provides the foundation) for step B.** Step B in turn prepares for Step C and so on. Some ways to understand the idea that A prepares for B are:

> **A is simpler or less demanding; B is more complex or more demanding.**
>
> For example, in Brooke Palmer's course, describing a mechanism is simpler than describing a process. In a grammar sequence, the present perfect tense is typically learned after the past tense because it is considered more complex linguistically (auxiliary + past participle) and conceptually (it is about the past as related to the present).
>
> **A is more controlled; B is more open-ended.**
>
> For example, in Toby Brody's newspaper course, learning to summarize an existing newspaper article is more controlled, while learning how to write an article is more open-ended.
>
> **A provides knowledge or skills required to do or understand B (or B builds on knowledge and skills provided by A).**
>
> The two examples above from Brooke's and Toby's course could also be used to illustrate this point. In Valarie Barnes' holiday course, learning the vocabulary for and then role-playing ordering in a restaurant provided knowledge and skills required for ordering in an actual restaurant.

Another basis for sequencing is the one Denise Maksail-Fine chose for her course: from the individual to the home to the community to the larger world. History and literature courses can follow a chronological sequence. Deciding over the span of the course how units should be sequenced is not an exact science, however, because different teachers will have different views of the relationship between A, B, and C. One teacher may reverse the process of a typical writing course in which students learn how to write paragraphs and then learn to write essays. Instead, students may be given the task of writing an essay first in order to diagnose their strengths and weaknesses. Subsequent lessons may break down the component skills in order to address the weaknesses. Students may first approach texts holistically before working with parts of them. Some teachers choose not to sequence their courses in advance, but work from a "menu" of units or strands and choose from them as the course progresses.

Ultimately, you need to be able to justify your reasons for how you decide to sequence the course content. The following investigation is designed to help you look at different sequencing possibilities and justifications for them.

7.5 *The lists below are drawn from the table of contents of three different English language textbooks. The first is a list of topics. The second is a list of grammar points. The third is a list of writing tasks. Do the following with each one separately:*

1. Work with a partner and decide the order in which you would teach the items on the list in a way that makes sense to both of you.
2. Compare your order with another pair and discuss the reasons for any differences.

For a similar activity using an actual textbook unit see Investigation 9.6, page 196.

Topics:	**Grammar points:**
people: education and childhood	simple present tense
cities: locations and directions	present continuous tense
food	subject pronouns
requests and complaints	yes/no questions
housing	questions with *which, how much*
travel and vacation	present tense of *be*
machines and appliances	frequency adverbs
holidays and customs	questions with *what*
changes and contrasts:	There is/are
life in past, present, future	future with *be going to*
movies, books and entertainment	count and non count nouns
buildings and landmarks	prepositions of location
money	past tense of *be*
people's abilities; jobs	
information about someone's past	

Writing tasks:

defining: writing about sleep problems
comparing and contrasting: writing about a car purchase
writing a memo: personal writing habits
persuasive writing: writing about subcultures within societies
classifying: writing about migrating to your community
collecting and reporting data: consumer habits
description and narrative: writing about personal success

Decisions about sequencing at the course level and at the unit level are similar. For Valarie Barnes, this is manifest on a weekly basis in the way the week is structured, with activities leading up to the field trip, and then the field trip itself as a prerequisite for the follow-up activities, and over the course as a whole, with the types of field trips each week. For Toby Brody, this is manifest in the weekly organization, where each task builds on the one before in order to culminate in the skill focus of the week, and in the course as a whole, where each focus is increasingly more complex and uses the skills learned or deepened the previous week. Toby describes her process this way:

Toby Brody

Once I had decided which pre-university skills students might need to develop or sharpen, [the "focuses"], I ordered these "Focus" items from simple to complex over the term of the course. The next step was to decide what specific tasks should be addressed in each "Focus," which tasks could be built on preceding ones, and which could be revisited in subsequent weeks. The spiraling of tasks such as summarizing, sequencing, reading for main ideas, formulating questions, etc. are woven throughout the eight week period.

The intensity of the course peaks at the end of the sixth and beginning of the seventh weeks, with students engaged in analyzing, inferencing, and problem solving. The lessons planned for the end of the seventh week are of a lighter variety and are intended to ease students into the creative fun of the final week, the students' own journalistic product.

Toby refers to **spiraling,** another principle of sequencing, also called **recycling.** This means that **something learned is reintroduced in connection with something else, so that it is both "reused" and learned in more depth.** The something may be knowledge (of vocabulary, for example) or a language-related skill (such as how to write a letter or how to make a phone call) or a classroom skill (such as how to work effectively in groups or how to give directions). In a reading skills course, different texts may be devoted to a similar topic, but with a more complex treatment each time. Ways to spiral and recycle include recycling something using a different skill (from reading to speaking, for example), recycling something in a different context (from a context provided in a text to one's own personal context, for example), recycling something using a different learning technique (categorizing a list of classroom behaviors as positive or negative, then using the vocabulary in a parent-teacher conference role play.) For example, in Valarie's course, the students categorize the food in menus on Tuesday of week two, followed by the chance to use the menu in a role play, followed by doing the role play using a different register, according to the context. Then on Thursday, they go to a restaurant and order from a menu. In Toby's course, the students predict main ideas from headlines in the first week (using reading and speaking skills), transform headlines into complete sentences in the fifth week (using grammar skills), and create their own headlines in the eighth week (using writing skills).

7.6 *Look at the complete course syllabuses for Denise Maksail-Fine's Spanish 3 course and for Toby Brody's Integrated Skills course in Appendix 7-1 on page 252 and 7-2 on page 256. What are some ways that each syllabus spirals or recycles previous material?*

The following investigation asks you to identify a possible sequence for the units of your course.

7.7 *Look over the list of possible units you drew up in Investigation 7.4.*

1. Consider the time frame of your course: how long it is (a month, a semester, a year); how often and for how long it meets; other scheduling factors such as an examination schedule or holidays. How many units could you realistically teach in that schedule?
2. What are some ways you could sequence the units? What is your basis for sequencing them in that way?

Unit content and organization

The fourth and fifth aspects of organizing a course are determining unit content (particular tasks, skills, functions, grammar, etc.) in accordance with the objectives for the unit, and determining how to organize the content within a unit. Let's look at Brooke Palmer's course syllabus again and see how she explains her approach to sequencing the course units and to organizing the content within each unit:

Brooke Palmer

An ESP Course for Professionals in the Sciences

Week 1: Introduction to ESP; Presentation Skills Workshop
Week 2: Amplified definitions
Week 3: Description of a mechanism
Week 4: Description of a process
Week 5: Classification
Week 6: Abstract writing
Week 7: Research reports
Week 8: Research reports
Week 9: Peer editing of research reports
Week 10: "Mini conference"—Presentations of research reports
Week 11: "Mini conference"—Presentations and peer evaluations
Week 12: Self evaluations and video evaluations of presentations

The course units build from the simple to the more complex. Though the content is based on technical writing products, they actually will serve as vehicles for developing other skills. Units run from two to six class periods depending on the level of sophistication of the writing product. Each product produced by the students is aimed to build upon the previous topic in general so that when the final research paper is due, students will not have to frantically begin from scratch. I based the units on technical writing elements found in *Science, Medicine, and Technology: English Grammar and Technical Writing* by Peter Anthony Master (1986).

Sequences within each unit are based on the materials design model from *English for Specific Purposes: A Learning Centred Approach* by Hutchinson and Waters (1986, pp. 108–109), which includes the following points:

- input
- content focus
- language focus
- writing task

Each sequence deals with the writing products from a what? how? and now what? approach, but I have chosen to take the process one step further and include public speaking and presentation tasks. Each time the students finish writing and peer-editing a product, they will then present it to the class for the development of their speaking and listening skills (and peer feedback). Presenting and speaking skills will be initially presented in the first week during an intensive workshop and thereafter addressed briefly before presentation time.

Unit content

If the organizing principle is topic or theme-based, the content of a unit will depend on the way you have conceptualized the course content and the goals and objectives for the course. For example, each unit in Denise Maksail-Fine's Spanish 3 course brings together vocabulary, grammar, culture, functions, and reading, writing, speaking, and listening skills, using the topic as the unifying focus. These elements—grammar, culture, functions, etc.—are the way Denise has conceptualized the content of her course, and they also appear in her goals and objectives. For example, one of her goals is for her students to develop speaking and listening skills and the objectives include being able to use grammar, vocabulary and functions appropriate to the topic. Denise's choices about what to put in her unit are governed by the way she conceptualized content and formulated goals and objectives.

See Chapter 5, page 91.

If the organizing principle of a course is a process or skill, rather than a topic or theme, then the unit content will be somewhat predictable because it will include the language, skills, and strategies needed to carry out the process or master the skill. For example, the organizing principle of Brooke Palmer's course is scientific texts, which students need to be able to understand and produce. The unit content will include the particular vocabulary, analytical skills, and writing skills students need to be able to produce the type of text that is the focus of the unit, such as the description of a mechanism.

However, Brooke's course does not only focus on writing skills. She formulated three goals for her course (which I have abbreviated here): for students to develop scientific and technical writing skills and strategies, to develop reading skills and strategies, and to develop speaking and listening skills and strategies. While the organizing principle was scientific texts such as amplified definitions and descriptions of a mechanism, she wanted her students not only to develop writing skills so that they could produce the texts, but also to develop reading

For her complete goals and objectives see Appendix 7-4 on page 260.

skills, using the text types as the basis for input, and presentation skills, using the information in their writing as a basis. Had she conceptualized content in a different way, for example as genre rather than skills, she would approach the texts differently and have somewhat different course goals.

See Chapter 4, page 48, re genre.

Regardless of what the organizing principle is, the unit content is derived from the way you have conceptualized content and articulated goals and objectives, which in turn are based on what you know about your context and your students' needs. Because course design is a multi-faceted process, you may find that you will want to modify or refine your goals and objectives because of discoveries you make as you organize the course and draw up a syllabus.

Unit organization

There are three complementary ways to organize the modules, units, or strands in a course: **a cycle, a matrix,** or a **combination** of the two. A **cycle** means that some elements occur in a predictable sequence and, once the sequence is completed, it starts all over again. For example, Brooke Palmer describes her unit organization as based on a cycle which begins with language input, followed by focus on content and focus on language, and ends with a writing task. To this cycle she has added a listening and speaking component based on the written product. In an academic writing course, students might follow a certain sequence for each type of essay, such as writing a rough draft, peer/teacher conferencing, editing, writing the final draft, publishing. Once they finish one type of essay, they begin the cycle all over again for the next type.

A **matrix** means that elements are selected from certain categories of content, but not in a predictable order. For example, in a theme-based course that integrates speaking, listening, reading, and writing, you could begin one unit with a listening exercise and then follow it with a reading and discussion. The next unit could begin with a reading, followed by a written response, followed by a speaking activity, and so on. The matrix is drawn from the way the teacher conceptualizes the content of the course, and may include skills, tasks, functions, grammatical items, vocabulary, and so on, which she or he draws from during each unit. Denise Maksail-Fine's course uses a matrix based on her goals and objectives (see Chapter 5).

A **combination** of a cycle and a matrix means that within a given unit, the course might follow a predictable sequence of learning activities, such as beginning each unit with a survey of what students know about a topic, ending each unit with students surveying others outside of class, and some learning activities that are drawn from a matrix.

The following diagram from the Australian Language Levels (ALL) curriculum guide *Pocket ALL* (Vale, Scarino and McKay 1996) provides a clear visual of a matrix approach to organizing unit content and shows how the unit content is chosen in order to achieve the unit objectives. The example given below is for upper secondary school students who are learning Italian. It is a unit called "Interviewing" within a larger syllabus module called "Self and others." The specific goals and general objectives of the unit are listed to the left. The general objectives are the focus of the activities at the center of the wheel. The specific objectives in the wheel encompass general knowledge, skills development, lan-

See Chapter 5, page 78, re goals and objectives in the Australian Language Levels.

Figure 7.6: Example of a Unit of Work for Upper Secondary Students

TABLE 14 Example of a unit of work derived from the Stage 4 syllabus module, *Self and others*

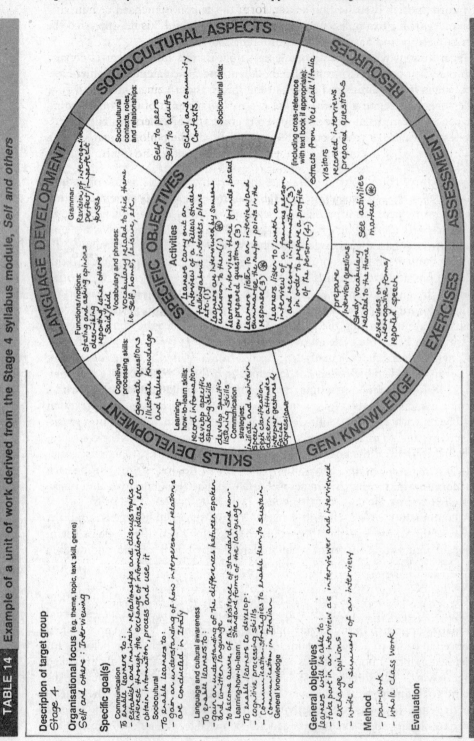

Description of target group
Stage 4

Organisational focus (e.g. theme, topic, text, skill, genre)
Self and others : Interviewing

Specific goal(s)

Communication
To enable learners to:
- establish and maintain relationships and discuss topics of interest through the exchange of information, ideas, etc
- obtain information, process and use it

Sociocultural
To enable learners to:
- gain an understanding of how interpersonal relations are conducted in Italy

Language and cultural awareness
To enable learners to:
- gain an understanding of the differences between spoken and written language
- to become aware of the existence of standard and non-standard forms of the language

Learning-how-to-learn
To enable learners to develop:
- cognitive processing skills
- communication strategies to enable them to sustain communication in Italian

General knowledge

General objectives
Learners will be able to:
- take part in an interview as interviewer and interviewed
- exchange opinions
- write a summary of an interview

Method
- pairwork
- whole class work

Evaluation

From *Developing Language Syllabuses and Programs: A K–12 Series of Syllabus Exemplars—Italian*

Pocket ALL, p. 59

guage development, and sociocultural aspects. These specific objectives, along with the activities listed in the center, form the matrix of what the unit will include. A blank copy of this matrix, called a "focus wheel," is in Appendix 7-5 on page 261.

There are some cycles that are the philosophical basis for the course and are, in a sense, the organizing principle for the course. The Language Experience Approach is one example of a cycle as the basis for organizing a course (Dixon 1990, Rigg 1989). The problem-posing cycle used as a part of the Participatory Approach is another example of a cycle (Auerbach and Wallerstein 1987). The experiential learning cycle (Kolb 1984) can also form the philosophical basis of a course. Below is a diagram representing Chris Conley's adaptation of the problem posing cycle for his Adult Education class:

Figure 7.6: Chris Conley's Adaptation of the Problem-posing Cycle

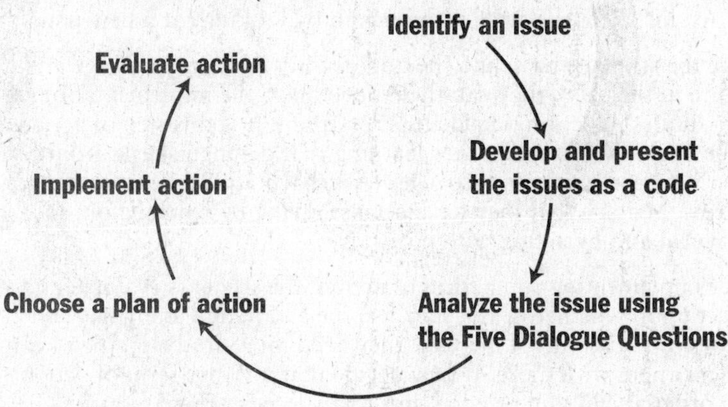

A code is a way of illustrating an issue so that it can be understood from a number of perspectives. For example, to illustrate approaches to job interviews, Chris used the code of two interviews, one appropriate and one not.

Chris describes the process:

Chris Conley

> The first steps in the cycle and sequence are to listen to the students' concerns and to identify issues they are facing. Once an issue is identified by the teacher or students, there is an option of waiting before addressing the issues or of immediately developing a code. If I decide to present the issue, I can develop a code around it, using a variety of presentation techniques to get students to identify the issue embedded in the code. I may use loaded pictures, phrases, stories, dialogues, writing from students or texts, videos or any other tool that will achieve the goal of delivering the issue to the students. I can also use an integration of other skills to present and practice the language of the code. In short, I can use just about any teaching tool or technique to present a code.
>
> Once a code and its language have been presented, it needs to be analyzed by addressing critical thinking questions (5 Dialogue questions):
>
> 1. Describe the issue
> 2. Ask students to define the issue
> 3. Personalize the issue

4. Look at the larger context
5. Address strategies for solutions

By asking these questions, the teacher is presenting a point of view that in order to improve our lives, we all must ask critical questions and question the status quo that exists. The teacher and students enter into a dialogue around the issue.

See pages 161–162 for a unit from Chris's course.

After the critical questions and dialogue, the students are called upon to make some decisions as to how they can use language to improve their lives and situations. What can students study or do in the classroom to resolve or address the issues presented in the code? Do they need to learn a new skill? More pronunciation? Rules of social conduct? Again, I am able to bring into play the integration of various language teaching techniques and methods to provide my students with choices that may help them in their decision. Or the students may not find the issue worth their while to study and let it die. At this point the cycle begins again by looking for a new issue.

Once the students have had the opportunity to study language and culture in the class, they can then move on to the implementation of their studies in action outside the classroom. It is this step of action in the process of participatory learning that distinguishes it from other learner-centered approaches (Auerbach 1993). Learners try to address the issue that they have been studying by reaching out to the world and by acting within it.

After implementing some form of action, the students evaluate and reflect upon whether or not they feel the action and study has had the desired outcome. If they feel they need more studying, then I can provide them with more. If they decide that another form of action is in order, then I will provide time and space for them to make choices. Or they may feel a sense of closure with the issue and want to move one. At this point, we begin the process again.

One of the challenges of developing a course based on a cycle or a process is how to integrate such language-based work with vocabulary, grammar, pronunciation, or specific functions. Chris Conley has integrated these aspects of language learning into his course by asking his students to identify language-specific aspects that might help them in dealing effectively with the issue they have identified.

7.8 *Consider Brooke Palmer's approach to unit content (see page 139), the Australian Language Levels Italian class exemplar in Figure 7.6, and Chris Conley's approach to unit content. Which approach to unit organization are you most drawn to? Why? Which are you least drawn to? Why? Discuss your answers with a colleague.*

We have investigated the work of five different teachers in this chapter. The way in which each teacher organized her or his course stems from the way in which the teacher has conceptualized the content and determined the goals and objectives for the course. Denise Maksail-Fine has conceptualized the content in terms of topics, grammar, and culture, and objectives in terms of development of the four skills, cultural awareness, and cooperative learning, using the topics as a vehicle. Toby Brody has conceptualized content based on what is found in the newspaper and in terms of specific skills such as proposing solutions that require the use of the four skills of speaking, listening, reading, and writing. She has included grammar and culture within each module as well.

The way the teacher has conceptualized content and determined goals and objectives depends in turn on the teacher's experience and the students' needs, or what the teacher knows about their needs. In Valarie Barnes' case, her knowledge of young adults on a holiday or vacation—that they have lots of energy and curiosity and do not want to study grammar—led her to develop a course organized around theme-based field trips. In Brooke Palmer's case, knowing that being able to write and deliver a scientific research paper was a priority for her students influenced her choices.

A teacher's beliefs also play an important role. Chris Conley believes that adult students should make decisions for themselves about their needs and has organized his course accordingly. The specific context in which the course takes place also determines how the course is organized, especially the amount of time, how often the class meets, and the resources available. Valarie's course lasts a month, and the students meet daily for up to six hours. In Denise's case, the course meets for a year, for approximately four hours a week. In some contexts, the schedule of examinations will play an important role in how the course is organized.

7.9 *Choose one of the units you listed in Investigation 7.4.*

1. Consider the way you have conceptualized the content of your course and your goals and objectives for the course. What are your objectives for the unit?

2. List the language learning components that will form the basis of activities in each unit so that the objectives for the unit are achieved.

Language components can include: grammar, vocabulary, pronunciation, communicative skills, tasks, intercultural skills, interpersonal skills, specific content, and so on.

3. Make a chart or mind map, or use a diagram similar to the one used for the Australian Language Levels in Figure 7. 6, in which you experiment with different ways to organize the content of the unit.

To close the chapter, I'd like to follow the process of a teacher as he works through the way he organizes his course. The teacher is Dylan Bate, and he is designing a course for Chinese university students who are studying to be English teachers. The course is organized around themes. Decisions about unit content—what to include in each unit relative to the theme—are governed by his goals. These goals are: for learners to develop autonomy, for learners to develop cultural awareness, and for learners to improve listening and speaking. Thus each unit will weave together work on learner strategies, cultural awareness, and listening and speaking skills.

Dylan Bate

> Originally, I envisioned a cyclical organization to my course on the daily, weekly and monthly level. I still see the course as following cycles, but now I see them as much more flexible, especially on the daily level. The week will also be adjustable, though having a more set routine, and the month will be pretty much as it was. The old plan looked like this:

See page 119 for Dylan's discussion of feedback.

> 1. Monday: introduction to the week's theme, structures and vocabulary.
> 2. Tuesday: storytelling activity, listening strategies, speaking strategies.
> 3. Wednesday: code-like activity, focus on Chinese/US culture, writing activities
> 4. Thursday: Silent Way and CLL activities, pronunciation, catch up, turning in speaking/listening logs
> 5. Friday: feedback, learning strategies, group work, games.

See Stevick (1998) for more on CLL, *Silent Way.*

See original grid in Appendix 7-6 on page 262.

> Each day followed a fairly strict form: warm-up activity, main activity, group/pair work, and feedback. I had worked out a grid with the four components of each day intersecting the schedule above to show how it would play out in a week using a week from the early part of the course as an example. This proved to be far too constricting for conceptualizing what would happen. I had jumped past the stage of putting each activity through the filter of my major goals for the course, a far more crucial step in a course that will have a lot of changes anyway when confronted by actual flesh and blood students. My thoughts were that if I could establish the actual time for each activity, and have the week fully planned, they would suggest their own inter-relatedness and their worthiness for inclusion in the course magically.
>
> In fact, I found myself spending an enormous amount of time trying to sequence and find the perfect set of activities by criteria that had no explicit connection to the central purposes for the course. The idea was that intuitively they would match up. Unfortunately, such a scheme, instead of justifying the unity of these activities, made me feel I would be teaching discrete, awkward pieces without relation to each other. I felt discouraged by the whole process.

At this point, Dylan came to me to talk about his course. He found that trying to explain his problem helped him realize what it was.

> My scheme had become too inflexible too fast, I had skipped an important step. I was reverting to my old mentality of "just get something concrete down." I think many teachers think in terms of what will happen in class on a given day; that is natural, but it is important to step back now and then and revise classroom planning in terms of the course goals.

I suggested that he use a grid format that could help him to see some of the relationships and connections he felt were missing. Dylan continues.

> I made the new grid with my goals at the top intersecting the activities of the week. They roughly fall in the order they might be taught. The actual order they are to follow, and the days they fall on, are subject to many variables, most of which will only become apparent at the time. With this in mind, I tried to realistically give enough material to fill the five hours of class time devoted to this unit.
>
> These changes are represented in the new improved chart. From these revisions came a looser and more serviceable cycle, informed on both ends by the course goals:

See grid in Appendix 7-7 on page 263.

Figure 7.8: The Cycle for Dylan Bate's Course Organization

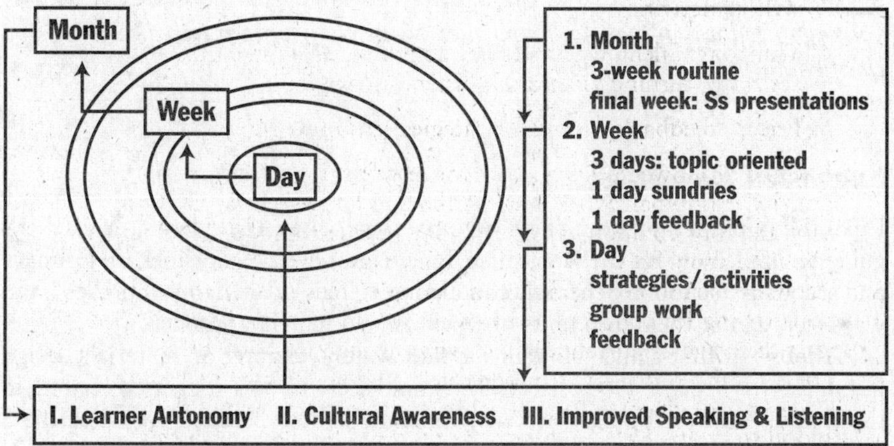

Dylan's narrative raises several points. First, organizing your course is not like putting a jigsaw puzzle together so that every piece falls neatly into place. There are two arguments against going about course design in that way. The first is that it is an exercise in abstraction that will end in frustration. I experienced this a few years ago when I was teaching a course to the non-native speakers of English in our undergraduate and graduate programs. I decided that I wanted it to have a four-skills focus and so devised a nice looking syllabus with the four skills evenly distributed. I had a video for listening, individual oral presentations for speaking, student selected texts for reading, and papers they had written for other classes for writing.

The course had no coherence because there was no organizing principle and so what the students did with each skill had no relation to the other. I had to drastically revise the syllabus so that I could save the course. We ended up using the video, which was on cultural differences in communication styles, as the vehicle for listening, vocabulary development, and discussion. The readings were chosen to link to the individual oral presentations given by the students. The course was somewhat better, but still disjointed. Were I to do the course over again, I would choose an organizing principle, such as topics. I would try to integrate the four skills around a few topics, such as communication styles, while still leaving room for student choice.

The second reason for not approaching course design as a jigsaw puzzle is that you leave out the students. When the course doesn't work, the tendency is to blame the students for not "getting it" rather than adjusting the course to their needs.

A second point raised in Dylan's narrative is the need to make choices and to justify them. Dylan's first tendency was to put everything he knew and wanted to try into the syllabus. The result was a mishmash that had no coherence. When he reminded himself of his three goals, they drove his syllabus and provided the basis for his choices. The conceptual container that supports your course must, ultimately, be based on what makes sense to you.

7.10 *Outline as much as you can of the syllabus for your course. Discuss why you organized it that way with a partner. Make changes to it based on what you clarified during the discussion*

Suggested Readings

I like the approach to organizing a course in *Pocket ALL* (1996), a teacher's guide to implementing the Australian Language Levels Guidelines for primary and secondary school teachers. It contains examples of "syllabus modules" and ways to organize them into units of work using a matrix approach.

Although at first glance Hutchinson and Waters' chapter on materials design in *English for Specific Purposes* (1987) would seem to be a suggested reading in the chapter on developing materials, I include it here because they describe a useful model for developing a unit of work, which Brooke Palmer refers to in this chapter in her reflections about her ESP course design.

For further ideas about criteria for sequencing, see the section titled "What Criteria May Be Used to Select, Grade, and Sequence Tasks?" on pages 96–98 in Numa Markee's book, *Managing Curricular Innovation* (1997).

8
Developing Materials

Materials development is the planning process by which a teacher creates units and lessons within those units to carry out the goals and objectives of the course. In a sense, it is the process of making your syllabus more and more specific. Materials development takes place on a continuum of decision-making and creativity which ranges from being given a textbook and a timetable in which to "cover it"—least responsibility and decision-making—to developing all the materials you will use in class "from scratch"—most responsibility and creativity. Neither extreme is desirable. When teachers are required to strictly adhere to a textbook and timetable there is little room for them to make decisions and to put to use what they have learned from experience, which, in effect, "deskills" the teacher (Apple 1986). The teacher is viewed as simply a technician and not a professional. On the other hand, the majority of teachers are not paid or do not have the time in their schedules to develop all the materials for every course they teach.

However, because a teacher does not have responsibility for choosing materials, does not mean that she cannot exercise creativity in using them. Teachers can be involved in materials development from the moment they pick up a textbook and teach from it. This is because a teacher will inevitably have to make decisions about how long to spend on certain activities, which ones to skip or assign for homework if there isn't enough time, which ones to modify so that they are relevant to that particular group of students. A teacher who changes the names of the people in a textbook exercise for practicing phone numbers to those of the students in the class is exercising responsibility and creativity. In Chapter 9 we will focus specifically on adapting a textbook. In this chapter we will focus on adapting existing materials and developing new materials as part of a coherent plan for teaching one's course.

The Scope of Materials Development

What are materials? What are techniques? Is there a difference between a technique and an activity? The boundaries between materials, techniques, and activities are blurred. On first reflection, one might say that materials are *what* a teacher uses, and techniques and activities are *how* she uses them. While that might have been true for language materials twenty years ago, it is no longer true. Part of the blurring of boundaries stems from the different ways which one can conceptualize content. If you conceptualize content as a skill—learning to write, for example—then materials will of necessity include activities. For example, Teli Pinheiro Franco, a teacher in Brazil, describes writing materials she developed for a teens' course, in terms of a series writing activities that result in a final piece of writing (1996). In a task-based course, the organizing unit is the task, which is focused on using language to get something done.

What is the difference between an activity and a technique? Again, the boundary is blurred. For me, the distinction is related to repertoire. When I teach language, there are certain types of activities that I rely on, regardless of the class I teach. In my case, this includes having students work in pairs and small groups for practice activities, using scrambled sentences and texts to work with syntax and discourse, categorizing for vocabulary learning, using my fingers to represent sentence elements for correction, using the "Human computer" (Rardin and Tranel 1988) and analysis techniques for pronunciation, rhythm, and intonation, having students give me regular feedback on the class, and so on. These activities comprise my repertoire of core techniques. I do add activities to my repertoire (and discard them), depending on what I have learned from the teachers I teach, from a presentation at the latest conference, from something I've read, or from something discovered by chance as I teach. (I also have a repertoire of core techniques for teaching teachers.) The basis on which a core technique becomes part of my repertoire depends on a variety of factors which include: what I want my students to learn, what role I want my students to play, my understanding of how people learn in general, and how they learn languages in particular, what I am comfortable doing, what I feel my students will be comfortable doing, and the resources available.

For a teacher designing a course, materials development means creating, choosing or adapting, and organizing materials and activities so that students can achieve the objectives that will help them reach the goals of the course. In order to understand the scope of materials development and where it fits within designing a course, we can refer to the flow chart for organizing a course from Chapter 7, Figure 7.1, page 125. For practical purposes, materials development takes place at the unit level, numbers 4 and 5 in the chart, and within a unit, at the lesson level. The chart is now expanded to include developing materials.

Figure 8.1: Five Aspects of Organizing a Course

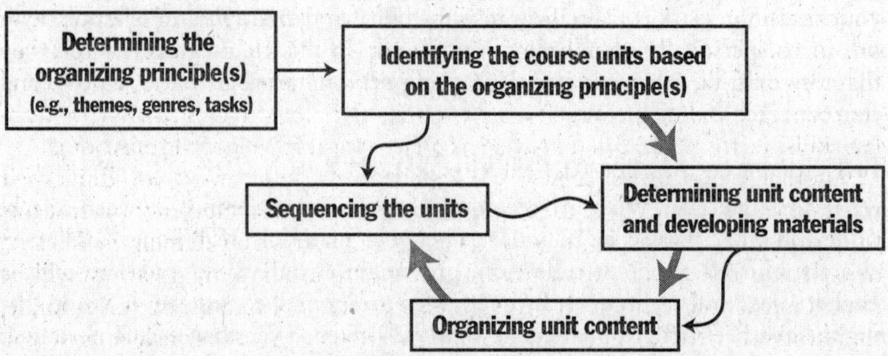

For the purposes of this book, materials development encompasses decisions about the actual materials you use—textbook, text, pictures, worksheets, video, and so on, as well as the activities students do, and how the materials and activities are organized into lessons. The materials you develop are influenced by your beliefs and understandings about teaching and learning languages as they apply to your particular course in its particular context. In this respect, the process of materials development involves deciding how to put your teaching principles into practice.

ON WHAT BASIS DOES ONE CHOOSE, ADAPT, OR DEVELOP MATERIALS?

8.1 *You have been given the following piece of authentic material (four housing ads from a United States newspaper) as the basis for creating a unit. You define the context for which you will create the materials for the unit. Sketch out a list of ideas for the materials. Then make a list of what you took into consideration as you sketched out your ideas.*

1. Studio. carpet, appls, gas and elec. incl. Near beach, on bus route. $395 . Month-to-month. 258-4135
2. House, quiet, country living only 40 miles from downtown. 3 bedrooms, backyard, garage, W/D HT and HW. Pets OK. Call 555-3980 after 6.
3. Furn 1 BR $450 + util. Conv loc near shopping, transportation. No pets. Sublet 6 months-1 year. 346-5967.
4. Duplex, 2 bedrooms, stove, frig, carport. $610. gas incl. Best schools. 3-year lease. Please call 246-8004

The list you make can help you get to the core of what you consider important in developing materials. To decide what to do with the ads you need to consider who the students are and whether they have a real need for finding a place to live. If they do, what are their needs regarding housing and how can learning to read housing ads help them in finding a place to live? Are they likely to encounter discrimination and, if they are, how will the activities address that?

If they don't have immediate needs related to housing, then other factors guide your decisions. One of those factors is the goals for your course. For example, if one of your goals is for students to develop cross-cultural awareness skills, then the ads could be used as a basis for understanding aspects of U.S. culture and contrasting it with their own. If one of your goals is for students to improve reading skills, then the ads could be used as a basis for different kinds of reading.

Another factor is your view of how students learn and what you think their role and yours should be in the classroom. If you feel it is important for students to take initiative in order to learn, then the activities you develop will reflect that. If you believe that students learn in multiple ways, then variety will be important. If you feel that students' affective needs are important, for example, that students need to build self confidence, then you will consider how you sequence the activities so that students can produce the language confidently. Additionally, you need to consider the types of activities they will do, for example, discussions or role plays, and the aspects of language they need to learn in order to carry out the activity successfully.

I have given these four ads to teachers in a variety of settings, notably groups of EFL teachers in Brazil and groups of mostly North American teachers in the United States. The following is a synthesis of their collective wisdom and ideas about what they considered when designing activities, why, and examples of activities or ways of organizing the activities.

The first one was the most frequent consideration:

1. **Activities should draw on what students know (their experience, their current situation) and be relevant to them**

   - to draw on what they know before moving to what is new;
   - to validate their experience;
   - to use what they know as the language basis for the lesson;
   - to engage their interest.

   Examples:

   Students make a list of what they consider when looking for a place to live.

   Students describe how to go about finding a place to live in their country or, if residents in another country, how they found the housing they have.

   Write "home" on board; make a word map in response to "What does it mean to you?"

   Students describe their housing as a basis for vocabulary.

The second one was raised mainly by teachers who taught immigrants in the United States. They also pointed out that if the students had literacy needs, the ads would not be appropriate:

2. **Activities should focus on students' outside of class needs, if appropriate**

   - so that needs can be met.

   Examples:

   Brainstorm issues and questions about their actual housing.

   Students make a list of what they need in housing.

This point addresses students' affective needs: how confident they feel about reading English, speaking English in front of their peers or outside of class; how they feel about making mistakes:

3. **Activities should build students' confidence**

   - so students can feel confident in transferring what learned outside of class.

   Examples:

   Sequence the activities so they provide enough practice.

   Narrow the focus of the activity so students can be successful.

This point addresses the teachers' view of how learners learn as well as student motivation:

4. **Activities should allow students to problem solve, discover, analyze**
   - so that students will be engaged;
   - so that students will use language.

   Examples:
   Abbreviations matching exercise.
   Analyze why housing ads are written the way they are.
   Students figure out in small groups then get together and share.
   Brainstorm questions to ask landlord.
   Students create own categories for housing information.

This point addresses how to ensure students learn skills which can be transferred to other learning contexts in or outside of the classroom, such as learning reading strategies:

5. **Activities should help students develop specific skills and strategies**
   - so that they can transfer skills to other learning situations.

   Examples:
   Read for main idea then read for specific information.
   Guess or match abbreviations.

This point addresses both the areas of the syllabus you want to cover as well as the need to provide the building blocks for writing, listening, reading, or speaking in real (or realistic) situations:

6. **Activities should help students develop specific language and skills they need for authentic communication**
   - so that students learn and practice vocabulary, grammar, functions, etc. that they can use in real situations.

   Examples:
   Work on vocabulary so they can access text and be able to speak.
   Do work on grammar and 4 skills before culture.
   Brainstorm questions to ask landlord prior to role play.

This point addresses a view of language and literacy as involving both oral and written channels in both receptive and productive modes:

7. **Activities should integrate the four skills of speaking, listening, reading, and writing**
   - because the four skills mutually reinforce each other.

   Examples:
   Follow up reading with telephone activity to answer ad; role-play renter/landlord.

Write an ad for their current apartment or home.

If teachers use authentic texts in their classes (spoken or written), students need to understand how they are constructed and why they are constructed that way.

8. **Activities should enable students to understand how a text is constructed**

   - so that students can gain access to similar texts.

   Examples:

   Analyze why housing ads are written the way they are.

   Use real newspapers to determine where to find this information.

9. **Activities should enable students to understand cultural context and cultural differences**

   - so they can have more confidence in target culture and understand own culture better.

   Examples:

   Discuss how housing is found in the United States vs. in their culture.

   Ensure they know how decisions are made and communicated in the United States vs. in their culture.

   Writing own ads: Would an ad like this be written in their culture? If so, how would it be different?

   Analyzing the ad: What does the way the ad is written tell you about U.S. culture?

10. **Activities should enable students to develop social awareness**

    - so they can navigate systems in target culture.

    Examples:

    Help students to know rights and responsibilities.

    Make sure students understand not only customs with respect to renting, but issues such as discrimination based on race, children, age.

11. **Activities should be as authentic as possible**

    - so that students see relationship with real language use;
    - so that students gain experience with real language use.

    Examples:

    Contextualize activities: friend is moving, what are friend's needs, choose an ad based on needs.

    What is process followed in the United States? Follow sequence.

    Provide authentic speaking practice: role-play talking to landlord over telephone; meeting with landlord.

    Provide newspapers and find other ads.

This point addresses two issues, one pedagogical, one social:

12. Activities should vary the roles and groupings

- within the class: so that students get different types of practice and responsibilities;
- with respect to social context: so that students experience /analyze different social roles.

Examples:

Students figure out (e.g., why housing ads are written the way they are) in small groups, then get together and share.
Students present what they know: students become teachers.
Students role-play renter and landlord.

13. Activities should be of various types and purposes

- to provide adequate practice.

Examples:

Students create own ad.

Students role-play.

14. Activities should use authentic texts or realia when possible

- so that students are familiar with/have access to language as used in "real world."

Example:

Bring in newspapers.

15. Activities should employ a variety of materials

- to engage students;
- to meet different learning needs.

Examples:
Visuals (pictures), print, audio, video, objects, realia.

I have summarized the fifteen considerations above on the following chart. I find it interesting that the chart, which is derived from the teachers' ideas, includes the three areas drawn from Stern (1992), which served as the framework for conceptualizing content in Chapter 4: language, learners and learning, and social context. In terms of social context, the sociolinguistic area is not explicitly mentioned by the teachers and could be added to the list. The chart includes two additional categories: "Activity/Task Types" and "Materials," which are specifically related to the process of materials development.

Figure 8.2: A List of Considerations for Developing Materials

Learners

1. make relevant to their experience and background
2. make relevant to their target needs (outside of class)
3. make relevant to their affective needs

Learning

4. engage in discovery, problem solving, analysis
5. develop specific skills and strategies

Language

6. target relevant aspects (grammar, functions, vocabulary, etc.)
7. integrate four skills of speaking, listening, reading, and writing
8. use/understand authentic texts

Social Context

9. provide intercultural focus
10. develop critical social awareness

Activity/Task Types

11. aim for authentic tasks
12. vary roles and groupings
13. vary activities and purposes

Materials

14. authentic (texts, realia)
15. varied (print, visuals, audio, etc.)

8.2 *Amend the list above based on the lists of ideas and considerations you developed in Investigation 8.1*

An important aspect of materials development is making choices. You can't target everything and so you need to make choices based on what you want your students to learn according to your goals and objectives and your syllabus focus. The word "authentic" appears several times on the chart above. Authentic material refers to spoken and written texts that are used by native speakers in the "real world" (Omaggio Hadley 1993). Authentic tasks are those that native speakers engage in in the "real world."

Using authentic material is problematic in the L2 classroom because it is not constructed to contain only the aspects of language the learner has encountered or learned up until that point and so may not be entirely accessible to the learner. There are good reasons to use pedagogically prepared material in order to provide the stepping stones to understanding and using authentic material. For example, the four advertisements, while they were taken from a newspaper, are not in the context of the newspaper. To be truly authentic, they would need to appear in the newspaper. In fact, the advertisements were chosen to show a range of housing possibilities. Thus, regarding authentic material, you have choices along the following continuum:

Material: pedagogically prepared ◄—semi-authentic—► authentic

There is a similar continuum of choices around the tasks or activities the learners engage in. The continuum looks like this:

Tasks/activities: pedagogical ◄—real world—► in the real world

In the case of using the advertisements, an "in the real world" task would be for students to call about an actual housing advertisement. This task would not be possible in EFL settings, and, even though feasible, might not be appropriate in an ESL setting. A "real world" task would be a role play of a telephone conversation with a landlord. A pedagogical task would be to read a scripted dialogue between a prospective tenant and a landlord.

The continuum of choice around language the learners produce (spoken or written) is similar:

Language output (by students): controlled ◄——► open-ended

Controlled language output would require students to practice certain grammatical structures or language functions or vocabulary items in order to gain mastery of them, often called a focus on accuracy. Open-ended language output allows students to use all the language in their repertoire to complete an activity. In some senses, of course, all language output is controlled by the context in which it is used. A more comprehensive way of looking at controlled versus open-ended language output that relates specifically to materials development is the distinction between an **activity** and an **exercise,** used in the Australian Language Levels guidelines. An activity is related to the open-ended output on the continuum above and involves "the purposeful and active use of language where learners are required to call upon their language resources to meet the needs of a given communicative situation." (Vale, Scarino and McKay 1991, p.94). An exercise is designed to help learners master specific aspects of communication in a more controlled fashion. "An exercise focuses on one or more elements of the communication process in order to promote learning of the items of language, knowledge, skills, and strategies in communication activities." When developing materials it is important to have a balance of activities and exercises. Too many exercises and too few activities will impede development of the ability to communicate in the real world, while too many activities and not enough exercises will deny students the opportunity to develop the language and skills they need to communicate effectively.

Examples of Materials

Below, we will look at a unit on Telephone Technology from Cyndy Thatcher-Fettig's speaking and listening course in a university intensive English program. The students are from different countries and are at a high intermediate/low advanced level. Classes meet five days a week for one and a half hours a day. Some activities are adapted from the book *Sound Ideas* in the Tapestry series (Heinle & Heinle 1995).

See pages 114–116 for Cyndy Thatcher-Fettig's approach to needs assessment.

8.3 *Study the following unit from Cyndy Thatcher-Fettig's speaking and listening course.*

1. What do you like about the unit and why? What don't you like and why not?
2. What can you infer from the unit about her goals and objectives for the course?
3. Which aspects of the list of considerations in Figure 8.1 above does she address?
4. Choose one of the continua on the preceding pages (for material, for tasks/activities and for language output) and find activities or materials in her unit that fall on different ends of the continuum.

Unit: Telephone Technology

***Monday:** Beginning of new unit—Telephone Technology*

(Students have been assigned the article "Voice Mail: not the answer?" prior to the unit and asked to be prepared to discuss questions based on the article. See Appendix 8-1 on page 264.)

I. Schema Activation:

Schema refers to one's background knowledge of a given subject.

- Activate students' schema on telephone technology by writing quote on the board—"One hundred years ago, the telephone was invented to allow people to talk to each other. Now it's being used to help people avoid talk."
- Students discuss quote in pairs—then as a whole class.
- Review vocabulary—voice mail, answering machine, call waiting, cellular phones, facsimile, technophobia, caller ID.

II. Communication Strategies:

- Review handout on clarifying and paraphrasing (see Appendix 8-2 on page 267).
- Students listen to a taped conversation and write down the instances of clarifying and paraphrasing.
- Student practice in pairs using strategic expressions during mini-conversations (two minutes) with a third student monitoring to see whether or not they're using the strategies.

III. Discussion

(Based on homework article "Voice Mail: not the answer?")

- Students establish a discussion leader (responsible for full group participation, and continuous movement of discussion).
- Students discuss homework questions in groups of five.
- Report findings or issues back to large group.

Homework: Listen to tape in the language laboratory—Chapter two: Listening Passage #2, parts A and B (see Appendix 8-1 on page 265).

Tuesday:

I. Warm-up:

- Students review cartoon and discuss questions in pairs (see Appendix 8-1 on page 266).
- Discuss meanings and reactions in large group.

II. Review Homework:

- Students briefly summarize the taped dialogues—Part A and Part B.
- Students share their descriptions.
- Discuss questions.

III. Simulation Preparation:

- Students brainstorm on board the pros and cons of having telephone technology in business.
- Students choose roles of simulation (pro/con see Appendix 8-4 on page 269) and get together with students that have their same role.
- Students talk about the stance they're going to take in the simulated office meeting, their reasons behind it, and how they're going to say it.

Homework: Practice part for the simulation.

Wednesday:

I. Simulation:

- Students break into their office meeting groups and begin simulation.
- Discuss results with other groups.

II. Functional Situations—Telephoning

- Discussion of telephoning fears—why it's difficult to talk on the telephone, why you don't like to, personal experiences, problems, etc.
- Students fill out as much of the blank handout (see Appendix 8-3 on page 268) as they can.
- Review expressions as a class (expressions, meaning, pronunciation).

Homework: Review telephone handout and finish filling the rest as best they can (possibly interviewing native speakers on the expressions they use).

Thursday:

I. Review of handout:

- Review telephone handout (new expressions, pronunciation)

II. Practice expressions:

- Practice with students (Teacher calling students, then teacher calling individual students, then students calling each other—back to back for full effect).
- Students listen to taped telephone conversations—focus on discrete information (fill in the blanks, questions).

III. Use:

- Students practice expressions with role-play cards (examples in Appendix 8-4 on page 269).

Homework: Call my house and ask for my fiancé. Leave a message.

Friday:

I. Review homework:

- Talk about general areas of success and things to work on when calling. Talk with individual students that need help privately after class.

II. Warm-up: Telephone situations

- Students read the situation (examples in Appendix 8-4 on page 269) in pairs and act it out.
- Discuss any questions, issues, concerns raised.

III. Calling for information:

- Discuss personal experiences about calling places to get information (bus schedules, store information, bank statement, bills, etc.)
- Review handout with students and practice pronunciation of set expressions (see Appendix 8-5 on page 270).
- Listen to taped telephone conversations of customers asking for information.
- Do practice situation in pairs.
- Have a few pairs demonstrate.

Homework: Call some place for information: store, bus depot, train station, telephone companies, travel agents, movie theaters, etc. Come prepared to share the information you received.

How is the unit above a realization of Cyndy's syllabus? In Chapter 7, we explored the idea that the basis for the content of a unit is the way you have conceptualized content and the goals and objectives for the course as they relate to the organizing principle. Cyndy's course is organized around weekly topics, each with associated functions. The aim of her course is for students to improve their listening and speaking skills so that they can function independently in both daily and academic contexts. To investigate specifically how her unit is a realization of her goals and objectives, consult Appendix 8-6 on page 271.

The unit above is clearly a realization of her syllabus, although she hasn't explicitly focused on daily versus academic uses of the telephone. Within the topic of telephone technology, she has targeted a variety of functions, some associated with using the telephone, some associated with negotiation. She has provided ample speaking and listening practice in a variety of contexts, including "in the real world." In terms of the chart in Figure 8.2, Cyndy has targeted all of the areas except, perhaps, the social context. For example, there is not an overt focus on the differences between the students' own cultures and that of the United States, although this may emerge in some of the activities such as on Wednesday when they talk about their individual experiences using the telephone.

It is clear from Cyndy's unit, that any given activity will account for more than one aspect of the chart in Figure 8.2. For example, the activity mentioned above, asking students about their individual experiences and fears with the telephone, makes the topic relevant (#1), and can surface needs, both target needs and affective needs (#s 2 and 3). The simulation on the same day, enables students to develop specific skills in negotiation (#5) while practicing the functions and vocabulary they have learned (#6), in different roles (#12).

We will now turn to a different course and course context. The following is a unit from Chris Conley's course for adult immigrants in which he shows one way to implement the action portion of his cycle (see Chapter 7).

8.4 *Study the following unit from Chris Conley's course.*

1. What appeals to you about the unit? Why? What doesn't appeal to you? Why not?
2. Which aspect of the chart in Figure 8.2 did he take into consideration in developing materials?
3. How are his materials similar to and how are they different from Cyndy Thatcher-Fettig's? What accounts for the differences?

A Plan of Action

The students in this adult ESL class are from the Dominican Republic, Vietnam, Guatemala, and countries in Eastern Europe. They are at the low intermediate-intermediate level. Based on work they have done in previous classes, students have decided that they would like to invite someone from the business community to present information to them about what they are studying.

Objectives:

Students will

- become aware of different styles of written invitations
- be able to identify some differences and similarities between cultural styles of inviting
- be able to recognize and identify the various components of a formal letter
- be able to write a formal invitation in English

Pre-writing

1. Teacher shows 4 types of invitations (see Appendix 8-7 on pages 272–274) and asks questions about them. Are they formal? informal? What is each invitation for? Is it an event? How is it presented—typed or handwritten? Is it personal? Professional?
2. Students get into same-culture groups and are told that they will invite someone from their culture to the class. They write in their language and style.

3. They present letters to the class. What are the components? Is it formal or informal? Personal? Typed or handwritten?
4. The teacher will post them on the walls for reference and reminders for the students to fall back on.
5. Students look at the 4 samples the teacher presented and choose the style which best fits their needs at the moment. It is hoped they will choose the formal business style invitation, although not certain.
6. They analyze why they chose this style.
7. The teacher posts this along with the other invitations on the wall as reference.

Writing

1. Students brainstorm the layout of the letter: what should go in it, the order, how long it should be.
2. Students form culturally mixed groups of 3 and as a group make a first draft of the invitation.
3. They present their invitation. The teacher makes notes of the different letters on poster paper so that they can compare and contrast what they have done.
4. The students discuss how to pull together information from all the invitations into one. The students dictate the letter to the teacher, who transcribes onto poster paper. The teacher is only the scribe. He does not add, subtract, or correct.

Post-writing

1. The teacher has the students read the letter out loud, one student taking one sentence. Then they read it silently.
2. Students are asked to consider how they would edit the letter: global changes in format or local changes in grammar.
3. Students copy the letter and read it at home for homework.

Next class

1. Students review the invitation and are asked for any additional changes.
2. Students type the letter.
3. Letter is mailed.

How is the lesson above related to Chris's conceptualization of his course as a whole? Here are his reflections:

Chris Conley

1. **Sequence of the cycle:** One theme or issue is presented at a time and it goes through the cycle as far as the students deem it necessary or beneficial for their life or English class. (See cycle in Chapter 7 page 143.)
2. **Action:** Study language and issues in the class; transform study to action in the classroom and in the real world.
3. **Throughout the course**—begin with more teacher-centered involvement and production of ideas and materials; then

move toward a more student-centered production (independence learning).

4. **Within a lesson:**

   A. Move from the objective (looking at an issue from another's viewpoint) to subjective (looking at the issue from the personal point of view).

   B. Begin with a focus more on language (grammar, pronunciation, etc.) and move toward the underlying cultural lesson (the issue that is embedded in the language).

   C. Begin with more controlled exercises of presentation and practice and move toward freer activities using the language.

SEQUENCING

Chris has raised the issue of sequencing activities within a unit. The same principles of sequencing, **building** and **recycling,** that apply to course organization apply to unit organization. At the unit level, building from step A to step B can be understood as:

Step A is simpler, step B is more complex.

For example, in Chris's unit, students write a letter in their own language prior to constructing one in the target language.

Step A is more controlled, step B is more open-ended, requires more initiative.

For example, in Cyndy's unit, on Friday, Sequence III, "Calling for information," students practice set expressions prior to practicing situations in pairs; the pair practice precedes the actual calling of a place for information.

Step A provides knowledge or skills required to do step B.

For example, in Chris's unit, students analyze examples of invitations in order to write their own invitations.

Step A uses receptive skills (listening/reading), step B uses productive skills (speaking /listening) [or input before action].

In Cyndy's unit, students listen to a taped telephone conversation, prior to producing their own. They read and study a handout with functional expressions prior to practicing them.

Step A uses productive skills to activate knowledge, Step B uses receptive skills to consolidate knowledge.

In Cyndy's unit, the students talk about what they know about telephone technology prior to studying vocabulary and expressions on a handout.

Other approaches to sequencing include:

- going from the **other** (another's viewpoint) to **self,** the **subjective** (one's own viewpoint).

In some classes, it is typical to use others' viewpoints or experiences as preparation for talking or writing about one's own. In Chris's unit, students write a letter in their language after they have read and analyzed four letters in English.

- or the steps could be reversed, from **personal** experience to **universal** experience.

In some classes, students' begin with their personal experiences in order to understand and make generalizations about the experiences of others.

As in the organization of a course, recycling is another important aspect of organizing and sequencing materials. Language acquisition is not a linear, discrete process, but an organic and unpredictable one (Larsen-Freeman 1997). Learners do not necessarily learn something the first time they encounter it, and so it is important to present material more than once and in different ways in order to aid the acquisition process. Recycling means that **something that has been introduced is then learned in connection with something else, so that it is both "reused" and learned in more depth.**

Ways to recycle include:

- recycling something **using a different skill.** In Cyndy's unit, students <u>listen</u> to taped phone conversations prior to <u>using oral skills</u> in a telephone role play
- recycling something **in a different context.** In Cyndy's unit, students call for information using <u>practice situations</u>, then call for information in a <u>real situation</u>.
- recycling something **using a different learning technique.** In Chris's unit, students <u>compare</u> letters they have written and then <u>dictate</u> one group letter to the teacher

Below we will look at Denise Maksail-Fine's plan for one of the units of her Spanish 3 course. This is a course she has taught for three years in an American high school in rural upstate New York. She is redesigning it to make it a more communicative and less grammar-based course.

8.5 *Look at Denise Maksail-Fine's materials for a unit in her syllabus for a Spanish 3 course in an American high school.*

1. What do you like about her approach to materials development? What don't you like?
2. Find examples from the unit which show how different activities build on each other and how material is recycled in the unit.

Unit 2: Family Life

Week 3

For information about the Natural Approach see Krashen and Terrell (1983).

Day 1 *Mind map "la familia"*

Natural Approach Listening Activity with visuals, follow-up questions

Create a class vocabulary list.

Day 2 *Warm-up: riddle*

Rod Activity "mi familia": volunteer student describes his/her family using rods; students take turns giving understanding responses; students query speaker. Repeat with another volunteer.

Concentration using local community members. Example: I am Bob Smith's mother's father. Who am I? Students match clues with names.

Day 3 *Warm-up: trivia question on Mexican Independence*

Readings (2) on Mexican Independence: Students are split into four equal groups. Two groups receive one reading, the other two receive the other reading. After reading, each group summarizes key points from their reading in writing, and then presents it to one of the groups who did the other reading.

Song: *La Cucaracha*

Day 4 *Warm-up: joke*

Picture Description: Large pictures of people are posted along chalkboard on newsprint.

Students come up one at a time and introduce people from the photos as family members. After identifying the individual(s), students write a short descriptive sentence underneath the picture in black marker. After each student has had a turn, students correct any noun-adjective agreement errors using green marker. Students other than the ones who have done the correcting are asked to state and restate any patterns they observe with regard to noun-adjective agreement.

Strip Sentence Competition: Students work in pairs; each pair is given a set of index card strips that contain elements of sentences. During a period of 5–7 minutes, students manipulate the strips to create as many different sentences as possible, making required agreement changes, and record each variation. The pair with the most correct sentences wins.

Day 5 *Warm-up: proverb*

Mind map: transition words

Whole Group Story Creation: students add sentences about family members' activities to Day 4's picture description sentences. Then, as a group, students take turns to create a story using the picture description sentences and adding transition words and sentences where appropriate.

Journal activity

Week 4

Day 6	*Warm-up: How was your weekend?* Reading: Typical Latino Families. Pre-reading-skim/scan activities. Students then read article once, restate key points for partner, reread, whole group summarization. Discussion: Key differences and similarities between Anglo-American and Latino Families.
Day 7	*Warm-up: riddle* Reread article on families from Day 6, paying particular attention to the use of definite and indefinite articles. Students deduce the most common uses from the reading, volunteering other uses not found in reading. Cloze Activities: articles
Day 8	*Warm-up: trivia question* Introduce parameters for process writing in Spanish class. Process Writing Activity: Students begin to gather and discuss and write ideas about their families (real or imaginary), what they are like, common family activities, how they are alike and/or different from Anglo-American families and Hispanic families.
Day 9	*Warm-up: joke* Continue Process Writing—grammatical focus: articles.
Day 10	*Warm-up: proverb* Continue Process Writing—grammatical focus: articles.

How Does One Develop Materials?

Decisions about developing materials are rooted in your beliefs, understandings, and experience. They also depend on your goals and objectives, the way you conceptualize the content of the course, the way you organize and sequence your course, and your understanding of your students' needs. Your experience has provided you with a basis for decision making as well as a repertoire of techniques. For example, some of the materials may already be in place in the form of routines you use such as warm ups; cycles such as process writing; or your method of assessment such as learning logs or portfolios. It helps to look at the course organization as a way of getting started—the organizing principle and unit content, as well as the time frame which provides the "temporal container" for the course.

It also helps to look at your goals and objectives. One teacher, John Kongsvik, developed an interesting technique to ensure that the materials he developed for his syllabus were, in fact, a realization of his goals and objectives. He had five goals, to each of which he assigned a different color. He drew up an initial course syllabus, outlining the activities on a day-by-day basis. He then went through his syllabus chart and underlined each activity according to which goal he felt it addressed. In some cases, an activity had more than one color under it. After he had gone through the entire syllabus chart, he was able to see the way in which each goal was or wasn't being addressed according to how often the color appeared.

8.6 *Develop the materials for a unit for your course. These include the texts, visuals, etc. as well as the activities students will do. (Refer to Cyndy Thatcher-Fettig's unit on pages 158–160, Chris Conley's unit on pages 161–163, and Denise Maksail-Fine's on pages 165–166.)*

1. Consider your course organization: what the unit focus is and what the unit content is, according to your goals and objectives. Refer to Investigation 7. 9 on page 145 in which you made a list of language components and skills you wanted to include. Consider your context: how long you have for the unit, who your students are, institutional givens.

As you develop the materials:

2. make a note of how you are taking into consideration the elements on the chart in Figure 8.2.
3. consider the continua on pages 156–157 and whether you have a balance of exercises that target specific language and skills, and activities that allow students to draw on the entirety of their language learning resources.
4. consider the ways in which the activities build on each other and recycle language and skills.

I'd like to end this chapter with Iris Broudy's description of her process in developing a unit for her theme-based course for adults offered at a university in Mexico.

Iris Broudy

> It's easy to get attached to your materials, especially when you have invested a lot of time and energy in developing them. That's what happened when I produced the two-week unit on the theme "Relationships."

She goes on to say that some of her aims in developing the unit were to integrate the four skills, use the Internet as a resource, and incorporate video. She continues:

> Soon I had a stack of possible activities. When it came time to sequence the materials, I paid attention to recycling and reinforcement and working in the various elements of my syllabus. I carefully divided each day's lesson plan into specified time chunks, with each activity leading nicely into the next. And before I knew it, I had two weeks filled with an interesting mix of grammar, vocabulary, functions, and skills—all integrated into lively, communicative activities.

But I felt uneasy about my beautiful product. It seemed too organized. It lacked spontaneity. The activities themselves were communicative, and I did leave some slots to work on grammar and pronunciation that might come up, but I had left almost nothing to chance—or to the students. Even if I was fairly certain what would interest this general student population, was I allowing much room for the actual learners to collaborate in their own learning process? No, not really.

After reflecting on this dilemma, Iris continues:

I still like most of the materials I developed for this module. However, they are only a resource, to be selected or adapted as it seems appropriate. I must remember that it is not the materials themselves, but what the students do with them that is important. At the same time, I need to keep reminding myself that materials can be developed without high-tech resources and hours of planning, and those may be the ones that best respond to the immediate needs of the students.

Following is a general plan and a set of materials for one module of English Conversation 600 (see pages 169–170). The theme, "Relationships," includes some subtopics that could be covered in the module. Others can be generated by the students. There are nine different types of materials, along with activities for each. I have also indicated the cultural, linguistic, and communicative elements that are integrated into these activities.

My objective was to provide a rich and engaging variety of activities that would relate to the different stages of the language acquisition process and connect with a wide variety of learning styles.

She then goes on to talk about sequencing.

On my first go-round, I interpreted sequencing to mean that every lesson plan should be perfectly planned out and timed. However, such preciseness makes the lessons too materials-centered and thus too rigid. Classroom management is important; good pacing and time use are essential for enjoyable, effective learning. However, as Stevick (1980) points out, there needs to be a proper balance between teacher control and student initiative. If I want to minimize teacher control, then I prefer to think of sequencing less as lesson planning and more in terms of language acquisition. My objective with these materials is first to familiarize students with a language form (or function, or strategy), then have them produce it in controlled exercises, and finally to begin producing it in free use. As for accuracy and fluency, I am still wrestling with what the balance should be and how and when to do error correction. Ongoing needs assessment (through feedback, dialogue journals, and teacher observation) and negotiation with the students will help me to form criteria in this area.

An Overview of One Module of English 600

Theme: Relationships

Possible subtopics: Friendship
Dating
Love/romance
Family
Social plans

Materials/activities for the module:

1. Dating Questionnaire
   - Phrasal verbs
   - Hypothetical conditional: controlled conversation
   - Look for potential dates through "the personals" (use realia)
   - Write and answer own personals
2. *The Rules: Time Tested Secrets for Capturing the Heart of Mr. Right*
   - Jigsaw reading/discussion of *Time* book review
   - Read/discuss consumer opinions from the Internet
   - Role plays: asking for a date (Mexico and the United States)
   - Students write own rules for "the dating game": create a book (with art)
3. Chris and Mike: written dialogue
   - Phrasal verbs of dating
   - Role plays: making casual social plans
4. "Late Again": jazz chant
5. What Time Will You Get There?: problem solving task
   - Fill out/discuss grid together
   - Role plays: what you say when you're late or kept waiting
6. Real invitations vs. polite chit-chat: four conversations
   - Identify language
7. "Mississippi Masala": film clips
   - Common language of invitations
   - Language of invitations: listen/identify
   - Produce and self-assess functional language
8. "Papa Don't Preach": Madonna song
   - True/false questions to elicit attitudes
   - Information gap listening activity
   - Controlled conversation: teenage pregnancy

9. "Something About the Nature of Midnight": short fiction
   - Reading skills/strategies
   - Free discussion: unwed motherhood
   - Writing personal opinion

The following elements are integrated into the above activities:

Functions:	Inviting; accepting/refusing invitations Complaining/apologizing Agreeing/disagreeing
Culture:	Dating customs Social relationships Male-female roles Concepts of time Social mores
Lexis:	Phrasal verbs (social plans + others) Lexicon of feminism, dating, relationships Slang/idioms
Grammar:	Hypothetical conditional Modal verbs
Phonology:	Reduced speech/schwa Stress/rhythm/intonation /g/in final position

8.7 *Look over the material you have developed for your unit. Is it organized in such a way that there is some flexibility depending on how your students respond to it? For example, does it follow a lock-step sequence, or can you vary the sequence? Are there activities that could be extended (and others omitted) if students needed more time? Is there student choice with respect to the activities themselves or the sequence of activities?*

At the beginning of the chapter I talked about materials development taking place on a continuum of creativity and responsibility. It is actually possible to be too creative and let the materials overwhelm the learning purposes they were designed to achieve. The teacher then loses the students as she or he rushes them through all the activities. Flexibility is important so that you can provide materials that are engaging and appropriate and also allow your students to use them productively in the classroom. Your decisions will also be affected by the resources and constraints of your context on the one hand and your objectives for your students on the other. Together they provide the parameters within which you can exercise your creativity: whatever you develop must be feasible and appropriate within the context. Your students can also be collaborators with you in choosing and developing material once they have a sense of what the course is about and how it is organized.

Suggested Readings

For ideas about developing materials, all of Penny Ur's books are gold mines. Her 1996 book, *A Course in Language Teaching,* brings together her ideas about materials (which in my definition include activities) for teaching the four skills of speaking, listening, reading, writing, as well as grammar, pronunciation, and vocabulary.

Alice Omaggio Hadley's book, *Teaching Language in Context* (1993), provides lots of examples of materials for different levels of proficiency in speaking, listening, reading, writing, but the layout is poor and not always easy to follow.

Each teaching-related book in the TESOL *New Ways* series, for example, *New Ways in Teaching Reading* (Day 1993), gives an abundance of teacher-developed and teacher-tested materials.

For further ideas regarding organizing and sequencing materials, see the suggestions at the end of Chapter 7.

9

ADAPTING A TEXTBOOK

In 1984 I had my first conversation with Susan Lanzano, an editor at Oxford University Press in New York, about the possibility of co-authoring a textbook series. My initial reaction was "I don't use textbooks in my teaching. Why would I want to write one?" Her response was that many teachers are required to use textbooks, a majority of teachers don't have the time or resources to prepare their own materials, and so textbooks are a necessity. "Wouldn't you like to write a textbook based on your experience for those teachers?" she asked. Some conversations later, I agreed to give it a try and started on a long and ultimately worthwhile journey. The journey resulted in a four book series called *East West.* I have since had the opportunity to teach with two of the books. I taught the intermediate level from cover to cover as part of a prescribed curriculum in a language institute in Brazil. I used different parts of the beginner's level in an adult education course here in the town where I live.

Each time I taught with the books, I made copious notes about what I would change in each of them, if writing a textbook were like a course and could be modified each time you taught it. In fact, the difference between writing a textbook and teaching from a textbook is that once a textbook is written, it is fixed, whereas when you teach with it, you can make changes in how you use it. The changes stem from your beliefs and understandings, your goals and objectives, your students' needs, and the requirements of your context. In this chapter we will look at the advantages and disadvantages of textbooks and how to exploit the advantages and overcome the disadvantages in order to use a textbook as a tool in course design. We will not look at how to choose a textbook or at specific techniques for teaching with a textbook. However, the investigations may provide insights that will help you evaluate textbooks and the teachers' voices may provide ideas for techniques.

See the list of readings at the end of the chapter for resources about techniques.

ADVANTAGES AND DISADVANTAGES OF USING A TEXTBOOK

After *East West* was published, I started going on author's tours to promote the series. I generally did two back-to-back presentations, one on a topic of general interest to teachers, such as how to motivate students, and one that focused specifically on the books. On these tours I was accompanied by someone from the publisher who would help set up the room, make introductions and so on. After one set of presentations on my first tour, the publisher's representative, who was actually a friend and had been a graduate student of mine, told me that I seemed very comfortable when giving the first, teaching-focused presentation but stilted when I gave the commercial presentation. I told him I felt awkward because I wasn't used to promoting something and, essentially, asking people to buy it. He said, "Kathleen, you have to realize that for teachers who use a textbook, it is the backbone of their courses. They want to get ideas about how to use it. Don't treat the book as a product, but as a teaching tool." In subsequent presentations, I learned to foreground the teaching issues, such as getting students to participate actively, and have the participants use the activities from the books to explore ways to address the teaching issue. At each presentation I would say something like, "This text is written for everyone and this text is written for no one." (The publisher's representatives probably cringed when they heard this.) We would then explore different ways to adapt the text so that it would meet the needs of their specific group of students. In retrospect I see that by exploring ways to adapt the text, I was asking them to become co-authors of the material. I would make notes of their ideas for adaptations so that I could include them, when appropriate, in future sessions.

In some presentations, the participants would begin by discussing what they saw as the advantages and disadvantages of using a textbook. We would spend some of the time analyzing the disadvantages and generating ideas for how to overcome or minimize them. I have made my own list below:

Some **advantages** of using a textbook:

- It provides a syllabus for the course because the authors have made decisions about what will be learned and in what order.
- It provides security for the students because they have a kind of road map of the course: they know what to expect, they know what is expected of them.
- It provides a set of visuals, activities, readings, etc., and so saves the teacher time in finding or developing such materials.
- It provides teachers with a basis for assessing students' learning. Some texts include tests or evaluation tools.
- It may include supporting materials (e.g., teacher's guide, cassettes, worksheets, video).
- It provides consistency within a program across a given level, if all teachers use the same textbook. If textbooks follow a sequence, as within a series, it provides consistency between levels.

Some **disadvantages** of using a textbook:

- The content or examples may not be relevant or appropriate to the group you are teaching.
- The content may not be at the right level.
- There may be too much focus on one or more aspects of language and not enough focus on others, or it may not include everything you want to include.
- There may not be the right mix of activities (too much of X, too little of Y.)

- The sequence is lockstep.
- The activities, readings, visuals, etc. may be boring.
- The material may go out of date.
- The timetable for completing the textbook or parts of it may be unrealistic.

9.1 *Think of a course in which you used a textbook (as a teacher or learner) and were satisfied and one in which you used a textbook and were not satisfied. What were some of the factors that accounted for the difference?*

Based on your experience as a teacher and learner, make a list of the advantages and a list of the disadvantages of using a textbook. Discuss your lists with a colleague.

Later investigations will ask you to examine a textbook you use or are considering using.

In Investigation 9.1, you made lists of the advantages and disadvantages of using a textbook. What you determined should go in each list depends a lot on your context and the students you teach, your own experience, beliefs, and understandings, and the type of textbook you have used. What one teacher considers an advantage in a textbook, another teacher may consider a disadvantage. For example, in one of the *East West* books, we wrote a suspense story, one episode at the end of each unit. I found that some teachers thought it was a wonderful aspect of the book and wanted to know why we hadn't written one for each of the levels. Other teachers said they simply skipped it. The list of disadvantages I have included above can all be overcome to some extent, if you view the textbook as a tool or instrument that you can mold and adapt to your particular group of students by changing, supplementing, eliminating, and resequencing the material in it. If you have to do so much work to adapt the textbook that you might as well develop your own materials, then it is probably worthwhile looking for another textbook.

How Can You Use a Textbook as a Course Tool?

To understand how a textbook is an instrument or a tool, we can compare it to a musical instrument, a piano, for example. The piano provides you with the means for producing music, but it cannot produce music on its own. The music is produced only when you play it. Playing well requires practice and familiarity with the piece. The more skilled you are, the more beautiful the music. Just as a piano does not play music, a textbook does not teach language. The textbook is a stimulus or instrument for teaching and learning. Clearly, the quality of the instrument also affects the quality of the music. However, if it is in tune, even the most humble piano can produce beautiful music in the hands of a skilled musician. The musical instrument analogy falls short because it involves only one performer, while success in teaching with a textbook depends also on the students who use it. Perhaps as teachers, we are called on to be not only musicians, but also piano tuners, composers, and conductors.

In working with teachers, I frequently come across the attitude that a textbook is sacred and not to be tampered with. In a previous chapter I said that we often give too much power to written documents such as our syllabuses or lesson plans, which in turn may prevent us from paying attention to *how* the students are using them. This is multiplied a hundredfold when it comes to a textbook. Such an attitude is detrimental both to the students and to the teacher because it assumes that the way teachers teach is uniform, and the way learners learn is predictable; that there is a certain way to teach a textbook, and that the results will be the same each time. Teachers' experiences disprove such assumptions repeatedly. The mental landscape of teaching is dotted with cries of "But it worked so well the last time I taught it."

A more disturbing aspect of such assumptions is the underlying notion that teaching doesn't involve decision making or skill based on our understandings, beliefs, and experience, which Michael Apple (1986) has called the "deskilling" of teachers. This deskilling is evident in the attitude that it is the textbook that teaches the students, rather than the teacher or the students themselves. One study of commercially prepared reading materials for elementary school students found that reading instruction was understood as students absorbing what was in the book rather than as a collaboration among author, teacher, and student. (Shannon 1987, p. 314). To reiterate the analogy with the musical instrument, just as the piano doesn't play the music, the textbook doesn't teach the language. A good textbook—one that meets students' needs, is at the right level, has interesting material, and so on—can be a boon to a teacher because it can free him or her to focus on what the students do with it. However, no textbook was written for your actual group of students, and so it will need to be adapted in some way.

There are two facets to understanding how to use a textbook. The first is the textbook itself: "getting inside it" so you can understand how it is constructed and why. The second is everything other than the textbook: the context, the students, and you, the teacher. The second facet is important, because when you evaluate a textbook, you generally use the lenses of your experience and context to evaluate it, and I think it is important to be aware of those lenses. The first facet, getting inside the textbook, is important so that you know *what* you are adapting or supplementing. The second facet helps you to be clear about *what* you are adapting it *to*.

The first step in using a textbook as a tool—getting inside it and understanding how it is put together and why—is actually a series of steps that includes three of the elements of designing a course: **conceptualizing content, formulating goals and objectives,** and **organizing the course.** In a sense, you retrace with the authors how they conceptualized content, what the organizing principle(s) is, how the text content is sequenced, what the objectives of each unit are, and how the units are organized. A good place to start is with the table of contents, since it lays out both what is in the book, how the units are sequenced, and, depending on the text, the content and organization of individual units.

In the following investigations, you will examine the tables of contents of three textbooks. The investigations will use the following framework as the basis for analysis.

Figure 9.1: A Framework for Investigating How a Textbook Is Put Together

How have the authors **conceptualized content,** i.e., what aspects of language, learning, and social context are being addressed? (Refer to the Chart in Figure 4.4 in Chapter 4.)

How is the **material organized,** i.e., what is the organizing principle(s)?

On what **basis** are the **units sequenced**?

What is the **content of a unit**?

What are the **objectives of the unit**? In other words, what should the students know or be able to do by the end of the unit?

How does the unit **content help to achieve the objectives**?

The first book you will investigate, *East West Basics,* is one I co-authored with Alison Rice. We conceptualized content in terms of grammar, topics and associated vocabulary, culture, communicative functions, pronunciation, speaking, and listening. With respect to the three dimensions of conceptualizing content—language, learning, and social context—outlined in Chapter 4, we focused primarily on language, although we did address sociocultural and sociolinguistic aspects of language. We did not include elements of learning, such as learning strategies and interpersonal skills.

The two organizing principles for the book were topics and grammar. We worked with lists of grammar and topics we felt were appropriate for a beginners' level. The units are sequenced on the basis of the grammar. We first developed a grammatical syllabus, since that was the easiest to sequence, and then looked for topics that would readily incorporate the grammar. For example, present tense of *be* is often linked with personal identification, *"My name is . . ., I'm . . .,"*

The order of the units changed as we developed the material within each unit, and different elements got moved around within a unit or from unit to unit. The culture and functions are related to the unit topics. There is a pronunciation syllabus for the book which includes work on the sound and syllable level as well as the word and sentence level. The speaking and listening activities are a combination of *exercises,* which focus on specific building blocks of language, and *activities,* which focus on purposeful communication (Vale, Scarino and McKay 1996.)

See Chapter 8, page 157, for definitions of exercises and activities.

9.2a *Look at the Table of Contents of* East West Basics *(Figure 9.2a).*

1. The authors conceptualized content in terms of: grammar, topics, pronunciation, culture, communicative functions, speaking and listening. Find examples of the first five aspects in the table of contents.

Figure 9.2a: Table of Contents from East West Basics

Contents

Unit	Topics	Functions	Grammar	Pronunciation	Put It Together Activity
1 Page 3	Names Occupations **Culture Capsule:** Titles: *Mr., Mrs., Miss,* and *Ms.*	Greetings Introductions Apologies	Present tense of *be* Yes/no questions	Word stress	Game: *Are you...?* Page 88
2 Page 9	Names Phone numbers Places **Culture Capsule:** Last names in English	Asking for spelling Making a phone call	Present tense of *be* Questions with *what* Personal pronouns	Sentence intonation	At a hotel Class phone book Page 90
3 Page 15	Family Numbers to 100 More occupations **Culture Capsule:** The American family today	Talking about family Asking about age Giving compliments	Present tense of *be* Questions with *who, how old* Possessives	Final -*s*	Game: *Number Olympics* Page 92
4 Page 21	Stores and places of business Telling time **Culture Capsule:** Opening and closing times	Asking for the time Asking about locations Expressing needs Prepositions of location	Questions with *where*	Vowel sounds	A map of your neighborhood Page 94
5 Page 27	Cities, countries, nationalities, and languages Favorite places **Culture Capsule:** American food is international food.	Asking where someone lives Talking about favorite places	Simple present tense Questions with *do* Questions with *how often, where* Expressions of frequency	Word stress	Class survey: *Good health* Page 96
6 Page 33	Sports Days of the week Leisure activities **Culture Capsule:** Sports in the US	Talking about likes and dislikes Talking about the past Giving an opinion	Past tense of *be* Past time expressions Questions with *how*	Reduced speech	Sports and games Page 98
7 Page 39	REVIEW UNIT				Pages 99–100

Unit	Topics	Functions	Grammar	Pronunciation	Put It Together Activity
8 Page 45	Leisure activities Music **Culture Capsule:** Conversation topics	Asking about others Talking about leisure activities Talking about likes and dislikes	Simple present tense Questions with *does*	Questions with *does* (reduced forms)	Class survey: Favorites Page 102
9 Page 51	Vacations Weather Seasons Months of the year **Culture Capsule:** Summer vacation	Talking about vacations Talking about the weather	Simple past tense Questions with *did* Questions with *how*	Past tense endings	November in New York Page 104
10 Page 57	Parties, invitations Dates, birthdays Food **Culture Capsule:** Parties	Describing present actions Asking about dates, birthdays Talking about food	Present continuous tense Count and noncount nouns	Vowels ending in *-r*	Let's have a party! Page 106
11 Page 63	Colors Clothing Shopping Gifts **Culture Capsule:** Giving gifts	Describing clothing Making suggestions Shopping for gifts	Questions with *which, how much* Object pronouns *it* and *them*	The rhythm of English sentences	Designing a catalogue page Page 108
12 Page 69	Future plans Invitations Ordering food in a restaurant **Culture Capsule:** Free time	Talking about future plans Inviting someone Ordering food in a restaurant	Future tense with *be going to* future time expression *would like*	Unstressed syllables	Make your own menu Page 110
13 Page 75	Rooms in a house Neighborhoods More place names **Culture Capsule:** Where people live	Describing one's home Describing one's neighborhood Informal greetings	*There is/are* Compound sentences with *and, but* More prepositions of location	Sentence and question intonation	Vacation in Alaska Page 112
14 Page 81	REVIEW UNIT				Pages 113–114
Word List Page 115					

K. Graves and A. Rice, Oxford University Press, 1994

Where do you think sociocultural and sociolinguistic aspects of language learning are addressed?

2. The organizing principles were topics and grammar. The rest of the areas clustered around those. Look for examples of how the areas clustered around topics and grammar.

3. If you were teaching beginning students, are there topics you would add? drop?

4. The units were sequenced on the basis of grammar. Do you feel that the sequence is logical? For example, do you feel that the present tense of *be* should be taught before the present tense of other verbs?

5. What do you like about the content of the book? Why? What don't you like? Why not?

The second book is *Modern Impressions* by Marie Hutchison Weidauer (1994). It is a writing text for advanced level students.

9.2b *Study the table of contents of* Modern Impressions *(Figure 9.2b).*

1. How did the author conceptualize content? In other words, what aspects of language, learning, and social context are included in the content of the book? Make a list with examples.

2. How is the content organized? On what basis do you think the units are sequenced?

3. If you could interview the author about how she put the book together, what questions would you ask her?

4. Read the preface to *Modern Impressions* (Figure 9.2c). Does it answer some of your questions?

The next investigation asks you to look at the table of contents of your own textbook or textbook you are considering using.

9.2c *Look at the table of contents of the textbook you use or are considering using.*

1. How has the author conceptualized content—i.e., what aspects of language, learning, and social context are being addressed? (See Figure 4.4 and Investigation 4.3a in Chapter 4.)

2. What can you say about how the material is organized? What is the organizing principle (s)? On what basis are the units sequenced?

Figure 9.2b: Table of Contents from Modern Impressions

xvii

xviii

Figure 9.2c: Preface from Modern Impressions

Modern Impressions: Writing in Our Times has been designed to guide the low-advanced ESL student into developing his capacity as an English writer as he comes to understand his beliefs about several institutions in society. While the social issues the student works with are presented in the U.S. context, they are applicable to other societies as well, as chapter exercises based on multicultural information and student writings attest to.

Just as any writer's purpose is to communicate a message, the students' purpose in the text is to find a message and succeed in communicating it. The chapters are very much content-driven; the more students learn about the topic and learn to recognize their own opinions on the topic, the more they have to say in their writing and the more they will care about saying it in a way which accurately reflects their opinions. As writing is a recursive process of discovery, the text gives students opportunities to discover knowledge and feelings about their topics and to craft, and re-craft, their writings. The text brings all of the students language skills together by encouraging them to receive input from reading and interactions with native speakers and each other while encouraging output not only through writing but speaking as well.

Modern Impressions has seven chapters, arranged in such a way that the major topic chapters (4, 5, 6, and 7) can be done in any order.

CHAPTERS 1, 2, AND 3

- Chapter 1 is designed as a "first day" group of activities to increase students' awareness of their preferred learning styles and their writing goals and acquaint them with other possibilities for both.
- Chapter 2 acquaints students with the basics of organizing essays. It may be done all at once or in conjunction with any of the major chapters.
- Chapter 3 gives students information about writing persuasive essays. In the major chapters, students are repeatedly given choices of essay topics reflecting

narrative, descriptive, analytic or persuasive modes of writing. Chapter 3 may be done early by students who want to launch into persuasive writing early; it may be done by the class as a whole when the teacher desires.

CHAPTERS 4, 5, 6, AND 7

There are four major topic chapters in *Modern Impressions.* They are conceived to constitute 12–15 hours of instruction spread out over approximately three weeks. Each chapter contains a choice of major essay assignments, several readings on the topic, writing skills instruction, language skills instruction, an editing strategy, a punctuation note, assessment of writing, sample student writings, and a writer's notebook. The skills are spiraled among each other in each chapter so that classes may work in the chapters in order of presentation of the materials. The chapters are designed in such a way that they support the revision process as students work their way through three drafts of a major essay and are referred back to these drafts to make changes using what they have just learned.

The Major Essay Assignments

Each major chapter offers students several choices for a major essay assignment (750–1000 words): a descriptive and/or narrative assignment, an analytic assignment, or a persuasive assignment. Students are encouraged to challenge themselves by choosing a topic which is a little bit harder than they are used to. Students continually work on drafts of this essay during the chapter and are repeatedly urged to revise or edit their drafts when they have learned a new writing or language skill.

The Readings

Each major chapter has one main topic centered on three or four readings. Each chapter begins with a short "Introductory Reading," which serves to orient students toward the topic, and continues with "In-Depth Readings" and "Further Readings" which are longer, provide many more details about the topic, and raise some of the most important issues associated with the topic. Teachers who prefer to assign less reading can choose from the readings or have students choose the reading(s) they prefer to read. Teachers who prefer to include more reading can send students to the library to find additional articles, an activity which has been found to be very successful in pilot use of this text. Each reading has several activities to support it and develop students' knowledge of the topic:

- Vocabulary Enrichment exercises help students learn new vocabulary, and a Vocabulary Checklist at the end of each chapter lets students record words they wish to remember for future use.
- Elaborating on the Reading helps students understand the points raised in the readings and come to grips with their own opinions on the topic. The exercises include question-answer, roleplay, simulation, and interviews in the community and may be written or oral.
- Short Writings of 150 to 200 words are designed to further students' knowledge of the topic and develop their writing skills. Short writings are often preceded by information about writing style, organization, or the writer's process. They may be assigned for homework or under time pressure in class as "quick writings."

The Writing Skills

Each major chapter also contains information and exercises to improve students' writing skills. These skills acquaint students with the process of writing, clear organization of writing, and techniques for clarifying or strengthening their writing. The organizational techniques that are introduced coordinate with the analytic major essay assignment for each chapter.

The Language Skills

Two types of language skills are developed in *Modern Impressions:* the skill to control or correct errors and the skill to write syntactically complex sentences. Most exercises are in context, consisting of paragraph-level discourse, in some cases essay level, for students to edit or manipulate in some way. Care has been taken to design exercises which approximate the actual process of revising or editing whenever possible. Students are continually referred back to their drafts to make changes based on the new language skills they have learned.

The Editing Strategy

Each major chapter contains one editing strategy which is independent of any particular topic or grammar point, one which they can use again and again in their writing in the future.

The Punctuation Note

Major chapters also contain a brief punctuation note coordinated with a teaching point raised with one of the language or writing skills.

The Assessment

In order for students to revise their drafts, the text promotes two types of assessment. Students assess their own work through Reflections on drafts one and three. Students assess each other's work in the Peer Responses for draft two. Both Reflections and Peer Responses are guided by a set of five questions. By using the Reflection and Peer Response techniques, students become more empowered writers because they improve their ability to read critically and depend more on themselves as they revise.

It is expected that a third mode of assessment includes teacher assessment. One successful technique for teacher assessment of ESL essays at the University of California, Irvine, has been to provide reactions to content and organization on the first draft, delay marking language problems until the second draft, and respond to the overall success of the essay and its revisions on the third draft. This gives students time to come to grips with the topic and their message while providing the guidance on language skill that they need at a time when it will not interfere with their writing processes.

The final mode of assessment is the Writer's Notebook, which gives students an opportunity to evaluate more broadly what they have been learning about writing and what they would still like to accomplish during this course. It is a type of "journal" of their writing development.

The Student Writings

Student writings are generally used twice per chapter: once as the basis for practicing the Peer Response of draft two, and once for further discussion or workshopping as students work on draft three. These writings have been chosen for the most part because they are good and because they provide interesting points of view on the chapter's topic, but they are not perfect. In addition, they have been ***lightly*** edited to remove grammatical errors.

Marie Hutchison Weidauer, 1994

Once you are familiar with the overall content and organization of the book, it is helpful to become familiar with one of the units—what the content of the unit is, what the objectives are, and how the content helps to achieve the objectives. There are several ways to do this. One is to make a mind-map or diagram of the unit. Another is to make lists of content, objectives, and the relationships between them. Another is to make a grid. In the next investigation you will analyze a unit from *East West Basics* and then your own textbook.

9.3a *Below you will find a mind map and a grid that lay out the content of Unit 1 of* East West Basics. *Each is an attempt to represent and link the content and the objectives. Study the unit in Appendix 9-3 on pages 277–280 and then study the mind map in Figure 9.3a and grid in Figure 9.3b.*

1. Do they help you see how the unit is put together?
2. Which do you find most helpful? Why? Which do you find least helpful? Why?

9.3b *Choose a unit from your textbook. Draw up a mind map, grid, or list that shows:*

- the content of the unit
- the objectives of the unit
- the way in which the content helps to achieve the objectives.

Figure 9.3a: Mind Map East West Basics Unit One

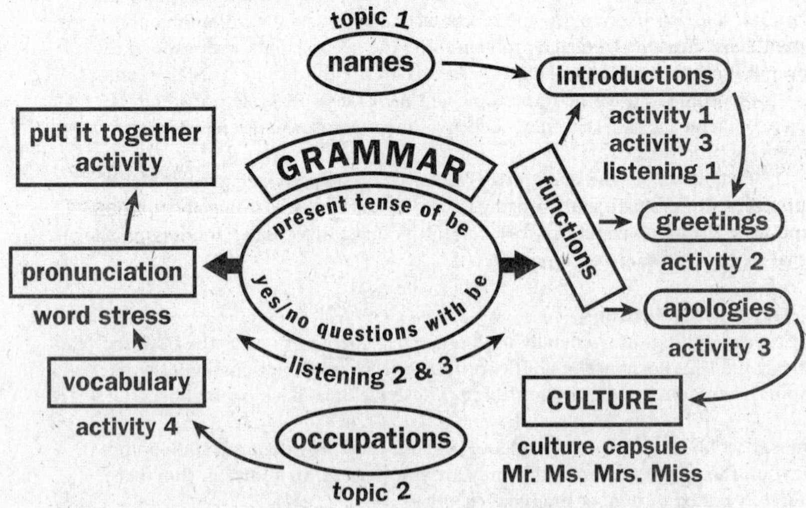

Figure 9.3b: Grid for East West Basics Unit One

Topics *Objectives:* Students will learn the occupations in the unit. Students will be able to give their names.	***Names*** Opening dialogue Speaking activities 1, 2, 3 Listening 1, 2, 3 Culture capsule	***Occupations*** Opening dialogue Speaking activity set 4 Listening 2, 3 Put It Together activity
Functions *Objectives:* Students will be able to introduce themselves to another person. Students will be able to greet each other informally. Students will be able to apologize using "I'm sorry."	***Introductions*** (Speaking activity set 1; Listening 1, 2) Greetings with names (Speaking activity set 2) Apologies (Activity set 3)	
Grammar *Objectives:* students will be able to use the present tense of *be* for 1st, 2nd, 3rd person. Students will be able to ask yes/no questions using the present tense of *be* for 1st, 2nd, 3rd person.	***Present tense of be*** (all activities) Yes/no questions (Activity set 3)	***Present tense of be*** (all activities) Yes/no questions (Put It Together activity)
Culture Students will learn that titles like Ms. go before last names only. Students will learn different titles for women: Ms., Miss, Mrs., and when to use them.	***Culture Capsule*** Mr., Mrs., Miss, Ms., and when to use them.	
Pronunciation Students will become aware that multisyllable words in English have major stress on one syllable.		***Word stress*** (in names of occupations)

Once you have "gotten inside" of the textbook and understood how its content is organized, you can consider how you want to adapt it. You have a range of choices about how much to adapt a textbook. You may stick to the syllabus and make adaptations at the **activity level.** You may stick to the syllabus and adapt at the **unit level** by doing the activities in a different order than in the book, changing, eliminating, or adding activities. You may adapt it at the **syllabus level** by adding new areas to the syllabus or eliminating parts of it. The adaptations are cumulative: adapting at the unit level involves adaptation at the activity level; adapting at the syllabus level involves adaptation at the unit level. Such choices depend on your experience with the textbook: it is easier to adapt a textbook once you have taught it. Those choices also depend on your context and your students' needs, which you will explore below.

Figure 9.4: A Range of Choices with Respect to Adapting a Textbook

The **activity** level: change, supplement, eliminate activities.

The **unit** level: change the order of activities and adapt existing activities.

The **book/syllabus** level: change, add to or eliminate parts of the syllabus.

Adapting at the Activity Level

One teacher at a language institute (ACBEU) in Riberão Preto, Brazil, Simone Machado Camillo, describes the way she makes adaptations at the activity level and why.

Simone Machado Camillo

> I have been developing activities to provide my students the opportunity to learn in a more pleasurable way. The activities are based on two books we use at ACBEU, *Touchdown* and *Intercom 2000*, although they could be adapted and used in any class since most of them are focused on grammar. My main concern was to develop activities that would focus on learners' needs, give some control to the students, allow for students' creativity and innovation to enhance students' sense of competence and self-worth.
>
> One of the best points of these activities is the suitability for the tight schedules we face at ACBEU, and I believe this is a situation many other teaching professionals face. I am very glad to see the activities fitting well in our schedule and making students more interested and active in the learning process. My students' feedback on questionnaires and in their journals has been a motivating strength that makes me even more enthusiastic and willing to continue the process of developing more activities.

Simone classifies the activities she has developed into four types: warm-up activities, presentation activities, practice activities, and consolidation activities. This classification will be familiar to teachers who have learned about a three stage lesson planning model such as presentation, practice, and production (Matthews et al. 1985). She describes the activity types as follows:

> A warm-up activity is usually based on previous topics. It can be considered a review activity. It is usually given in the beginning of a class. It can be a creative way to start a class or break the routine of a class.
>
> A presentation is based on new topics. It is given with the books closed. It is a preparation for the book activities.
>
> A practice activity should be given after the presentation. It can be developed before bookwork, during it, or after it. It is a more meaningful opportunity for the student where he can practice the taught material in a more realistic and meaningful context.
>
> A consolidation activity is developed after the practice. It reinforces the topics that were already taught. It can be used as a review activity as well. It is usually a game. Students have fun while they review what was taught previously.

Simone developed a system for enhancing what was in the textbook and adapting it for her students so that they could be more active learners. She chose to weave her activities into the existing framework of the books based on contextual factors which included the course schedule as well as student expectations. She found that the younger students enjoyed the activities and wrote comments in their journals such as, "I like to play in our English classes." "I loved the 'give-receive' activity." "Have you noticed, Simone, I didn't sleep today . . ." With some of the older students (young adults) there was some resistance to departing from the book. She writes:

> Developing activities for young adults was a great challenge. Breaking their routine of learning was a very hard task. In the beginning, some students refused to stand up, mime, take a more active role in their learning process. They felt strange and didn't like to be on the spot. Students had to feel at ease so that they would get into the mood of the activities. Most students would rather have the "traditional" class. During one of my classes I told my students we were going to play Bingo. One student said, "Don't you have a more useful activity to do?" I thought it was a harsh comment, but I answered his question calmly and he seemed to be convinced by my arguments. I told him it was a very useful activity and my purpose was to reinforce a topic that had already been taught. It seemed that showing my purpose was a key to my student's understanding of the importance of fun in learning.

Here are two examples of Simone's adaptations of unit 13 of *Intercom 2000 Book 1* (Chamot et al. 1991). The unit begins with a dialogue between Toshio Ito, a flight attendant from Japan, and the Logans, friends he is visiting in the United States. The introduction to the dialogue includes contrasts between the present and past such as *"Last week he was in Hong Kong and Tokyo." "This week he is in Winfield at the home of his friends, the Logans."* On the next page there is a grammar explanation that shows the past of the verb *be*. Simone's first activity is a presentation activity. It is done before the students open their books.

See Appendix 9-1, page 275, for the original pages of the unit.

Time Trip (presentation activity)

Time: About 15 minutes.

Grammar: Past tense of verb *to be (was/were)*

1. Divide the board into two columns (present/past).
2. Write sentences about yourself and your family in the columns.

Past	*Present*
I _____ a student in 1976.	I _____ a teacher at ACBEU.
I _____ 7 years old in 1977.	I _____ 25 years old.
My parents _____ single in 1968.	My parents _____ married.
In 1985, my sister _____ a student at UNAERP.	My sister _____ a lawyer.

3. Ask students to try to complete the blanks using the verb *to be* in the past and present. If they can't, help them or provide the answers.
4. Pair students up and ask them to write sentences about themselves and their parents in the present and in the past to be shared with their partners.
5. Students ask questions about their classmates.

   A: I was a/an ________ in _____. What about you?

   B: I was a/an ________.

   B: My parents were ________ in _____. What about yours?

   A: ___________.

   A: My sister was ________ in _____. What about yours?

   B: ___________.

Simone's second activity is done in place of what is in the book. The exercise in the book shows a chart with examples like the following:

The Logans/New York City/last month.

A: The Logans were in New York City last month.

B: That's right.

Simone comments: I didn't use the exercise in the book because it was not meaningful enough. I have adapted it using more realistic examples.

Right or Wrong (practice activity)

Time: about 20 minutes

Grammar: past tense of verb *to be (was/were)*

1. Give students slips of paper with some cues that will help them to make some sentences using *was/were*.

   e.g., Brazil / discovered / in 1984.

FHC / in Brasilia / last week. (FHC are the initials of the president of Brazil, Fernando Henrique Cardoso)

2. Divide the class into two groups.
3. A student from group A reads his or her sentence, for example, "Brazil was discovered in 1984."
4. A student from group B will accept it saying *"That's right."* or will correct the statement saying, for example, *"No, it wasn't. It was . . ."* or *"No, they weren't. They were . . ."*
5. Continue the practice with the whole class.

Simone's belief in the importance of student participation as a vehicle for learning motivated her to adapt the textbook to provide more opportunities for interaction. She personalized the activities so that they would be relevant to the students. Each activity challenged the students to think about the meaning of a given statement or response. The activities were structured so that students would interact with each other. In some cases, she bypassed the book activity entirely. Her understanding of what her students needed in order to be able to participate in these activities—feeling at ease, understanding why they were being asked to work in a different way—was a key factor in the success of her course.

9.4 *Choose an activity or activity sequence from a textbook you have used or are considering using. Do the investigation with a particular group of students in mind.*

Choose and answer one of the questions below that is appropriate for the activity or sequence of activities you have chosen.

1. How would you adapt it to make it more challenging (so that students have to think about what they are doing or have to solve a problem)?
2. How would you adapt the activity or sequence to make it more personal (to draw on the students' experience)?
3. How would you adapt it so that the students never opened the book to do it?
4. How would you adapt it so that it integrated the four skills of speaking, reading, listening, and writing?
5. How would you adapt it so that the students could do it with you out of the room?

Adapting at the Unit Level

In Investigation 9.4 you looked at ways to adapt individual activities or a sequence of activities in a textbook. The next level of adaptation is at the unit level. Below we will hear about Michael Gatto's experience adapting a textbook unit. Michael taught in El Salvador at a language institute. After he returned from El Salvador, he took a course design seminar with me in which

See Michael Gatto's description of his context on page 14, Chapter 2.

he chose to redesign the course he taught in El Salvador, which required a textbook. During the seminar he raised the issue that most teachers don't have a semester to write goals and objectives, draw mind maps, develop materials, and so on. In El Salvador, as a newly arrived teacher, he was given the textbook the night before he was to begin teaching it. He writes about how he ultimately redesigned the course.

Michael Gatto

Hey! In real life you were only given one day to "design" this course—so how would you do it if you really had to? Of course, it made perfect sense. Here I had been losing sleep over my half-baked goals and objectives when what I had to do was realize that my style dictates that I have to be knee deep into the project before the goals, objectives, and all the other parts of a course are visible.

Luckily that week Kathleen Graves had given us a demonstration on how we can resequence the textbooks we use to fit the courses we're teaching. She just photocopied a unit from an English textbook, took out a pair of scissors, chopped away, and then had us resequence the unit and then give our rationale for resequencing it that way. I was stunned because I had always viewed these texts as being set in stone—unmovable. Here we've been talking all year about developing a teaching "tool box" and the most useful one I found was a pair of scissors!

I put my mind maps away and took out *East West Basics,* the textbook that the binational center required its teachers to use, and photocopied the first unit. At first it was with great reservation that I started making a jigsaw puzzle out of it because it just so happened that this book was written by Kathleen Graves, the person who would be evaluating the results. Well, I got over that uneasiness quickly because it was too much fun cutting, resequencing, pasting, repasting, writing, and rewriting that evening. About four hours later I had the first week of my course designed and well thought out. The goals and objectives were clearer than they had ever been. What was even more important was that for the first time since I started teaching, my beliefs about learning, teaching, and language acquisition were clearly defined in the way I rationalized why I sequenced various aspects of the course the way I did. It was like looking in a mirror and seeing the reflection of a true professional.

Here I had spent most of my teaching career angry every time the institute I was working for handed me a new book and said, "Here, teach this." Finally, I had found a way to satisfy the students' needs, the institute's needs, and my needs as a teacher. The fact that this realization only took four hours after weeks of frustration made me realize the importance of keeping one's head out of the clouds when designing a course.

The following pages are copies from the original sequencing activity that I did that night. I would like to point out that my own sequencing of the unit is subject to change. After all, if it isn't working for the students, then it isn't working for anybody.

The sequence and Michael's rationale follow. The unit introductory material and unit as they appear in the textbook are in Appendix 9-2, page 276 and Appendix 9-3, pages 277–280.

Michael Gatto
BCC Course 8:00 am - 9:40 am M-F
22 Students
East West Basics Units 1-3

Unit One

Topics: Names, Occupations, Titles (Mr., Mrs., Miss, and Ms.)

Functions: Greetings, Introductions, Apologies

Grammar: Present tense of *be,* Yes/no questions

Pronunciation: Word stress

Monday:

1. *Speaking Exercise 1: Introducing yourself*

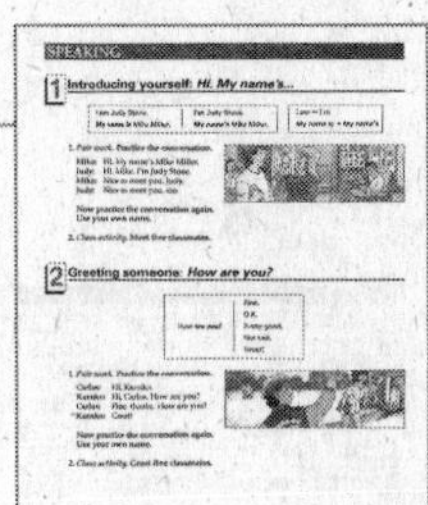

Why did I choose to put this one first? One of my main concerns in starting a class is building community. I think that most would agree that having students know each other's name is a good start. This will be reinforced later on with the help of other activities.

2. *Speaking Exercise 2: Greeting someone*

I think this is a good follow up to the first speaking exercise. Even though this is a beginners' course, I believe that many already know these introductions and greetings. I want them to feel comfortable with the very first exercise.

3. *Classroom Language*

I chose to do this for the second part of the class because it contains a lot of important vocabulary that the students will be hearing me say every day. What I did here was choose the imperatives from the book's list (listen, write, read, open/close your book) and add four of my own that I know I'll use a lot (stand up, rotate, sit down, stop). Instead of showing the students the words in the book right away, I chose to teach them a la TPR. I also wanted to do this activity because it is fun and will continue to help the students build community.

TPR refers to Total Physical Response, in which students watch the teacher demonstrate an action and then respond to commands from the teacher to do the action (Asher 1982).

4. *Students Dialogue Journal explanation*

This is where I break down and recruit a Spanish speaker who also understands English to come and help me. This is what I want my students to know about the SDJ:

1. They need to buy a small notebook.
2. They are to turn the journals in to me twice a week (Group A: Mon/Wed, Group B: Tues/Thurs).
3. They can write about anything they want. Some of the topics they might choose are: family, school, work, their feelings about the class.
4. They should try to write everything in English, only using Spanish when all else fails.

5. The journals can be anything from one sentence to 1000 pages—it's up to them.
6. I'm not going to correct their errors. Instead I'm simply going to write them back. They should think of this as a "pen pal" exercise.
7. This will count as part of their homework grade. All they have to do is turn it in on time twice a week, and they will have an automatic perfect score.

Tuesday

1. Review speaking exercises 1–2.

I think it's always a good idea to review. Again, I believe that students are more comfortable starting a class with something they have already been exposed to. I will probably have them go around the class and introduce themselves to as many people as they can in 5 minutes. The next five minutes can be spent on Exercise 2, where they have to go back to the same people and greet them.

Review Classroom language TPR

Again, a quick review —could be student-led.

2. Useful expressions

For the first part of this exercise, I have only chosen three expressions for the students to work on (How do you say ___ in English? How do you spell ___? and How do you say this word?). I did this because they are somewhat related and probably the most useful for students at the beginning level. After looking at this and reflecting on how poorly it was presented to the class I taught during my internship, I decided to turn this into an activity, which I consciously made as communicative as possible. For the first activity the students would work in pairs. Student A receives a sheet of paper of ten pictures with its word after every other one (only five words). Student B receives the same except that he has the words that student A doesn't. Here they have to say things like, "How do you say 'gato' in English?" "How do you spell cat?" and then write them down. I hope to make it clear to them that the expressions are the main focus of this activity, not the vocabulary.

Briefly cover expressions 4 and 5 . . . maybe as a group with me talking too fast or mumbling.

3. Poster making session

See Stevick (1998) for information about Lozanov.

Here the students will make mini-posters for the classroom walls with the imperatives we learned with the TPR Classroom Language and the Useful Expressions. This helps to build community since they are expected to complete these in small groups. I also believe it helps the students feel more invested in the class by helping to decorate it. I like Lozanov's idea of having a lot of peripheral materials, so why not have it made by the students? It also gives them practice reading and writing.

Wednesday

1. Speaking exercise 3: Identifying someone

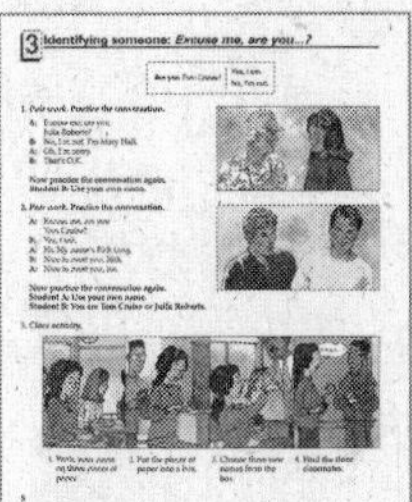

I think that this works out well in the sequencing of this course because it allows students to build on the English skills they have acquired this week, especially those dealing with introductions. Here the students get the chance to try to remember everybody's name. The class activity should be a lot of fun!

2. Conversation

It seems logical for me to put this here since I want it to serve as a support to what the students have been working on up to this point, and the dialogues cover it all. The presentation would include using Natural Approach techniques and playing the tape. For practice I would have the students do the dialogues in pairs and then move into groups of four where two students are facing each other with their books closed. The other two will be behind them and will feed them the dialogue.

3. Cocktail Party

This is a suggested additional activity which I think works well here because students can have fun taking another identity (of a famous person) and *use* the language they've been learning.

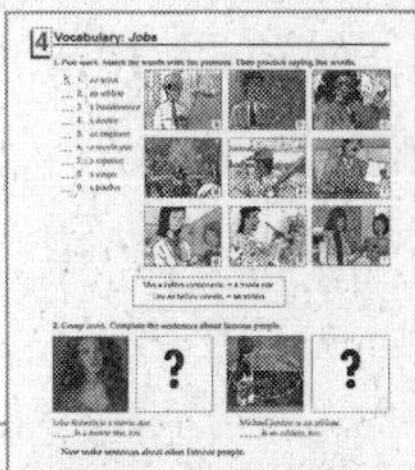

4. Jobs: Speaking Exercise 4 and pronunciation: word stress
(do the group work activity from Exercise 2 after word stress.)

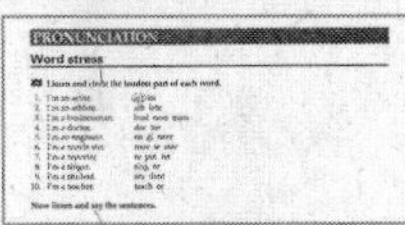

Combine these related exercises so that students become aware of word stress.

Thursday

1. Listening Exercises

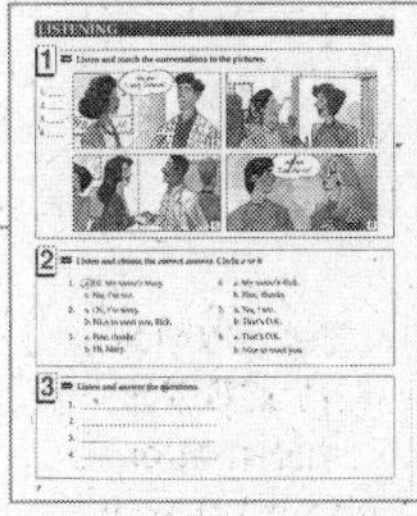

Students will listen and figure out the answers in teams.

2. Culture Capsule

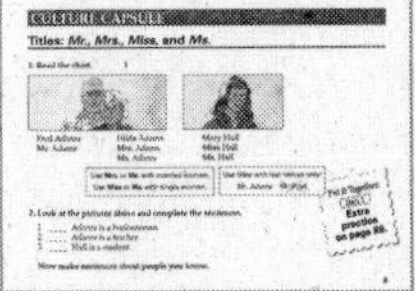

Presentation: I will use what is in the book as the presentation.

Practice:

1. Bring in many pictures of people (adults, men and women) including well-known celebrities—Salvadoran, Latin American. Have the students categorize them according to Mr., Mrs., Miss, Ms.
2. Have students form Mr., Mrs., Miss, Ms. clubs. Make name tags using only family names. Go back to Speaking Exercise 3 ("Excuse me, are you Mr. Gonzalez?").

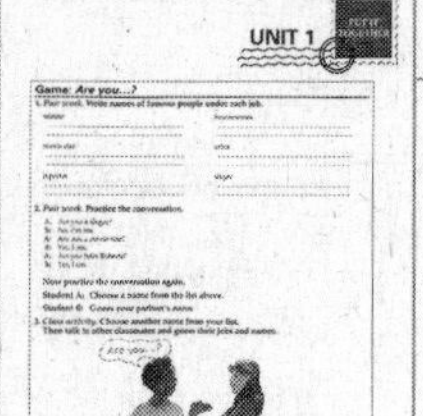
UNIT 1

Game: Are you ...?

3. Put It Together

Follow the activity as is.

4. Assign Workbook Unit 1, due tomorrow.

It will be covered in Review Station 1.

Friday

1. Review Stations

1. Workbook
2. Useful expressions
3. Classroom language (TPR)
4. Culture Capsule
5. Speaking Exercises 1–4

2. Poster making session

There will be three groups. Each one will make a poster titled "What we've learned this week." These will be put on the walls and serve as peripheral materials for the rest of the course.

3. Explain Monday's quiz

9.5 *What do you like about the way Michael has outlined his first week? Why? What would you do differently? Why?*

What can you infer about Michael's beliefs and understandings or what he feels is important with respect to language, learning, and social context?

What information will Michael be able to learn about his students' needs during the week?

The next investigation looks at the unit as a whole and how to adapt a textbook at the unit level. It is designed to demonstrate both how the sequence within a textbook unit can become flexible, and how your beliefs and understandings about how people learn affect decisions about sequencing.

9.6 *The material for this investigation is a unit from* New Interchange 3, *which is intended for the high intermediate level. The material is in Appendix 9-4 on pages 281–285. It is in reduced form and in an order different from the original.*

1. Photocopy the pages and cut up the activities. Work with a partner and sequence the activities in a way that makes sense to you. As you work, discuss the reasoning behind your choices.
2. Show your sequence to another pair and explain why you sequenced it the way you did. Discuss the differences you see between the two sequences.

I have done this investigation in different contexts with different groups of teachers. The unit has twelve different activities which focus on speaking, listening, reading, and writing, as well as vocabulary and grammar. Every time I have done this (with up to ten small groups) there have never been two identical sequences, and never one that matches the original. In each case, the teachers have good reasons for sequencing the activities the way they do. The reasons have to do with their views of what language learners need to know and be able to do in order to practice and master different aspects of language, views of how the four skills interact and should be learned, and views of how activities build on each other.

Adapting at the Syllabus Level

Thus far, we have heard two teachers, Simone Machado Camillo and Michael Gatto, describe how they adapted a textbook at the activity and unit level. Below, we will hear from a teacher who adapted a textbook at the syllabus level by adding two components important to her: community building and cultural understanding. The teacher is Mary Patten. The course she describes took place in Rabat, Morocco.

Mary Patten

> The course which I taught at the ALC (American Language Center) and chose to redesign is Intermediate 1. It met three times per week for 50 minutes each session. The textbook assigned to this level was *Crosscurrents 1*, co-authored by Marcia Fisk Ong, Kathleen Harrington, and Donald Occhiuzzo. It is a skills based textbook which is driven by unit themes. Only the first four units of the book were covered in this level.
>
> Due to the fact that my course had an existing text in place, my choice regarding selection of materials was limited. I focused on finding and developing supplementary materials that I could use in conjunction with the text and adapting areas of the text to provide a wider array of activities for my students to work with. I strongly believe that students should be able to experience a variety of materials from different sources, not only to provide opportunities for exposure to these sources, but also as a means of addressing the varied needs, interests, and intelligences (Gardner 1983) of the students.
>
> I also feel that it is important to integrate the individual into the learning process in ways that allow the learner to make the learning personally meaningful. A further extension of this idea is that learning in a classroom situation means that a learning community exists, and as such, it can be utilized as a resource. However, in

order to make it a resource, the members must be aware of what it is and must be willing to explore its dynamics together. This idea leads into my desire to provide the students with opportunities to explore the aspect of culture. As students of English, and more specifically American English, they are being exposed to not only the language, but the culture as well, yet the cultural aspects addressed by the textbook do not really allow the learners to explore and analyze what is being presented and then bring their own experiences into play—at least not in depth. . . . Therefore, I created two new components in my redesign to address the areas of community building and culture.

Crosscurrents presents material in the form of theme-based units, which provided a wonderful unifying agent to my development of secondary materials. It also allowed me to integrate my objectives regarding culture and community around the themes when planning various activities. When I first began teaching the course, I was puzzled as to how I would be able to incorporate the individual in the learning process; but as I began working with the unit themes, I found that they provided the key. I discovered that I could create opportunities for individual expression, exploration, and meaningfulness through activities centered around the themes. I created two component areas dealing with the aspects of community building and culture, which were easily woven in to the unit themes and forms that were to be addressed in the four skill areas.

Mary developed a grid for the four units covered in her course, shown in Figure 9.5. The grid represents the content of each unit and includes the two additional components of community building and culture.

Figure 9.5: Course Design for Intermediate 1

American Language Center
Rabat, Morocco
Mary D. Patten

(Syllabus based on Unit 1–4 material from *Crosscurrents 1,* the assigned text for this level)
f=forms; **s**=skills; **t**=topics

Unit Themes:	**Unit 1** ***Communication***	**Unit 2** ***Male and Female***	**Unit 3** ***Animals***	**Unit 4** ***Solutions***
Topics:	Gestures, customs, learning attitudes, expectations, and strategies	Stereotypes, professions, gender-based differences, family and classroom roles	Pets, hunting, endangered animals, imaginary animals, monsters	Disagreements with neighbors and relatives, sticky situations, worries
Grammar:	Verb tense review: simple present, pres. cont., pres. perf., simple past	Contrasting tenses: simple pres./pres. cont., simple past/ pres. perf.; adj. clauses with **that**	Verbs of perception + **like** for comparison, real (first) conditional sentences	Imaginative future (second conditionals), sentences with **hope**

Speaking/ Conversational	**forms:** story-telling, discussion **skills:** story openers, showing interest, relating personal information, comparing and contrasting	**f:** dialogues, discussion **s:** sharing news, stating opinions, comparing and contrasting	**f:** presentations, dialogues, discussions **s:** expressing disbelief, emphasizing a point	**f:** dialogues, presentations, discussions **s:** relating personal experiences, suggesting solutions to a problem, avoiding misunderstanding
Listening	**forms:** dialogues, stories, discussions **skills:** listening for details, listening for gist	**f:** dialogues, discussion **s:** listening for details	**f:** presentations, dialogues, discussions **s:** listening for gist, predicting, listening for details, listening for speaker's attitude	**f:** songs, dialogues, discussions **s:** predicting, listening for specific information, listening for words
Reading:	**forms:** textbook passages, personal letters, illustrations **skills:** getting meaning through context, getting background from illustrations	**f:** textbook passages, magazine articles, student generated paragraphs, lyrics **s:** predicting, reading for gist, applying topic to oneself	**f:** textbook passages, magazine articles, student generated paragraphs **s:** skimming, reading for gist, guessing word meanings from context	**f:** song lyrics, textbook passages **s:** pre-reading discussion of topic, reading for gist
Writing:	**forms:** personal letters **skills:** brain-storming ideas, writing first draft, revising	**f:** paragraph **s:** brainstorming ideas, topic sentence, supporting sentences, revising	**f:** paragraph **s:** transitional phrases, editing, revising	**f:** paragraph **s:** brainstorming to generate ideas, subject/verb agreement, transitional phrases
Community Building:	**topics:** class-mates' names, attitudes about and preferred styles for learning English	**t:** group dynamics	**t:** personal stories, non-judgmental acceptance	**t:** problems of the course's structure and possible solutions
Cultural:	**topics:** Moroccan and American forms of communication	**t:** interpretation and observation	**t:** treatment of animals in American and Moroccan cultures	**t:** intercultural problems and strategies for developing solutions

> As I have already stated, I was concerned with building community and bringing a deeper focus on the aspect of culture in the classroom in ways that allowed students to incorporate their own experiences in the learning process. The first step in looking at how I wanted to do this was to look at what each unit already had. From here I modified, adapted, expanded, and created materials that would allow for individual expression within a fixed thematic unit, while making sure that the objectives for each skill were being addressed.

Mary made a mind map for the second unit, "Male and Female," which centered around the theme of gender. She also made notes on the first page of the unit about how to adapt it. The mind map and notes are in Appendixes 9-5 on page 286 and 9-6 on page 287. She experimented with the sequencing of the various activities in the unit.

> Though several activities follow the sequence presented in *Crosscurrents 1,* many of them have been modified, and some have been replaced by other materials. This particular unit included what I saw as gender biased material, and I therefore sought materials which could balance this bias.

The sequence is in Appendix 9-7 on pages 288–289.

> My mind map provides the overall layout of the unit, and how I conceptualized progressing through it. Although it is somewhat abstract, it makes sense to me and conjures up more through its images than mere words could. However, I recognize that details and explanations for sequencing are also important in providing a rationale for the plan. For this reason I have made a sequencing chart for the second unit, although its primary focus is on community building and culture. I have not detailed all the activities for each day, such as the grammar presentations and practice activities, though the grammar is implicitly incorporated into several of the activities that I have included in the sequencing.

Mary has described a process of becoming clear about what is important to her, based on her beliefs about how people learn languages, that is not included in the textbook or adequately addressed in the syllabus. She "gets inside" the units and finds ways to incorporate these additional elements. She finds that the theme based approach is helpful.

The Hidden Curriculum of Textbooks

Mary raises the point that she feels the material is gender biased, something she seeks to balance by bringing in additional materials. Textbooks represent a view of language, learning, and social context held by authors and editors. In some cases the view may be compatible with your own, in other cases not. An important part of investigating a textbook is to become aware of these views, which are embedded in the aspects of language addressed in the textbook, who and what are portrayed in the visuals, readings, and dialogues, and how students are asked to work with the material.

9.7 *Look at the first page of the unit of* Crosscurrents *and Mary's notes on the unit in Appendix 9-6 on page 287. Why do think Mary felt the material was gender biased? Do you agree with her? Why or why not?*

Authors are not always aware that the choices they make reflect certain views of students and language. In the mid 1980s, Elsa Auerbach and Denise Burgess analyzed a number of textbooks and curriculum guides written for adult learners in the United States and found a "hidden curriculum," whose choice of topics, functions, and activities treated the learners as recipients of language and learners of behaviors that supported the status quo, rather than as adults capable of analyzing their situations and proposing solutions. For example, they pointed out that "Language functions in most survival texts include asking for approval, clarification, reassurance, permission, and so on, but not praising, criticizing, complaining, refusing, or disagreeing." (1987, p. 159). Although it may not have been the authors' intention to write material that would equip students only to acquiesce to the status quo, that was, in effect, what happened.

In a later study, Karen Grady (1997) analyzed the assumptions underlying many textbooks whose goal is to develop communicative competence. She used *Intercom 2000* as an example. (We saw examples of how Simone Camillo adapted activities in *Intercom 2000 Book 1* earlier in this chapter on pages 188–191.) Grady points out that the way characters are portrayed, what they do and discuss, trivializes both characters' and—by extension—students' lives. For example, work is portrayed as an optional activity, not as necessary for survival. Emphasis is on the grammatical correctness of an utterance, not necessarily on its content. For example, a discussion about elections is used as a basis for disagreement using emphatic *do* as in *He does help poor people,* rather than as a basis for a discussion about poverty.

I don't exempt myself from such criticism. My own experience writing a textbook for an international market confirms the tendency to choose uncontroversial topics, to treat them in a supposedly neutral fashion, and to write about characters who are middle class, in the interest of reaching a wider market. I am concerned, however, about how far the critiques cited above, which are written from an ESL perspective in which English is a matter of survival and acceptance, can be applied to EFL settings. For example, how far can an American teacher in Japan pursue an issue such as gender inequality in a way that does not presume that her intention is to bring her students around to her views?

The following questions and investigation are designed to help you explore the assumptions underlying the textbook you use. Being clear about your own beliefs about the role you want your learners to take in their learning, and about the skills and strategies you want them to learn, can help you to be aware of the beliefs underlying the texts you use. Your ability to adapt the textbook so that it aligns with your beliefs and purposes will depend on clarity about those beliefs and your own role, and comfort with bringing to the fore and dealing with issues that are ideologically based.

Questions to ask in analyzing a text:

People: Whom does the text portray with respect to gender, culture, socio-economic background, family make-up, and so on? How are they portrayed?

Topics: How are topics in the text treated? Are they seen only as a basis for learning language-specific elements such as vocabulary, functions, and grammar, or are they also seen as means for learners to explore their own experience? Do they promote a single view of the topic or allow for a multiplicity of views?

Language and skills: Do the language (grammar, vocabulary, functions) or skills (speaking, reading, writing, listening) in the text provide the means for learners to express their needs, to solve problems, to make decisions? Do the examples of language favor a view of gender, class, race, culture?

Visual material: Does the visual material in the text favor a view of gender, class, race, culture?

Tasks and activities: Do the tasks and activities in the text give learners opportunities for reflection, problem-solving, and decision making?

Text: If there are readings (authentic or pedagogically prepared) in the text, whose point of view do they represent? Why were they chosen? How are the students asked to relate to the readings: as examples of language, as information to be learned, as texts to be challenged?

9.8 *Choose a unit from your textbook and analyze it in terms of two or three of the areas and questions listed above.*

Are there views that are incompatible with your own? What are some ways you could adapt the textbook so that it is more compatible with your own views? For example, initiating a discussion about stereotypes and whether the characters represent stereotypes; bringing in supplementary material, as Mary Patten proposed to do, in order to provide alternative views of a topic; posing questions similar to the ones above, that ask students to view the text critically.

Discuss your findings with a colleague.

Factors Other than the Textbook Itself

In the last investigation, your beliefs and understandings about how people learn played an important role in your interpretation of the text. In order to make decisions about how to adapt a textbook at the activity, unit, or syllabus level, it is important to be aware of your **beliefs and understandings**, the **givens of your context,** and what you know about **students and their needs.**

Figure 9.6: Factors to Consider in Adapting a Textbook

The givens of your context

e.g., institutional latitude with respect to adapting a text, schedule, examination system, number and level of students, time of day.

Your beliefs and understandings about how people learn languages

e.g., through interaction or introspection, by using all four skills, by identifying problems and proposing solutions.

Your students' needs and interests

e.g., their level, whether they will use the language in specific contexts, whether they have certain expectations about how they will be taught.

Your beliefs and understandings play a key role because they can help you make decisions about what is core and what is not, according to what you deem important with respect to what the students are learning and how you want them to learn. These beliefs and understandings can also help you make decisions about what to add and what to change. We have seen above how Simone Camillo's belief in student involvement as a key to learning influenced her decisions about how to adapt the activities. We also saw how one teacher, Mary Patten, adapted a textbook to give it both a group dynamics and an intercultural focus, because of her beliefs about how people learn.

Your students' needs and interests also play a major role in decisions about adapting a textbook. My students in Brazil, for example, told me they wanted more practice with functional language and less emphasis on grammar, and felt that role plays were an ideal way to practice the functions. Their input helped me make decisions about which exercises to emphasize and spend more time on and which ones to drop or assign for homework.

The institutional context in which you work plays a crucial role in decisions about adapting a text. In some contexts, teachers have a great deal of latitude as far as what they do in the classroom. In other contexts, teachers may need to be sensitive to institutional and cultural constraints with respect to what, how, and how much they can adapt the textbook. Another important given of your context is time: how often, for how long each time, and how long overall you meet with your students. Depending on time factors, you may not be able to do all the activities in a textbook and so will need to determine which aspects are core and should be addressed and which are not core and can be left out. Conversely, you may have more time and be expected to supplement the activities.

9.9 *This can be done as a mind map or in list form. Essentially, you want to clarify:*

1. what you know about the context that will have an impact on how you use a textbook, such as schedule, class size, and examinations. (You may have done this in Chapter 2, Investigation 2.3.)

2. what you feel is important in learning languages based on your beliefs and understandings (You may have done this in Chapter 3, Investigation 3.6.)

3. what you know about your students and their needs (You may have done this in Chapter 6, Investigation 6.4.)

Pare each list down to its essentials: key phrases, words, and images that will help you as you investigate the textbook.

In the last investigation you will draw up a plan for adapting the unit you have worked on in previous investigations for your particular context. The process of figuring out how to adapt this one unit will prepare you for adapting other units. You have prepared the way through the work you have done in:

- Investigation 9.3b in which you made a map, grid, or chart of the unit
- Investigation 9.6 in which you resequenced a unit from another textbook
- Investigation 9.8 in which you analyzed the assumptions underlying the language and activities in the unit
- Investigation 9.9 in which you wrote the key phrases, words or images that would help you consider contextual factors, students' needs, and your own beliefs and understandings.

9.10 *Draw up a plan for how you would teach the unit based on what you know about your context, your students' needs, and your own beliefs and understandings. You have several options as to how to do this.*

1. Draw up a mind map, as Mary Patten did.
2. Cut up the unit, resequence it, and write notes on it, as Michael Gatto did.
3. Write comments in the textbook itself.
4. Use a format that works for you.

The Cycle of Textbook Adaptation

The plan you have drawn up in the preceding investigation is only the first part in the cycle of adapting a textbook. This follows the same cycle as course development: **planning** how to teach with the text, **teaching,** (all the while adjusting as you plan and teach), **replanning** based on evaluating the teaching and the text, **reteaching** with the text.

Figure 9.7: The Cycle of Textbook Adaptation

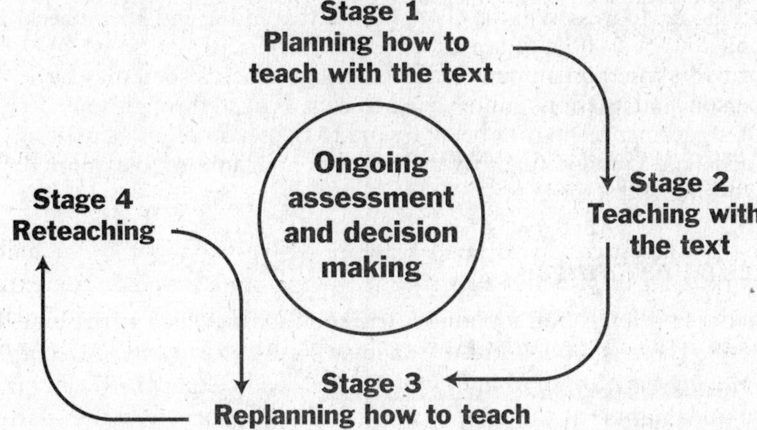

The work you have done to plan a unit in the investigations above provides a basis for further changes, once you have had a chance to teach with the textbook. In stage two, teaching the book, you may choose to ask your students to express their views of how effective the textbook and your adaptations of it are with respect to their needs and their learning. In the next chapter we will look at designing an assessment plan. Each aspect of the plan, needs assessment (addressed in Chapter 6), assessment of language learning, and course evaluation, can also be part of a course built around a textbook. In Chapter 10, we will see how Mary Patten designed assessment activities for her unit.

See pages 231–232 for Mary Patten's assessment activities.

A teacher in Taiwan provided a good example of how the cycle worked for her. She came up to me after a presentation I had given on using textbooks. She had a copy of one of the books I had co-authored. She riffled through the pages of the book, which were covered with little yellow "post it" notes on which she had written notes to herself. She said "Your book was hard to teach the first time, much easier to teach the second time." She showed me how the notes had helped her to make changes and adaptations. To return to the piano analogy, the first time she played the piece of music, it was new to her and not necessarily easy to play. With practice and familiarity, however, she could play it with more confidence and skill. Each time she went through the cycle of planning, teaching, replanning, and reteaching, she became more comfortable making choices about what to emphasize, what to leave out, and where to supplement and personalize the material. She was using the textbook as a resource for her students' learning. In terms of adapting the textbook to her particular students in her particular context, her yellow post-it notes and what they represented—reflecting and learning how to make the text work for her and her students—had allowed her to become, in effect, a co-author of the book.

I'd like to close the chapter with Mary Patten's summary of her experience learning to adapt a textbook:

Mary Patten

Although the textbook was a constraint as far as allowing for student choice (or teacher choice for that matter) on what themes would be addressed in the class, I think that in the end I have been able to look at how to use a text as a sort of skeletal form which provides a certain amount of structure but which also allows for personal adaptation. I am excited to have broken through some of my former feelings of being bound to the textbook in its existing form, and I am looking forward to new opportunities to explore working with other texts.

Suggested Readings

I haven't seen a lot about adapting a textbook, particularly at the unit or syllabus level. There is a book in the Longman *Keys to Language Teaching* series called *Making the Most of Your Textbook,* by Neville Grant (1987), but it views textbook adaptation at the activity level, and so its focus is rather narrow. It does provide examples of how to make activities more communicative, and is useful as a materials development tool. Penny Ur's chapters on "Materials" and "Topic Content" in her book, *A Course in Language Teaching* (1996), provide ideas for how to adapt a textbook, again, mainly at the activity level, and her unit, "Underlying Messages," provides some good activities for investigating textbook bias.

Karen Grady's article, "Critically Reading an ESL Textbook" (1997), is thoughtful and thought provoking, and she provides clear examples to illustrate each of her points.

10

DESIGNING AN ASSESSMENT PLAN

To get started in thinking about assessment, I'd like to use an excerpt from one of the teacher's voices from Kathleen Bailey's book in this series, *Learning About Language Assessment: Dilemmas, Decisions, and Directions.* The voice is Pete Rogan's and he is describing his experience teaching English in two high schools in Poland, which took place early in his career.

Pete Rogan

> With [some of the] classes, I was responsible for the full range of course design, including evaluation. Learning that a failing grade in my course (or in any course) would mean that a student would need to repeat the whole year of schooling, I became intimidated by evaluation. For most of the semester, I avoided the issue, freed the students of the anxiety of test-taking and forged ahead. As the semester drew to a close, however, it became clear that I had little evidence to support decisions about course grades. Now I was in the situation that whatever test or task I designed would carry an immense weight by itself in the semester evaluation. This was the nightmare I had dreaded all along—one-shot, indirect, inauthentic assessment. (p. 205)

10.1 *Read about Pete Rogan's situation in Poland.*

What advice would you give him about assessment so that he would not find himself faced with the dilemma he describes? Discuss your ideas with a colleague.

To find out what he did, consult *Learning About Language Assessment: Dilemmas, Decisions, and Directions,* page 206.

Now, think back to a course you have taught or in which you were a learner What role did assessment, as you understand it, play in the course?

THE ROLE OF ASSESSMENT IN COURSE DESIGN

Assessment plays three interrelated and overlapping roles in course design. The first is **assessing needs,** the second is **assessing students' learning,** and the third is **evaluating the course** itself. Needs assessment is the subject of Chapter 6. This chapter will look at plans for assessing students' learning and evaluating the course itself, as well as their relationship to needs assessment. Broadly speaking, needs assessment can help to answer the question *What (and how) do students need to learn with respect to ____?* Language learning assessment answers the question *What have students learned with respect to ____?* Course evaluation answers the question *How effective is/was the course in helping them learn ____?* An assessment plan for a course should take into account these three different types of assessment.

Assessment can be both **formative** and **summative.** Formative assessment takes place as the course is in progress and provides information about how well the students are doing—what they have achieved, what they need to work on, and how well the course is meeting their needs. The teacher uses the information to guide her decisions as the course unfolds. Summative assessment is done at the end of a course and provides information about the students' overall achievement as well as the overall effectiveness of the course. There is a parallel between assessing the students' learning and evaluating the course. When you assess students' learning, you assess what they have achieved with respect to what they have been learning in the course. When you evaluate the course, you assess what your course design has achieved with respect to your intentions in designing it.

In the pedagogical grammar course I teach, my assessment plan includes ongoing needs assessment, assessment of learning, and course evaluation. I will first describe my learning assessment plan and my course evaluation plan and then explain how ongoing needs assessment is embedded in them.

The course has three units: phonology, lexicon, and an introduction to syntax and transformational grammar. The last unit is divided into sub-units. My learning assessment plan for each unit has three parts: pre- and post-reflective questions about the unit material, tests, and lesson plans. The reflective questions at the beginning of each unit ask students to articulate what they know about the unit content as well as to list questions they have about it. They reread their answers at the end of the unit and write about how their thinking has changed, what they've learned, as well as which questions they have (or still have). I respond to their questions with answers or suggestions for further resources.

For the unit take home tests, which I call "reviews," students have to answer questions related to the content of the unit. They answer the questions once through "from their heads." The second time, they use a different pen and answer the questions with the help of notes, books, and/or peers. (For a complete description of how these tests are conducted, see "Self-tests," pp. 60–63, in *New Ways in Teacher Education,* Freeman and Cornwell, eds., TESOL 1993.) I read and make notes on each test before handing it back. Some students are asked to make revisions, if there are incorrect answers or unanswered questions.

Students also have to prepare and teach a lesson related to the unit content. After teaching the lessons outside of class, they bring in the written plan and reflection on teaching it to class, present it to their peers in small groups, and then hand in the lesson to me. I return the lessons with questions, comments, and suggestions. Lesson plans may need to be rethought and revised if I feel they have missed the point of the particular aspect of grammar, vocabulary, or pronunciation teaching.

My course evaluation plan includes periodic feedback on the course and a summative course and teacher evaluation. My questions for the periodic feedback are usually phrased as "What's working for you in the course?" "What isn't working for you?" "What suggestions do you have for changes?" Sometimes I hand out index cards and they write answers using a different side for each question. I compile the feedback in two columns (positive, negative + suggestions), give an oral summary in the next class, with responses to their suggestions, and post the summary on the bulletin board. At other times, I conduct the feedback orally. I usually have an end-of-course feedback session in which I ask particular questions that I am interested in about the effectiveness of the course, for example about materials used, the reviews, the sequence. The written end of course evaluation by the students is one that the program administers; it includes numerical scales as well as room for comments. I see these once I have handed in my grades.

Needs assessment is linked to both assessment of learning and course evaluation. The questions the students list at the beginning of each unit with respect to the content of the unit give me a picture of their needs, and I try to include ways to address these in my lessons, if possible or appropriate. Some of the questions are similar each year, some are unique to a given group. The periodic feedback gives me information about their affective and learning needs such as whether they feel the pace is appropriate, how they feel about small and large group work, whether learning the terminology is intimidating or empowering, and so on. The tests and lesson plans show me what they have learned and can apply and also where there are gaps and more work is needed. I keep a record of their questions, their feedback, and how they do on the tests and the lesson plans. Overall, students know what is expected of them and are held accountable. Students also know what I expect of myself, and I ask them to hold me accountable.

Assessing Students' Learning

Kathi Bailey's *Learning About Language Assessment: Dilemmas, Decisions, and Directions,* referred to at the beginning of this chapter, is devoted to assessing students' language learning. In this chapter, we focus on how this type of assessment fits into the overall framework of course design. For more in depth treatment of assessment and testing, with examples of different kinds of assessment instruments including direct and indirect tests, multiple choice tests, role plays, authentic tests and portfolios, please refer to Bailey's book and to the suggested readings in her bibliography.

10.2 *Do the following investigation either before reading the next section to articulate what you know and provide a basis for comparison, or after you read it, as a means of summarizing your understanding.*

Answer the following questions about assessing students' learning and compare them with a colleague's answers.

Assessing students' learning

Who assesses students' learning?

What is assessed?

Why assess students' learning?

How can you assess students' learning?

When can you assess students' learning?

What is done with the results of assessment?

Who assesses students' learning? Possible answers are the teacher, the student, the students, the institution. In traditional thinking, the teacher or the institution makes the decisions about what, why, how, and when to assess. However, as we shall see in the examples that follow, the students can share in some—or many—of those responsibilities, depending on the teacher's goals for the course, his beliefs about the roles of learners in learning, and feasibility within the context.

What is assessed? *What* includes both a global and a specific answer. The global answer depends on the way you have conceptualized the content of the course and the way that conceptualization has been articulated in goals and objectives. For example, if you are teaching a speaking and listening course whose objectives include being able to speak in "real world" situations, then your assessment plan will include ways to assess students' ability to speak in those situations. For example, a group of business people who are learning how to participate in meetings in the target language will be assessed on that ability. A group of students who plan to use the target language in tourist settings will be assessed accordingly. If you are teaching a content-based history course for high school students whose objectives include the ability to read and analyze history texts as well as the development of strategies to do so, then your assessment plan will include ways to assess your students' development of strategies as well as their reading and analytical skills. If you are designing an integrated skills course for adult immigrants whose objectives include developing literacy skills, then you will assess those skills. Your goals and objectives for the course provide a guide for what you assess.

The specific answer to what you assess has to do with the criteria for assessment. In her thesis on learner-centered assessment, Sally Cavanough writes, "A critical role in the assessment process is deciding which criteria to use." (1995) I have found this point to be the most important and the most problematic for teachers. In his introduction to *New Ways of Classroom Assessment* (1998, p. vi), J. D. Brown points out that assessment activities (as distinct from tests), while they may look like normal classroom activities, are different because "they provide a way of observing or scoring students' performances and giving feedback in the form of a score or other information (e.g., notes in the margin, written prose reactions, oral critiques, teacher conferences) that can enlighten the students and teachers about the effectiveness of the language learning and teaching involved." The basis on which the students are scored or on which feedback is given are the criteria Sally mentions above. For example, a teacher may have as a goal "Students will be able to give effective business presentations." In order to assess whether students are able to give effective presentations, she or he needs to have criteria for what is meant by "effective." Those criteria need to be communicated to and understood by the students. Furthermore, the students need to learn how to meet the criteria. The criteria could be a set of guidelines, which, in effect, constitute one set of objectives to meet the goal. A teacher who has not developed criteria will simply have the students give presentations. However, it is not enough to provide students with opportunities for such presentations. Without criteria for what an effective presentation involves, teachers can neither teach nor assess the requisite skills.

The processes of conceptualizing content, formulating goals and objectives, and developing a syllabus constitute an important foundation for being able to develop criteria for assessment. For one thing, they help to narrow the arena for what will be assessed. Formulating goals and objectives for an integrated skills course will help the teacher make decisions about which skills and topics will be addressed and therefore can be assessed.

Why Do You Assess Students' Learning?

The following figure, adapted from Kathi Bailey's book on assessment, captures the major purposes for assessing students' language abilities and learning in course design:

Compare to page 39 of Bailey's book.

Figure 10.1: Four Major Purposes for Assessing Learning in Course Design

Assessing proficiency	**Diagnosing ability/needs**	**Assessing Progress**	**Assessing Achievement**
pre course: to place students appropriately *post course:* may be done to assess achievement	*pre and during course:* in order to identify and meet needs	*during course:* to assess progress	*at end of course or unit:* in order to assess what has been learned and/or assign a grade

Below is a simplified overview of how the four purposes outlined above relate to course design. The examples of teachers' assessment plans that follow will, I hope, show how these purposes are carried out within the context of a course.

We assess **proficiency** in order to find out in a broad sense what the learner or learners are able to do in the language. Proficiency can be assessed with respect to speaking, listening, reading, and writing. For example, the ACTFL proficiency guidelines (1986), which were developed by the American Council on the Teaching of Foreign Languages, provide a systematic set of criteria for assessing proficiency in each of these areas. As Bailey points out in her book, proficiency testing has nothing to do with how the person reached that level of proficiency (1998, p. 38). Assessment of proficiency provides us with a starting point as the learner embarks on the course because it gives us an idea of his or her ability level with respect to what was assessed. It is important for course design so that we can be sure that the goals and objectives and materials of the course are appropriate with respect to level of difficulty in the targeted skills.

Proficiency testing may be done formally as part of the placement process or may be assessed informally as part of initial needs assessment. An initial proficiency assessment tool, such as an interview, can also be used at the end of the course to assess achievement. Some teachers record the initial and end-of-course interviews so that the students can literally hear the progress they have made. Some programs use a standard proficiency test as a pre-test for placement purposes and a post-test for achievement purposes. One problem with using proficiency tests for achievement purposes is that they may violate a cardinal rule of achievement testing: teachers should test what has been taught. If there are elements of the proficiency test that have not been addressed in the course, then they are not good indicators of achievement.

Diagnostic assessment is designed to find out what learners can and can't do with respect to a skill, task, or content area. The skill or task is derived from the content and objectives of the course. For example, if one objective of a writing course is that students will be able to write business letters, then a diagnostic assessment could involve assigning them the task of writing a business letter within certain parameters (e.g., the company and purpose for writing the letter). Comparing their letters to target examples (by fluent or native speakers) will provide a picture of what they know how to do (abilities) and what they don't know how to do (needs). This type of assessment can be viewed as part of ongoing needs assessment.

Assessing progress means finding out what the learner has learned with respect to what has been taught at different points in the course. To continue with the business letter example: as students are taught how to write effective business letters, each letter they write can be viewed in relation to the first one they wrote and in relation to the target, showing the progress they have made—what they have achieved—and where they still need to work. One of the principles of assessing progress is that you should assess only what has been taught. If one of the objectives of a speaking and listening course is for students to be able to give effective presentations, then the syllabus and materials will target and teach that skill, criteria will be developed, and students will be assessed on their ability to give an effective presentation. If the teacher simply has students give presentations without teaching them what is involved and how to improve their skills, then they should not be tested on their ability to give presentations. Additionally, the modality used to test should be the one that is being tested: an assessment tool which asks students to write a report about their presentation would be inappropriate since it does not test their oral abilities.

Assessing achievement is a summative form of assessment, since it is designed to find out what the students have mastered with respect to the knowledge and skills that have been taught in the course or unit. Assessing achievement can also be used as one of the bases for giving grades. If you are expected to give grades, then your assessment plan must include the bases on which grades are given. Part of that plan may be achievement tests or activities. The plan may also include factors such as participation, project work, completion of individual assignments, and so on. If a requirement for passing your course is a certain score on a standardized test, your course content will be influenced by the test requirements.

How do you assess students' learning? What instruments or activities will you use to assess them? In practice, as long as the students are actively engaged in learning (as opposed to watching the teacher do all the work) you can assess students' learning continuously by observing them as they learn, according to your criteria. However, a comprehensive assessment plan includes assessment activities which are designed for the specific purposes outlined above. As with needs assessment, these activities can take myriad forms. Tests, authentic tasks, portfolios, role plays, written assignments, student-made tests, student-developed rubrics or standards, and peer evaluations are some of the tools for assessing learning. An important point to keep in mind is that students need to learn how to use any assessment instrument, whether it is peer feedback or a multiple choice test.

10.3 *Refer back to Cyndy Thatcher-Fettig's one week plan in Chapter 8, pages 158–160. Which activities give her an opportunity to assess students' learning? What can she assess? What could be used as the criteria for assessment?*

When can you assess students' learning? The answer to this question depends on your context: how long the course is, whether and when you have to assign grades, how the course units are constructed. Assessment can take place at any time, with any frequency. The important thing is to have a plan for both formative and, if appropriate or necessary, summative assessment.

What is done with the results of assessment? Proficiency assessment helps you to choose or modify the materials so that they are appropriately challenging for the students. Diagnostic assessments help you to know what your students' needs are, to evaluate the appropriateness of the goals and objectives with respect to their needs, and to design materials that will meet them. Progress and achievement assessment help you and the students to get a sense of what they have learned and how the course is successfully helping them to make progress. If assessing achievement shows they are not doing well, then the goals and objectives may need to be examined to make sure they are appropriate. The syllabus may need to be reorganized.

10.4 *Think of a course you have taught recently. List the ways in which you assessed students' learning. Why did you use those ways? Did you think they were effective? Why? Why not?*

If you have not taught a course, then think of a course in which you were a learner or observer. In what ways was learning assessed? Did you think they were effective? Why? Why not?

Evaluating the Course

10.5 *Do the following investigation either before reading the next section to articulate what you know and provide a basis for comparison, or after you read it, as a means of summarizing your understanding.*

How would you answer the questions below? Compare your answers with a colleague.

Evaluating the course

1. Who evaluates the course?
2. What can be evaluated?
3. Why evaluate the course?
4. How can you evaluate it? (What are some ways to evaluate it?)
5. When can you evaluate it?
6. What is done with the results of evaluation?

Who evaluates the course? In formative evaluation of the course, it is usually the teacher and the students who evaluate its effectiveness. In summative evaluation, in addition to the teacher and students, the institution may have an official means of evaluating the effectiveness of a course.

What is evaluated? Each aspect of the course design can be assessed and evaluated:

- *the goals and objectives:* Are/were they realistic? appropriate? achievable? How should they be changed?
- *the course content:* Is/was it what the students need/ed? at the right level? comprehensive enough? focused enough?
- *the needs assessment:* Did it provide the needed information? the right amount of information? in a timely way? Did the students understand it? Was it appropriately and effectively responded to?
- *the way the course is organized:* Does it flow from unit to unit and within units? Do students perceive a sensible progression? Is the course content woven together in a balanced way? Is material recycled throughout the course?
- *the materials and methods:* Are they at the right level? Is the material engaging? Do the students have enough opportunities to learn what they need to? Is the material relevant? Are the students comfortable with their roles? the teacher's role?
- *the learning assessment plan:* Do students understand how they will be assessed and why? Do assessment activities assess what has been learned? Do they help students diagnose needs? measure progress or achievement? Are they timely?

- *the course evaluation plan:* Do students understand how the course is being evaluated and their role? Do they understand the purpose? Is the formative evaluation timely? Does it provide useful information?

Why evaluate the course? The purposes of formative evaluation are: to evaluate what is effective and to change what isn't so that the course effectively meets students' needs (as negotiated within the course context); to give students a voice in their learning; to provide information for the redesign of the course. The purposes of summative evaluation are: to make decisions about whether the course should continue or not; to assess the "achievement" of the course; to provide information for the redesign of the course.

How can you evaluate the course? You can evaluate the course through systematic observation, feedback (oral or written, individual or group), questionnaires, dialogue journals, ranking activities, and so on.

When can you evaluate the course? You can evaluate the course periodically, at natural intervals (end of week, unit); at the midterm, or at the end of the course; when problems arise.

What is done with the results of evaluation? Formative evaluation information is used to retain effective aspects of the course and to change ineffective aspects while teaching it. Summative information is used to improve it for next time.

The course development cycle introduced in Chapter 1 captures the way in which evaluation of the course works. The course is evaluated throughout Stage 2 in order to make improvements as it is being taught. Information from both formative and summative evaluation informs Stages 3 and 4.

Figure 10.2: The Course Development Cycle

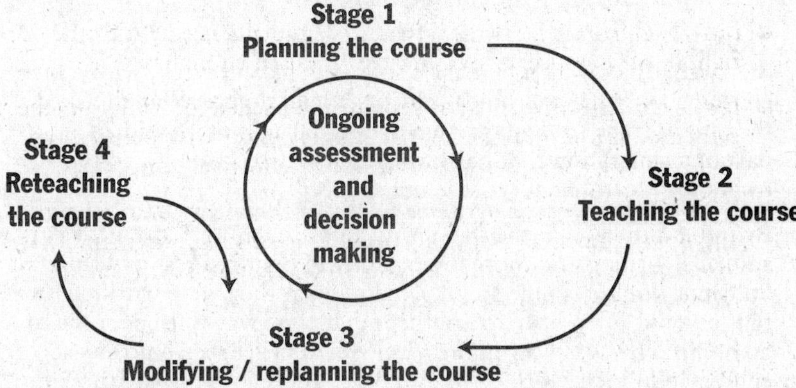

Thus the purpose of evaluating the course is to help you make decisions on both an ongoing and final basis about the course. Ongoing needs assessment and formative course evaluation overlap, since they help to gauge students' affective needs, learning needs, and language needs while the course is in progress so that the course can be modified, as appropriate, to promote learning. For example, if students assess the activities they have done in a given week in terms of which they felt most effective for their learning, the teacher has information he or she can use to improve the course. Teachers can also gain this information from systematic observation of students' work in class and in the course while it is in progress.

10.6 *What were the ways in which you evaluated the effectiveness of the last course you taught? Was the evaluation formative or summative? How did the information help you?*

If you have not taught a course, choose a course in which you were a learner. How and when was the effectiveness of the course evaluated?

What Are Some Ways to Design an Assessment Plan?

See Appendix 5-1, pages 239–241, for David Thomson's goals and objectives.

We will look at five assessment plans below. The first is David Thomson's plan for his course "Writing using computers" in an intensive English program in the United States. The second is Sally Cavanough's plan for a low-intermediate general English course in a university in Japan. The third is Sally's plan for assessing writing in an EAP (English for Academic Purposes) setting in Australia. The fourth is Denise Maksail-Fine's plan for her Spanish 3 course in a rural high school in the United States, and the fifth is Mary Patten's plan for assessing her students' learning of the material in a textbook unit she taught in Morocco.

David Thomson's assessment plan for the writing component of his course for high intermediate level ESL students "Writing Using Computers" is part of a redesign of a similar course he had taught twice before. It is an elective course given in the afternoons in an intensive English program in the United States. There are 12 students from different cultures. Their level of English is high intermediate to advanced. He writes about the course:

David Thomson

> Though some of the students had never used computers before, they were quickly able to learn and by the second week, with a little coaching from me and other students, could do everything I asked them to do. The students were between the ages of 15 and 24, part of a generation that has grown up using technology, so the technology learning curve was not so steep.
>
> By the end of each of the two terms, I noticed an improvement in students' writing and more importantly in their interest in writing. Students would become so involved in what they were working on that I would often have to tell them that class was finished, time to go home. This was very impressive—I had never seen students so engrossed in their work. What was even more impressive , though, was the self-direction they showed. . . . I had given them the assignments at the beginning of the term, and most were able and willing to proceed with little more than minimal instruction. It was watching the students get involved with what they were doing and watching them take responsibility for their studies that made me want to work more on developing this course.

His assessment plan follows. Some parts of the plan were retained from the old course, some were new.

10.7 *Read through David Thomson's assessment plan and his reflections on it.*

1. Which parts of his plan assess students' needs? Which parts of his plan assess students' learning? Which parts of his plan evaluate the effectiveness of the course?
2. What do you like about his plan? What don't you like? Why?
3. As this is David's plan prior to teaching, (in other words, he hasn't been able to "test" it in practice), what advice would you give him about what to take into consideration as he tries out his plan?

David Thomson's Assessment Plan

1. *Student letter:* Students write a letter about writing in English in which they write about their past experiences with writing, their future needs, the problems they have encountered, what they hope to work on in class. They also include two goals they would like to accomplish during the course.
2. *Error correction symbol sheet:* Students review a composite list of their errors from the writing sample during the placement tests. They use an "Error Correction Symbols" handout to help them understand how the errors are coded and how to correct them. By doing this, they also gain practice with the symbols sheet as an assessment tool. (See Appendix 10-1 page 290.)
3. *Self-rating forms:* Students rate themselves as writers. They rate themselves according to a "Types of Writing" form which includes examples of the types of writing referenced in the ACTFL Advanced Writing section. They then rate themselves on four "Writing Evaluation" forms. (The forms are in Appendix 10-2 on pages 291–294.)

The ACTFL guidelines were developed by the American Council on the Teaching of Foreign Languages.

David comments on the "Types of Writing" form:

> These are the kinds of writing advanced level students are expected to do competently. This form and the self-assessment process are discussed in class, then students are asked to try to be objective and rate their ability to do these kinds of writing. This same form will also be used at the end of the second week and at the end of the fourth week so students can see if they made progress during the term.

He comments on the "Writing Evaluation" forms:

> The other forms—"Writing Evaluation" forms—list a variety of writing skills under four general categories (I. Content/Organization, II. Vocabulary/Word Choice, III. Language Use, IV. Mechanics). Students review the forms to make sure they understand the various categories and skills. They discuss the forms with a partner and then with the class as a whole. For homework they are to rate themselves on each continuum and then put a date next to the rating. Additionally, they choose two skill areas from each sheet that they want to focus on during that term.

Listed below each skill area are several blank lines for "strategies." I will work with students throughout the term to help facilitate their awareness of the various strategies they can use to improve in each of the skill areas. Students will record the different strategies they have tried or want to try on this part of the form.

Below the lines for strategies are descriptions of what "excellent" is for each of the skills. Here students are given a definition of one pole on the continuum and are told the other (poor) means "having no ability in this area."

I have included one of the forms below. Please note that the actual form is two pages with a lot more space between lines and sections.

Writing Evaluation Forms

I. Content/Organization

A. Introduction/Thesis Statement

I________ I________ I________ I________ I________

poor fair good very good excellent

Strategies: ______________________________

EXCELLENT: The writing has an introduction that clearly frames and establishes the purpose of the paper, and gets the reader's attention. For multi-paragraph assignments, a clear thesis statement has been written to inform the reader of the gist (perhaps point of view, theme, primary point of argument, etc.) of the paper.

B. Topic Sentence(s)/Supporting Details

I________ I________ I________ I________ I________

poor fair good very good excellent

Strategies: ______________________________

EXCELLENT: Each paragraph has a clearly stated topic sentence that is followed by supporting information, details, facts, or opinions. The writer's ideas and/or opinions are well developed and supported.

C. Logical Sequencing/Connection of Ideas and Information / Cohesion

I________ I________ I________ I________ I________

poor fair good very good excellent

Strategies: ______________________________

EXCELLENT: The writing is well organized at all levels. Information flows in a logical sequence (from general to specific, from most important to least important, chronologically, etc.). Information in the paragraph is directly related to the topic sentence. Appropriate transition words are used throughout. The writer effectively uses pronouns and other referential links.

D. Conclusion

| ________ | ________ | ________ | ________ | ________
poor fair good very good excellent

Strategies: ____

____

EXCELLENT: The main points of the writing assignment have been briefly reiterated or summarized in a conclusion.

David comments on the rating sheets:

> Each time students write a paper they will rate their writing, (i.e., that specific piece) on each of the same continua by marking the date. At the end of the course, students will have a record to show their progress during the term.

4. *Portfolios:* Each of the forms and each draft of a writing assignment is kept in a portfolio.

David comments on the portfolio:

> A portfolio is a collection of the students' work done during the term. By the end of the course students will have rated themselves on each of the forms so they will have a sense of their successes and the areas that still require work. I, too, will use the forms—the same kind of forms used by the students—to rate them on each assignment. At the end of the term, they will have two copies of each form—one filled out by them, the other by me.

5. *Grammar/Vocabulary Log:* In this log students record new vocabulary, grammar structures, idioms, collocations they learn. The log is kept in their portfolio.
6. Teacher-student *dialogue journals*

David comments on the dialogue journal:

> This is my way to keep in touch with the students individually. My intent is to get them to express themselves to me. I encourage them to ask me questions about any subject they are interested in. Sometimes the questions are about language, sometimes about life in the United States, sometimes about frustrations with the program. I will answer their questions and often ask them my own. I only correct their mistakes if they ask me to. I want them to feel comfortable writing and feel they have a teacher with whom they can communicate freely without fear of criticism or censure.
>
> This is also my main way to evaluate the course, to see what is important to students and what is of little consequence. Throughout the term I ask students to give me feedback on what we are doing and also tell me what they would like to be doing or would rather be doing. At the end of the term, this information will be used to determine the effectiveness of the course and to decide what should be changed the following term.

7. *End of course letter:* In this letter students write about what they learned during the term and what they feel they still need to work on. They review their original goals and evaluate how close they came to reaching them.

8. *A final self-rating:* Students use the rating sheets to assess their writing skills based on the writing evaluation forms.

9. *A read aloud:* Students choose the writing they are most proud of and read it aloud to their classmates.

I'd like to analyze David Thomson's writing plan according to the WH Question framework.

Who assesses? The main assessors in the course are the students themselves: they set goals and rate each piece of writing. They assess progress. The teacher also rates their writing.

What is assessed? The global answer is the students' writing. The specific answer lies in his evaluation sheets, which are based on the ACTFL proficiency guidelines. These sheets carefully spell out the criteria for good writing at that level. The criteria provide the basis for diagnosis and improvement. The students will need to learn to use the rating sheets in order for them to be successful assessment tools.

Regarding the course, David has not specified which aspects of the course he will ask students to evaluate in their dialogue journals.

Why? For what purposes? The initial rating is a subjective one in which students determine their entry proficiency level and also try to diagnose needs. Diagnosis then happens on a regular basis with each of their compositions. The diagnosis is done by both teacher and students. Progress is measured by dating each assessment and comparing over time. Achievement assessment is done with a final rating using the scales, and at the end students choose their best piece to read aloud. The initial and end-of-course letters also provide a means for assessing achievement.

How? Assessment take several forms: the pieces of writing and the rating scales, which are kept in a portfolio; the first and last day letters; the error correction sheets, which are a tool for diagnosing and assessing errors; the learning logs, which are records of learning, a form of achievement. The dialogue journals are used for course evaluation rather than assessment of learning.

When? Assessment starts on the first day and is ongoing. Although there is a summative assessment in the form of the final rating, letter, and read aloud, students have been given and learned how to use tools which will enable them to continue to assess their own writing beyond the classroom.

What is done with the results of assessment? Each of the assessment tools is meant to provide students with a means to understand and assess their own work in an ongoing way, both within the class and after they leave the class.

Sally Cavanough

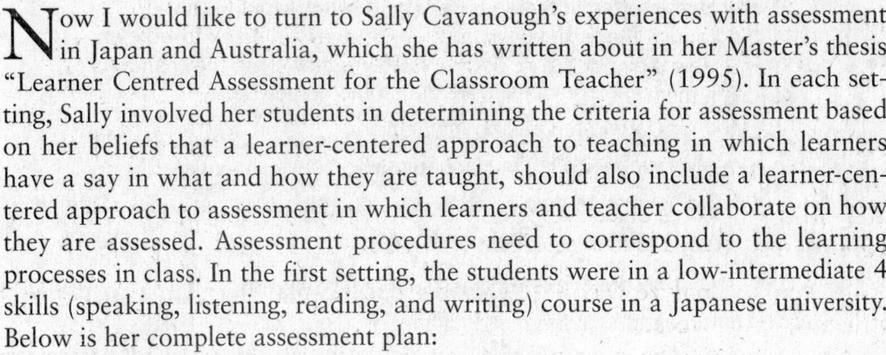

Now I would like to turn to Sally Cavanough's experiences with assessment in Japan and Australia, which she has written about in her Master's thesis "Learner Centred Assessment for the Classroom Teacher" (1995). In each setting, Sally involved her students in determining the criteria for assessment based on her beliefs that a learner-centered approach to teaching in which learners have a say in what and how they are taught, should also include a learner-centered approach to assessment in which learners and teacher collaborate on how they are assessed. Assessment procedures need to correspond to the learning processes in class. In the first setting, the students were in a low-intermediate 4 skills (speaking, listening, reading, and writing) course in a Japanese university. Below is her complete assessment plan:

IE7 Class Assessment Plan

This is how you will be assessed during the semester:

What	*How*	*Percent of grade*
Attendance	daily count	20%
Participation	4 observations each	20%
Coursework:		
■ Text/classwork	1 student-made quiz	15%
■ Projects:		
Brazil Tour	tasks/group presentations	15%
Mixed Projects	tasks	20%
■ Conversation skills	oral assessment	10%

1. *Attendance.* There are 48 classes this semester. If you only miss two classes, you will get an A.

   A 48–46 (2 absences)   C 43–42 (6 absences)

   B 45–44 (4 absences)   F 41– (7 or more absences)

2. *Participation.* Your participation grade is based on the following Table of Standards that we made in class:

   5. ■ completes all classwork and homework
      ■ always eager and interested to learn English
      ■ speaks only English in class
      ■ often volunteers opinions and asks questions
      ■ works very well in pairs and groups

   4. ■ completes most classwork and homework
      ■ usually eager and interested to learn English
      ■ usually speaks only English in class; occasionally speaks Japanese
      ■ sometimes volunteers opinions and asks questions
      ■ works well in pairs and groups

   3. ■ completes most classwork and homework
      ■ interested, but not very eager to learn English
      ■ sometimes speaks English in class, but often speaks Japanese

- occasionally volunteers opinions and asks questions
- works OK in pairs and groups

2. - seldom completes classwork and some homework
   - not very interested in learning English
   - rarely speaks English in class, usually speaks Japanese
   - rarely volunteers opinions and asks questions
   - doesn't work very well in pairs and groups

1. - almost never completes classwork and homework
   - not interested in learning English
   - almost never speaks English in class, always Japanese
   - never volunteers opinions and asks questions
   - doesn't work well in pairs and groups

How will you be evaluated on the above Table of Standards?

- This is a subjective opinion made by me.
- I will observe four students each day during the semester.
- I will observe you each four times.
- I will randomly choose whom I observe. You will not know that I am observing you.
- If you are absent that day, you will receive a zero grade (unless you have a doctor's certificate, etc.).

3. *Teacher assessment.* In class, you wrote down the following ideas about a "good teacher." I will ask you to evaluate me on the below points during the semester.
   - does not get angry
   - is kind
   - cheerful, smiling
   - tried to understand Ss (students)
   - has a sense of humor
   - is friendly
   - corrects Ss mistakes
   - speaks English loudly and clearly
   - talks to all the students fairly
   - speaks at a natural speed
   - has an interesting class
   - lectures are understandable
   - tries to know Ss ability
   - teaches Ss what they need most
   - is always on time
   - writes clearly on the board
   - is well prepared for class

Sally writes about the way she negotiated the assessment plan with her students:

> At the end of the second week of the semester, I led class discussions which determined the assessment procedures for attendance, participation, and coursework. For coursework, we concentrated on how to assess what was learned from the text and other classwork. I explained the difference between exams and quizzes. I pointed out that unlike assessing participation, written tests are objective, that is, they have a correct answer. The students decided that they preferred a quiz. The students took one quiz on the coursework to aid in the overall student assessment profile. The material for the quiz was taken directly from class activities during the first six weeks of the semester.
>
> To continue the spirit of learner-centered assessment, the students wrote the quiz themselves. First, basics of test construction were taught (Heaton 1988), including how to write a matching item, a true/false item, and a short-answer question. Guidelines to do this were handed to the students and discussed in class as another learning activity. Students got into small groups to review the semester's materials, then chose what was important and wrote items to test knowledge in that area. Several dozen items were produced in a short time. I chose 15 of the best items, added five of my own, and created the quiz.
>
> After working on oral and project assessment criteria, the last stage of the process was to finalize the assessment framework. This included writing in how to evaluate next to each category. . . . I asked students what percentage of each category should be awarded and wrote the responses on the board. My role here was to serve as co-ordinator and to help mediate suggestions to assure they followed university guidelines. . . . Though not all students were satisfied with the final tabulations, I felt confident that each had participated somewhat in the process and, more importantly, understood the decisions required to create an assessment framework.

10.8 *What do you like about Sally's assessment plan? What don't you like about it? Why?*

How would Sally answer the WH questions for assessment?

One interesting feature of Sally's assessment plan is that a careful reading of the students' ideas about a "good teacher" under Teacher Assessment provides insights into some of the students' affective and learning needs. The systematic assessment of participation also provides information about students' needs that help her to make the course more responsive to them. Sally writes:

> I assessed students' class participation on a daily basis. Although the process was laborious, the information gained was diagnostic, and it helped to improve my teaching and the students' learning.

> In the process, I observed four students each day, using the criteria established with the students. Each student was observed four times during the semester. After each class, I filled in a report sheet which I gave to the individual during the next class. Over the semester, I noticed that I became much more conscious of each student's performance in class, and, as a result, I was able to direct my teaching more toward the students' needs. At the same time, the students were able to receive immediate feedback on their progress in class which enabled them to direct their learning more effectively.

Sally later taught academic writing in Australia. One place she taught was the Centre for English Language Learning at the Royal Melbourne Institute of Technology. She co-taught an EAP class for advanced level students and was responsible for the writing component which was designed around four written assessment tasks. These tasks were a cause and effect essay, an argument essay, and a group report, each on assigned topics, as well as a research essay on one's own topic. The first time Sally taught the course, she involved her students in designing assessment criteria for the tasks, in the form of three descriptive grading bands: 8–10, 6–8, and 5, similar to the Table of Standards in the Japanese setting. Each band included criteria for presentation, content, form, and organization. The grading system is explained below:

Cause and Effect Essay

Discuss poverty in your own country. Focus on one major cause, eg., lack of education, and discuss the effects.

Due: Friday, August 12

Requirements:

- 500–700 words
- Double-space your text, type if possible
- Include two references
- Include a cover page and list of references

Grading:
Your essay will be graded on the following criteria that we made in class.

8–10

- The author's handwriting is clear, the author appropriately paraphrases and references other authors' written material, the author includes a cover page and a correctly-formatted list of references.
- The author develops original ideas, offers interesting and thoughtful opinions, incorporates appropriate materials and sources in a way that is clear and logical.
- The author's grammar, vocabulary, and use of connectives, transition signals, and so on are accurate.

- The paper is well organised with an introduction, body, and conclusion. The introduction provides a clear outline of the essay (a thesis statement). Each paragraph has a topic sentence. The conclusion clearly summarises the issues and includes any relevant recommendations.

6-7

- The author's handwriting is generally clear, but sometimes difficult to read. The author appropriately paraphrases and references most of the ideas taken from other authors' written material. The author includes a cover page and a list of references; however, there are a few mistakes in the style.
- The author develops some original ideas, offers some interesting and thoughtful opinions, incorporates appropriate materials and sources in a way that is mostly clear and logical.
- The author's grammar, vocabulary, and use of connectives, transition signals, and so on are good, but with some mistakes that do not prevent communication.
- The paper has an introduction, body, and conclusion. The introduction provides an outline of the essay (a thesis statement). Most paragraphs have a topic sentence. The conclusion summarises the issues and includes recommendations.

5

- The author's handwriting is not very clear and is difficult to read. The author does not paraphrase and reference ideas taken from other authors' written material. The author includes a cover page and a list of references; however there are many mistakes in style.
- The author develops few original ideas, and only offers a few interesting and thoughtful opinions; does not incorporate appropriate materials and sources very logically.
- The author's grammar, vocabulary, and use of connectives, transition signals, and so on are OK, but with some mistakes that sometimes prevent communication.
- The paper has an introduction, body, and conclusion. The introduction does not have an outline of the essay (a thesis statement). Not all paragraphs have a topic sentence. The conclusion does not clearly summarise the issues.

Sally found, however, that the bands were problematic. She writes:

> As we were grading the essays, various issues emerged. The criteria, divided into three descriptive bands, were difficult to apply. For example, a student met all the requirements for form, content, and organization in the "6–7" range, but her presentation was poor. Our dilemma was deciding whether the student's grade should be dropped to "5." Considering the above situation, we agreed that the descriptive bands, written as they were, were difficult to use.

Additionally, Sally administered a final course evaluation, which included 31 items that asked students to evaluate the course, the grading system, the teaching, and themselves. (The form is in Appendix 10-3 on pages 295–297.) She comments:

> Below are some views on the grading system garnered from the survey:
>
> - 37% agreed that their overall understanding of the class assessment plan was clear from the beginning of the course
> - 37% agreed that the grades that they received assessed their work fairly
> - 50% agreed that they understood their teachers' method of grading their work.

The negative results of the survey and her experience with trying to use the three assessment bands provided her with a basis for improving her assessment plan in the next course she taught, which was similar to the previous one, except that a "compare and contrast" essay replaced the "cause and effect" essay. This time she and her co-teacher took a more systematic approach to assessment. She writes:

> Before we met with the students, we looked at the feedback from E6 (the previous class), and reviewed our own interpretations. In the light of the previous class, we spent more time in the planning process, and handouts were distributed to students indicating course objectives, the assessment plan, and a list of hurdle requirements for the written assessment tasks.
>
> At the beginning of Week 1, I started planning how to grade the first written assignment, the comparison and contrast essay. I reviewed the chapter "Compare and Contrast," from the writing text we were using in class and reviewed how a comparison and contrast essay is organised, and what comparison and contrast structure words and phrases are used.

She then followed a similar procedure for getting students to generate criteria for grading the essay, except this time, rather than developing descriptive numerical bands, they developed criteria for the categories of *requirements, form, content,* and *organization.* She asked the students to think about their previous experience with having their essays graded as a basis for deciding what should go in each category. She writes:

> In groups of three, I assigned each group one of the four categories: requirements, form, content, and organization. On large pieces of butcher paper, each group listed criteria for that category. To help the students, I referred them to their notes and handouts reviewing what we had covered in class [about comparison and contrast essays.] We put the completed lists on the floor, and looking at each list, filled in what was missing, and clarified anything that was unclear. I typed up the criteria and distributed the handouts to the students, asking them to use the criteria as a guide to writing their essays.

> The criteria were organized into categories; but instead of writing descriptive bands, I typed up the student-developed criteria as descriptive statements. I hoped to avoid the problem we had in the previous course where we had difficulty assigning grades, because the descriptions of each grade band did not accommodate those students whose essays were in the "8–10" range for form, content, and organization, but were in the "5" range for presentation." (See Appendix 10-4, pages 298–299, for the criteria for the comparison and contrast essay.)

This time around the assessment plan was a more integral part of the course. Students were involved in developing the assessment criteria as soon as the course started so that it was part of the course. Students developed the criteria based on material they had learned about that type of essay. Sally found that some students still did not meet all the requirements. Part of this could be due to the fact that students needed to learn how to use the criteria. In other words, if having students generate assessment criteria is one of your course objectives, then you need to teach them how to use the criteria as part of the syllabus.

The next essay Sally taught was the argument essay. She writes,

> I had difficulty deciding on the best way to teach argument; the information regarding this genre varies considerably. I finally decided on a model that was adapted from two texts. By deciding what to teach, I had a much clearer picture of what to grade.

This last statement is important for understanding the role of assessment in course design. What you teach and what you assess each influence the other. What you teach is the basis for what you assess. In Sally's case, how she conceptualized the argument essay—how she taught it—provided the basis for what was assessed. Conversely, your criteria for assessment can be used as the basis for what you will teach. Sally followed a similar process for having her students generate assessment criteria in the four categories above. This time, all of the essays had followed the hurdle requirements and none needed to be resubmitted. Additionally, the responses to a mid-term course evaluation were much more positive than the previous term's class.

- 88% agreed that they understood the assessment plan clearly;
- 77% agreed that the grades that they had received so far had assessed their work fairly
- 77% agreed that they understood their teachers' method of grading their work

She concludes:

> The results reflect more positive percentages than those from the previous class. This is probably due to a number of factors. First of all, the feedback from E6 (the previous term class) prompted us to be more organised from the beginning of the course, preparing an assessment plan together with hurdle requirements. Secondly, my confidence in developing the student-developed criteria

increased with time, and the process served to give clear guidelines for students to follow. And lastly, the students, especially those from the previous class, E6, were now familiar with the process of writing an academic paper.

The criteria for the argument essay are in Appendix 10-5 on pages 300–301.

10.9 *What appeals to you about Sally's approach to assessing writing? What doesn't appeal to you? Why?*

How does Sally's approach to assessing writing differ from David Thomson's approach?

The following assessment plan is Denise Maksail-Fine's plan for her year-long Spanish 3 class in a rural high school in upstate New York. This is the third year of Spanish for her high school students. In addition to periodic quizzes and unit tests, she outlines the following:

Denise Maksail-Fine

See Chapter 4, page 61, for Maksail-Fine's mind maps; Appendix 5-2, page242, for her goals and objectives; Chapter 7, pages 128–129, for her course syllabus; and Chapter 8, page 165, for a unit plan.

Assessment Plan

Learning Assessment Tool #1:
New York State Comprehensive Regents Examination

This first assessment tool is not one of my own creation, yet it is probably the primary tool to measure student achievement and teacher effectiveness within any given school district in New York State. The Regents Comprehensive Examination in Spanish is a statewide, standardized exam administered at the completion of the third full year of Spanish study, and its successful completion is required in partial satisfaction of the NYS Regents Diploma requirements. Students must achieve a score of 65% or higher in order to successfully pass the exam.

It is summative in nature in that it is administered at the end of this course. It is also a course evaluation tool because, by doing an item analysis of the exam after it is administered, I will be able to ascertain in which areas my students' strengths and weaknesses lay and adjust my curriculum planning for the following year accordingly. It also provides me with an idea of my students' achievement in relation to their peers statewide, which is one of the realities of teaching in a public school district in New York State.

The examination is divided into four sections, each section testing one of the four skills. Part I tests the student's ability to speak in the target language. Within a specified time frame before the examination date, Part 1 is individually administered to students by me. It is similar to the ACTFL Oral Proficiency Interview.

The other three sections of the exam are administered statewide on a designated date. Part 2 tests students' listening comprehension. Part 3 assesses reading comprehension and Part 4 assesses writing. Although I have my own personal misgivings about some of the content that appears on the exam, I believe it is a fairly accurate measure of the four skills when viewed within the context of standardized testing in general.

Assessment Tool #2: Portfolios

A portfolio provides a different form of both student assessment and program evaluation from the Regents exam. The Regents exam provides an external, standardized measure of the Spanish 3 course in relation to other programs statewide. While such exams are often an integral part of public school instruction, my personal belief is that they also often heavily emphasize product and form. I feel that it is necessary to provide students with an alternative form of assessment that offsets the stress on form and product by designing an assessment tool that emphasizes process, creativity, and reflection.

Although at the time of this writing I am unsure as to what, specifically, I want the portfolios to contain, I envision them as a tool that documents individual student progress in the areas of the four skills as well as cultural awareness. I have built time into the syllabus (week 34) for portfolio presentations. I would like the students to invite their parents in and present their work to them. This is because I believe that it is important for parents to see exactly what their children have been doing throughout the year and for students to have ownership over their progress.

I see this tool as mainly summative in nature. My hope is that it will assist my students and me in determining how, exactly, students have been working toward the course goals and objectives, and, therefore, provide insight into how the program may need to be modified in the future to better meet those goals and objectives.

Assessment Tool #3: Situational Role Plays

Speaking can often be very stressful for the students I teach, especially if they know they are being assessed in some way. I try to counteract this in a few different ways. First, I have them speak as much as possible, even when they are not being assessed. I have found that this eventually assists students in becoming more spontaneous with their speech. Second, I try to have students do different role-play activities in order to prepare them for the speaking situations that they will face on their exam at the end of the year. The variations can include: working with each other, with puppets, or with me; prepared presentations or impromptu performances; etc. Third, instead of creating the rubric for assessment myself, I often take class time to create one with students for use throughout the year. Not only do they create the criteria, they also vote on the final rubric as a class. I have found that by assessing them in this way, there is much less cause for complaint, whining, accusations of unfairness, or claims of ignorance. The following rubric is an example created by a former Spanish 3 class:

Sample Role-play Rubric:

Pronunciation	*Presentation*	*Content*
0 fails to communicate	fails to communicate	fails to communicate
1 barely comprehensible	no eye contact; inaudible at times; uses some English	some incomplete and/or inaccurate information; repetitive vocabulary
2 sometimes exhibits adequate pronunciation	minimal eye contact; voice is monotone	adequate information; little variety of vocabulary
3 demonstrates correct pronunciation most of the time	occasional eye contact; adequate voice tone and volume	appropriate information and variety of vocabulary most of the time
4 consistently accurate pronunciation	consistently makes eye contact; effective use of voice tone and volume	precise, detailed, accurate information; wide variety of vocabulary

Course Evaluation Tool #1: Student Feedback Questionnaire

This evaluation tool is an end-of-unit questionnaire that will be administered in class to each student at the end of each unit.

This tool will be formative in that it will be an ongoing, periodic evaluation of the individual units that will assist me in modifying future units based on the feedback that I receive from students, so that the remainder of the course is tailored to their needs and expectations.

It will also be summative in nature in that it will provide me with an overall view of the progression of the course from beginning to end as perceived by my students. This will provide me with some of the documentation that I will need in order to reflect on the year as a whole and decide which changes I wish to implement for the upcoming year with the intent of making the program more effective in meeting my (and the school district's) goals and objectives. This also includes re-evaluating the goals and objectives themselves to decide whether or not they are actually appropriate and realistic for the students.

Sample Questionnaire:

Name: ____________________ Unit: ____________________

1. What activity or activities did you find most worthwhile in this unit? What was it specifically that made them worthwhile?
2. What activity or activities did you find least worthwhile in this unit? What was it specifically that made them less worthwhile than the other activities?
3. What specifically would you suggest to improve the activities that you listed in #2?

10.10 *What do you like about Denise Maksail-Fine's assessment plan? What don't you like? Why?*

Which parts of the plan assess students' needs? Which parts of the plan assess students' learning? Which parts evaluate the effectiveness of the course?

The last assessment plan we will look at is Mary Patten's plan for assessing her students' learning with respect to a unit from the textbook she is teaching. The course takes place at a language institute in Rabat, Morocco. The students are at an intermediate level. There is an end of term exam, which is prepared by the institute. We read about Mary's approach to textbook adaptation in Chapter 9 in which she describes adding two areas to the syllabus: a culture focus and a group dynamics focus (see pages 197–199). The following quiz is for the unit she described in chapter 9, whose theme was Women and Men.

Intermediate 1: Unit 2 Quiz

Name: ____________

Theme: Women and Men

I. Write five sentences about things you have learned regarding the theme of this unit.

1.
2.
3.
4.
5.

II. Complete the following paragraph with the correct forms of the verbs in parentheses.

Roger only works part-time now, but he ____(have+be) in the restaurant business for more than 40 years. He ____ (start) his first restaurant almost as a hobby. He is almost 70 years old, but still ____ (go) to work every day. These days he ____(talk) about retiring, but he's afraid he's going to be bored. He ____ (be+look) forward to taking a vacation next month, because he ____ (miss) his grandchildren who live far away. Roger _____(wish) he could see them more often, but he doesn't want to move. Roger_____ (like) his town, and the friends he _____ (have+make) over the years.

III. Express your opinion about someone you admire or someone you do not admire. Then write a few sentences which explain your opinion.

IV. List four classroom roles.

1.
2.
3
4.

Mary writes about the quizzes she prepared:

Mary Patten

> The purposes of the quizzes were manifold. One reason was to provide the students with test-like procedures and formats, which were reflective of the final exit text at the end of the course. Another reason was to help the students track their own progress with the material that was being covered in class, as they would be tested on it in the final test. The quizzes were not graded, but served to provide me with additional information as to their test taking skills and their progress with the material, at least in written form. The quizzes allowed me to note individual and group problem areas, and to plan for more review in those areas. They also served as review sheets for the students.
>
> The students were a little wary of the first quiz, but once they realized my objectives in giving it, and saw that it was not going to be graded but instead was meant to be used as a learning tool, they became excited about taking the quizzes and trying to do their best. One day, an activity went overtime and we didn't have enough time left for the quiz so I told them we would have to wait until the next class to do it. Several of the students started whining and talking about how they were ready to take it then, and really wanted to do it even though they would have to stay late to finish it! However, the businessmen said they couldn't stay, so the class decided to take it during the next class. It was really amazing to see them get so emotional about the quiz—in such a positive way!
>
> The unit quizzes were only one means of evaluation used in the course. I often did more informal types of formative evaluation in which I tried to obtain information not only on how students were doing with the required technical aspects of the course, but what they were feeling and thinking about the learning process and the course itself. Interviews, both formal and informal, general and specific opportunities for oral and written feedback, and careful observation of student interactions and body language in class provided a lot of useful information, and certainly helped me try to evaluate how my course was going.

10.11 *What do you like about Mary's approach to the quizzes? What don't you like?*

What kind of information does the quiz on page 231 give Mary about her students' learning? How does the quiz reflect her addition of a group dynamics and an explicit cultural focus to the syllabus?

To summarize, your assessment plan should allow you to assess students' needs, to assess their learning, and to evaluate the effectiveness of the course. It should include formative assessment activities so that you can adjust the course as you teach it, and provide summative information so that you can look back retrospectively in order to redesign it. How you answer the WH questions of *who, what, when, how,* and *why* will depend on your context and its requirements, on what you consider important, and on your students. David Thomson's, Sally Cavanough's, Denise Maksail-Fine's and Mary Patten's assessment plans reflect the demands of their context and their beliefs and understandings about how students learn, how their learning should be assessed, and how the course should address their learning needs. Your assessment plan will reflect the uniqueness of your institutional and sociocultural context, your students, and your beliefs and understandings about language, learning, and teaching.

10.12 *Draw up an assessment plan for your course using the guidelines in the chapter.*

Discuss your plan with a colleague. As you discuss it, note areas that aren't clear, as well as activities that can be used for more than one assessment purpose.

The last investigation of the book is one that I learned from Barbara Fujiwara, a friend and colleague in Japan (see Fujiwara 1996). It is a letter to the students about the course. The letter, in fact, usually conveys more than information about assessment. It can include information about the content and organization of the course, its goals and objectives, the roles of teacher and learners, and the teacher's hopes and expectations for the course. Writing to your students requires clarity about the course and clear language to describe it. It also allows you to give a snapshot of the course, to emphasize what you feel is important, and to set a tone for the course. In some cases, teachers have included the voices or advice of former students in the letter.

10.13 *Read David Thomson's letter to his class (below). Which parts of the letter provide information about: assessment? goals and objectives? course content? the way the course is organized? roles of teachers and learners?*

Write a letter to your students explaining to them the purposes of the course and how they will be assessed.

If you would like to broaden the scope of the letter, you can include any other information about the course you feel would be useful to your students.

David Thomson wrote the following letter to his students about his course:

David Thomson

> Dear Student:
>
> Greetings and welcome to: "Writing: Using Computers."
> I'm happy you chose this course and look forward to working with you throughout your stay at ISE Vermont. My goal is to help you find ways to improve your writing and also show you how to use the computer for a variety of writing purposes. "Writing: Using Computers" is a new course and I want to make it a success for each of us.

I'm sure some of you are a little concerned because you've never used a computer before. Please don't worry. We'll start right after this term begins and I think you'll be surprised at how easy they are to use. Those of you who already have some computer skills understand that the best way to learn to operate a computer is to just sit down and do it! I would like to ask those of you who already have good computer skills to work with your classmates who are new to them and help them get started.

By the end of the course each of you will have a good understanding of computers. You'll be able to use the keyboard and a variety of word processing tools and functions. You will have selected e-mail partners (keypals) and corresponded with them. I think you are going to like meeting new friends from around the world and will be able to learn a lot about them, their countries, and their ESL experiences. I also think you're going to like using the Internet and will find many interesting and fun sites on it. I want you to be able to learn things about computers that you can take with you when you leave here and use in your job or at school or maybe at home.

We're going to do a lot of writing in this class. You've chosen to be here, which says to me that you're interested in writing, and I'm going to do everything I can to help you. I'm going to help you directly by reviewing your writing and offering suggestions for ways to improve it. But—and this might be more important—I also want you to find ways to be the best judge of your writing. I want you to develop skills and strategies that will help you get started writing, help you while you're writing, and help you edit your writing. I want you to become aware of what you're doing well and of the areas in which you need improvement.

One of the ways you're going to develop an awareness of your writing is through using "portfolios." I won't try to tell you about them now—we'll talk about them in depth on the first day of class—but I do want you to go to the bookstore and buy a file folder for the portfolio. (You can find them with the supplies.)

We're going to be doing a lot of writing and we'll start by writing a couple of paragraphs. We will work together as a class to write these paragraphs. I want you to learn to work closely with other students, and I want you to see how important it is to have someone else to talk to about your writing.

As I mentioned earlier, you're going to find keypals and write to them on a regular basis. Using e-mail, you and I will also communicate on a regular basis through a dialogue journal. I'll let you decide what topics to discuss in these journals. The final assignment—the big one for this course—is a research project. For this, you'll choose a topic that is of interest to you and then go to the Internet and find at least three sources from which to get information about your topic. I want you to enjoy this assignment and encourage you to start thinking now about what you would like to research.

I'm sure you have lots of questions. If you can't wait until the first day of class you can stop by my office and see me. If you want to use e-mail, you can reach me at ________. I'm really excited about this term and I hope you are, too. I'm looking forward to seeing you in class!

See you soon,
David Thomson

To close this chapter and the book, I'd like to return to some of the ideas in the beginning of Chapter 1. The first investigation in the book asked you to complete the sentence "Designing a language course involves . . ." I said that the way I would complete the sentence was both assured, because of what I know about course design, and tentative, because I feel that there are many ways to arrive at an answer. I hope that you have affirmed, challenged, and expanded your own answer as you read about the ways the teachers in the book approached the design of their courses, and that your own approach to course design is more assured, while leaving room for flexibility as you approach each new group of students.

Suggested Readings

As I have made clear in the chapter, I would go out and buy Kathi Bailey's book in this series, *Learning about Language Assessment: Dilemmas, Decisions, and Directions* (1998). She writes in an engaging and accessible style about a subject that intimidates many teachers. She, in turn, provides ideas for further reading. I also like *New Ways of Classroom Assessment* (1998), edited by J. D. Brown and published by TESOL, because it contains over a hundred activities developed by teachers to assess their students' learning.

With respect to course evaluation, "Planning an Advanced Listening Comprehension Elective for Japanese College Students" by Barbara Fujiwara (1996) includes her midterm evaluation and her thoughts on her students' responses, as well as her end-of-course evaluation. It also includes her pre-course letter to her students, which I have since added to my own repertoire of curriculum products.

Appendix

(There are no appendix entries for Chapters 1–4.)

Chapter Five

5–1 *Goals and objectives for David Thomson's 4-week course, "Teaching Writing Using Computers" for high intermediate students in an intensive English program in the United States.* *(See pages 80, 84.)*

Awareness

Goal 1. By the end of the course, students will have become more aware of their writing in general and be able to identify the specific areas in which improvement is needed.

Objective 1a. Each student will maintain a portfolio which will include his/her personal goals and objectives, self-assessments, teacher assessments, reflective writings, and all writing done by him/her during the course.

Objective 1b. Students will be able to use the ACTFL scale to rate their own writing level.

Objective 1c. Students will be able to write reflectively about their sense of their writing ability and level, what they have been learning, and their feelings about writing.

Objective 1d. Students will learn how to work in pairs and small groups to learn to give and receive feedback on writing.

Objective 1e. Teacher will provide students with guidelines and tools to assess their writing and will work closely with students to apprise them of their progress in general and of specific areas needing improvement.

Objective 1f. Students will use teacher-provided tools to assess their writing.

Teacher

Goal 2. Throughout the course, teacher will clearly communicate to students what his standards are for successful completion of tasks.

Objective 2a. Teacher will give students straightforward instructions and feedback during all stages of assignments.

Objective 2b. Teacher will adjust the pace of the class and his level of involvement consistent with the needs of the students.

Objective 2c. Teacher will review students' work on an ongoing basis and help them develop ways to review and revise on their own.

Objective 2d. Teacher will work closely with students to facilitate their awareness of the writing process.

Goal 3. By the end of the course, the teacher will have developed a greater understanding of student needs and will make adjustments to ensure these needs can be met in the next (following) course.

> ***Objective 3a.*** Teacher will conduct action research and will maintain a personal journal throughout the course.
>
> ***Objective 3b.*** Teacher will maintain a dialogue with students throughout the course.

ATTITUDE

Goal 4. By the end of the course, students will have developed a positive attitude toward writing.

> ***Objective 4a.*** Students will become more confident in their ability to write by developing and improving writing skills and strategies.
>
> ***Objective 4b.*** Students will recognize that writing to a "keypal" in a foreign country is engaging and can be entertaining.
>
> ***Objective 4c.*** Students will realize a greater sense of self-understanding and increased self-esteem by expressing themselves creatively and critically in purposeful writing tasks.

SKILLS

Goal 5. By the end of the course, students will have developed the ability to use the computer for a variety of purposes.

> ***Objective 5a.*** Students will be able to efficiently use keyboard functions and word processing tools/functions.
>
> ***Objective 5b.*** Students will be able to communicate via e-mail with other students in the class and with ESL students in other geographic areas.
>
> ***Objective 5c.*** Students will be able to use the Internet to find information.
>
> ***Objective 5d.*** Students will be able to make use of a variety of functions that enable them to use the Internet for an assortment of purposes.
>
> ***Objective 5e.*** Students will acquire computer skills they can transfer to and use in other areas of their life (i.e., work, school, personal).

Goal 6. By the end of the course, students will improve their writing to the next level on the ACTFL Proficiency Guideline's writing scale.

Objective 6a. Students will develop strategies to help them get started writing.

Objective 6b. Students will develop better language resources (i.e., vocabulary, syntax, grammar, etc.) so they can focus on conveying meaning rather than form when they write.

Objective 6c. Students will develop a set of writing skills and have strategies for knowing when and how to use them.

Objective 6d. Students will be able to write single paragraph and multi-paragraph compositions that show a good understanding of underlying organization.

Objective 6e. Students will know how to use appropriate review techniques to correct composing problems.

Knowledge

Goal 7. By the end of the course, students will be able to understand the elements of and what constitutes "good writing."

Objective 7a. Students will have an overall understanding of the ACTFL rating system.

Objective 7b. Students will be able to determine which ACTFL level most appropriately describes their level.

Objective 7c. Students will have sufficient knowledge of their writing to be able to determine when their writing is good and when it needs further work.

Goal 8. By the end of the course, students will be able to understand the appropriateness of using computers for different writing and research purposes.

Objective 8a. Students will know when and why to use the different computer functions.

Objective 8b. Students will know how and when to use the Internet to find information.

5-2 *Goals and objectives for Denise Maksail-Fine's year-long (36-week) third year high school Spanish course in the United States.* *(See pages 82, 91.)*

NYS LOTE (language other than English) Standard 1: Students will be able to use a language other than English for communication.

NYS LOTE Standard 2: Students will develop cross-cultural skills and understandings.

Goal 1. Students will be able to utilize the skills of listening and speaking for the purposes of: socializing, providing and obtaining information, expressing personal feelings and opinions, persuading others to adopt a course of action, in the targeted topic* areas.

*Objectives*** Students will be able to:

1.1 comprehend messages and short conversations when listening to peers, familiar adults, and providers of public services in face-to-face interactions.

1.2 understand the main idea and some discrete information in television, radio, or live presentations.

1.3 initiate and sustain conversations, face-to-face, with native speakers or more fluent individuals.

1.4 select vocabulary appropriate to a range of topics, employing simple and complex sentences in present, past, or future time frames, and expressing details and nuances by using appropriate modifiers.

1.5 exhibit spontaneity in their interactions, particularly when the topic is familiar, but often relying on familiar utterances.

Goal 2. Students will be able to utilize the skills of reading and writing for the purposes of: socializing, providing and obtaining information, expressing personal feelings and opinions, persuading others to adopt a course of action, in the targeted topic* areas.

*Objectives*** Students will be able to:

2.1 read and comprehend materials written for native speakers when the topic and language are familiar.

2.2 read simple materials independently, but may have to guess at meanings of longer or more complex material.

2.3 write short notes, uncomplicated personal and business letters, brief journals, and short reports.

2.4 write brief analyses of more complex content when given the opportunity for organization and advance preparation, though errors may occur more frequently.

2.5 produce written narratives and expressions of opinion about radio and television programs, newspaper and magazine articles, and selected stories, songs, and literature of the target language.

Goal 3. Students will develop cross-cultural skills and understandings of perceptions, gestures, folklore, and family and community dynamics.

*Objectives*** Students will be able to:

3.1 demonstrate an awareness of their own native culture and identify specific cultural traits.

3.2 exhibit comprehensive knowledge of cultural traits and patterns.

3.3 draw comparisons between societies.

3.4 demonstrate an understanding that there are important linguistic and cultural variations among groups that speak the same target language.

3.5 understand how words, body language, rituals, and social interactions influence communication.

Goal 4. Students will develop skills that enable them to work together cooperatively.

*Objectives*** Students will be able to:

4.1 demonstrate the ability to listen actively to speakers within the classroom setting.

4.2 restate and summarize material for the benefit of classmates

4.3 demonstrate the ability to provide others with constructive feedback

4.4 identify traits of appropriate and inappropriate classroom interactions and possible consequences.

4.5 develop an awareness and repertoire of language learning strategies.

---

* *targeted topic areas: personal identification, house/home, services/repairs, family life, community and neighborhood, physical environment, mealtaking, health/welfare, education, earning a living, leisure, public and private services, shopping, travel, current events.*

** *criterion: student-produced written work and spoken utterances must be of the level that they can be understood by a native speaker of the L2, who speaks no English but is used to dealing with non-native L2 speakers and writers.*

5–3 *Goals and objectives for Denise Lawson's 10-week advanced composition course. (See pages 81, 93.)*

I. Proficiency.

Students will develop effective writing skills transferable to any context.

Activity

- Students will use a five-step process writing model to write three paragraphs: descriptive, personal narrative (memory), and expository; two essays; and a group research paper.
- Students will use assessment forms to evaluate their own and their peers' writing.
- Students will annotate their reading and maintain reading logs.

Involvement

Students will develop criteria for a well-written paragraph, essay, and short research paper.

- Students will work with peers to generate ideas, get feedback, and to write a research paper.

Mastery

- Students will be able to use a process writing model.
- Students will be able to assess writing (their own and others') based on criteria for good writing.

Critical thinking

- Students will be able to determine and articulate characteristics of a well-written paragraph, essay, and short research paper.

II. Cognitive

Students will gain an awareness of the influence of sociocultural issues on their writing.

Activity

- Students will read Fan Shen essay "The Classroom and the Wider Culture: Identity as a Key to Learning English Composition."

Involvement

- Students will brainstorm issues which may affect their experience writing in English.
- Students will reflect in their daybooks and interview each other regarding their experiences writing in English.

Mastery/Critical thinking

- Students will be able to write short reflections regarding the sociocultural issues that affect their writing and their response to these issues.

III. Affective

Students will develop confidence in their ability to write in English.

Students will develop an appreciation for the contribution their knowledge and experience (and that of their peers) make to the learning process.

Activity

- Students will compose "authority" lists (topics on which they have some knowledge or expertise)
- Students will document their strengths as writers, highlighting areas in which they can serve as "teachers" to other students.
- Students will use assessment forms to evaluate their own and their peers' writing.

Involvement

- Students will discuss their authority lists and writing strengths with peers, forming writing groups with complementary abilities.
- Students will practice giving and receiving feedback on their writing, discussing with peers kinds of feedback which are/are not helpful.

Mastery

- Students will be able to write narrative assessments of their own and their peers' writing.

Critical thinking

- Students will be able to articulate particular areas of knowledge and experience, and how they can draw on these strengths to improve their writing.
- Students will be able to articulate how they can use feedback from their peers to improve their writing.

IV. Transfer

Students will gain an understanding of how they can continue to improve their writing skills.

Activity

- Students will maintain a daybook in which they record their writing history, explore their attitudes toward writing, take notes on strategies for improvement, and track their progress.

Involvement

- On an ongoing basis, students will brainstorm ideas regarding strategies for improving writing skills, and will share and discuss their daybook entries with their peers.

Mastery

- Students will develop an awareness of the importance of becoming managers of their own learning.
- Students will learn how to use self-reflection and consultation with others as tools to improve their learning.

Critical thinking

- Students will be able to describe their current strengths as writers and what they need to do to continue improving their writing skills.

Chapter Six

6–1 *Denise Lawson's "Letter to Students" in her advanced composition course.* *(See page 107.)*

Welcome to the advanced writing course!

I am looking forward to working together during the next ten weeks. I would like to outline my design for the course, and extend an invitation to you to offer feedback so that the course will be relevant to your needs and interests. In addition, I will describe the writing process we will use and introduce my goal of creating a community of writers.

Course Design

My responsibility: I have attached a course syllabus which describes the goals and objectives, assignments, schedule, and methods of assessment.

Your responsibility: The syllabus is an outline; you will have an opportunity to shape the course in a number of ways. For example, you will set goals and objectives for your own learning, and will reflect on your progress in a daybook. In addition, you will select what you write (topic), and—with your peers—determine the criteria by which your writing will be evaluated.

Feedback

My responsibility: Communication will be an important part of our work together. I encourage you to give feedback throughout the course, and I will provide a variety of ways for you to do this, including in-class discussion, feedback cards, and brief questionnaires. I will respond to your comments.

Your responsibility: Please feel free to comment on any aspect of the course at any time. Part of taking charge of your own learning involves noticing what takes place in the course, observing your response to it, and letting me know what aspects of the course are most and least useful for you. If you do not have experience engaging in this kind of reflection, don't worry: we will discuss how to do this in class.

Writing Process

We are all accustomed to looking at final drafts: books, newspapers, and research papers are some examples. Final drafts look polished, with ideas clearly and logically presented, and without any grammatical or spelling errors. However, we are not accustomed to looking at rough drafts—the writing that preceded these seamless, published versions.

In this class we will examine the process of writing by looking at each other's drafts-in-progress. We will break down the process of composing a final draft into five steps. (You may not use all of the steps in each of your writing assignments—now or in the future—but you will learn how to use the steps and will determine which ones are most productive for you.)

Community of Writers

By now, you have completed your first writing assignment of the course (five minute freewrite); by definition, you are a writer. Together we form a community of writers. Each of us has different experiences, backgrounds, strengths, and points of view. This class provides an opportunity to share our commonalities and differences, and to learn from and with each other. You will have an opportunity to work together as a whole group, in small groups, and in pairs. I encourage you to participate fully in class, and to form writing groups outside of class as well. The more you contribute the more you will learn.

6–2 *Chris Conley's "Find Someone Who . . ." needs assessment activity for intermediate adult learners in a community adult education program in the United States.* *(See page 108.)*

Find Someone Who

Ask other students the questions. When someone says "Yes," write his or her name on the line. Use a name only once. Good luck!

Name

1. . . . plays a musical instrument.
   Question: Do you play . . . . ? __________
2. . . . likes spicy food.
   Question: Do you like . . . . ? __________
3. . . . lived in a small town.
   Question: Did you . . . . ? __________
4. . . . felt angry recently.
   Question: Did you . . . . ? __________
5. . . . can cook well.
   Question: Can you . . . . ? __________
6. . . . can use a computer.
   Question: Can . . . . ? __________
7. . . . is happy today.
   Question: Are you . . . . ? __________
8. . . . is <u>not</u> younger than 25.
   Question: Are you . . . . ? __________
9. . . . was in Boston last week.
   Question: Were you . . . . ? __________
10. . . . was sick last week.
    Question: . . . . ? __________
11. . . . has learned a new skill recently.
    Question: Have you . . . . ? __________
12. . . . had a scary dream recently.
    Question: Did you have . . . . ? __________
13. . . . has an interesting job.
    Question: . . . . ? __________
14. . . . enjoys working alone.
    Question: . . . . ? __________
15. Write your own question.
    Question: . . . . ? __________

6–3 *Chris Conley's "Letter of Explanation" as part of needs assessment for intermediate adult learners in community adult education programs in the United States.* *(See page 109.)*

Dear Students,

Welcome to our class! It is nice to see that you are here and that you wish to study English. I would like to explain to you about our class.

Our class is going to study the English language and American culture. We will study about topics and issues that are around us, like our families, our feelings, and how we came to this city. We will study issues in English by using our skills in speaking, writing, reading, and listening.

You have many important roles to play in our class. First, you are a representative of your community and country. It is one goal of our course for you to tell us about your country and its culture. Second, you also will be a researcher of your life and your community. It is important to learn about yourself and to tell the members of our class what you know. Third, I hope that you will feel free to tell our class what you need and want to learn. I also hope that you will report to our class about what you like or do not like about our studying. Fourth, in our class we will study about topics and issues around us. It will be necessary for us to not only study these issues but also to make a plan of action to attempt to change these issues. With our class, we have the power to influence other people in order to make our community a nicer place to live.

My role will be to provide you with choices. I will give you many options on how to study, options on what to study, and options on how to make a plan of action. I will assist you in your studies of English and American culture so that you learn what you need or want to learn. I will give you information (feedback) on your studying when you want me to do so. I hope that I will be a good resource for you as you study and learn English and the community around you.

I hope that you will see that we are all teachers and learners. I can teach you something about my culture and language, and I know that you can teach me something about your culture and language. I am very excited about our class. If you have any questions, please ask them to me anytime. I enjoy talking to you and answering your questions.

Sincerely,

Chris Conley

6–4 *Cyndy Thatcher-Fettig's Learning Style Survey.* *(See page 116.)*

Learning Style Survey

This survey is to help you and your teacher understand the way you usually like to work on assignments, projects, and activities in class. Please read each statement and decide whether you agree or disagree with each statement, then give a reason for your answer.

1. I enjoy having opportunities to share opinions, experiences, compare answers, and solve problems with classmates.
   Agree Disagree
   Why? ____________________

2. I like to work with a partner or a small group. I feel that I learn more and I do a better job on the project.
   Agree Disagree
   Why? ____________________

3. When I work by myself in class I think that I do a better job.
   Agree Disagree
   Why? ____________________

4. When I work by myself in class I often feel bored or frustrated.
   Agree Disagree
   Why? ____________________

5. I prefer working with a single partner than with a large group.
   Agree Disagree
   Why? ____________________

6. I feel more comfortable working in groups when I can choose the group members.
   Agree Disagree
   Why? ____________________

7. I like it when the teacher decides who I will work with.
   Agree Disagree
   Why? ____________________

8. I prefer to work in a mixed level group.
   Agree Disagree
   Why? ____________________

9. I like to work in a group when the teacher assigns roles to the group.
   Agree Disagree
   Why? ____________________

10. I like it when the teacher allows the students to think of the topics and questions for discussion.
    Agree Disagree
    Why? ____________________

Chapter Seven

7–1 *Course syllabus for Denise Maksail-Fine's year-long (36-week) third year Spanish course in the United States.* *(See page 129.)*

Week 1: **Personal Identification**
(Sept) Biographical Data
Introductions, Greetings, Leavetaking, Common Courtesy
Review: Present tense verbs

Week 2: **Personal Identification**
(Sept) Physical Characteristics,
Psychological Characteristics
Review: Present tense verbs

Week 3: **Family Life**
(Sept) Family Members
Family Activities
Cultural Awareness: Día de Independencia (México)
Review: Noun-adjective agreement, articles

Week 4: **Family Life**
(Sept) Roles and Responsibilities
Cultural Awareness: Hispanic vs. U.S.A. Families
Review: Noun-adjective agreement, articles

Week 5: **House and Home**
(Oct) Types of Lodging
Review: Prepositions

Week 6: **House and Home**
(Oct) Rooms, Furnishing, Appliances
Review: Prepositions

Week 7: **House and Home**
(Oct) Routine Household Chores
Housing in Latin America
Cultural Awareness: Día de la Raza
Review: Imperative

Week 8: **Services and Repairs**
(Oct) Repairs of Household Goods
Review: Prepositions

Week 9: **Community and Neighborhood**
(Nov) Local Stores, Facilities
Recreational Opportunities
Cultural Awareness: Día de los Muertos
Review: Imperative

Week 10: **Private and Public Services**
(Nov) Communications: Telephone, Mail, E-mail
Review: Imperative

Week 11: **Private and Public Services**
(Nov) Government Agencies: Post Office, Customs, Police, Embassies
Review: Imperative

Week 12: **Private and Public Services**
(Nov) Finances: Banks, Currency Exchange

Week 13: **Shopping**
(Dec) Shopping Facilities and Goods
Review: Subjunctive, Direct and Indirect Object Pronouns

Week 14: **Shopping**
(Dec) Shopping Patterns: Hours, Ordinary Purchases, Modes of Payment, Measurements and Sizes
Cultural Awareness: Las Posadas, Día de la Virgen de Guadalupe
Review: Subjunctive, Direct and Indirect Object Pronouns

Week 15: **Shopping**
(Dec) Information: Prices, Advertisements, Labels
Cultural Awareness: La Navidad, Día de los Inocentes
Review: Subjunctive, Direct and Indirect Object Pronouns

Week 16: **Mealtaking**
(Jan) Types of Food and Drink
Cultural Awareness: Año Nuevo
Review: Preterite

Week 17: **Mealtaking**
(Jan) Types of Food and Drink
Cultural Awareness: Los Reyes Magos
Review: Preterite

Week 18: **Mealtaking**
(Jan) Mealtime Interaction
Eating Out
Cultural Awareness: Platos Típicos
Review: Preterite

Week 19: **Leisure**
(Jan) Leisure Activities: Sports
Cultural Awareness: Jai Alai, Fútbol, Corrida de Toros
Review: Imperfect

Week 20: **Leisure**
(Feb) Leisure Activities: Music, Hobbies, Media
Cultural Awareness: Día de la Constitución (México)
Review: Preterite vs. Imperfect

Week 21: **Leisure**
(Feb) Special Occasions: Traditions, Customs
Cultural Awareness: Día de la Bandera (México), Día del Santo, Quinceañera
Review: Preterite vs. Imperfect

Week 22: **Education**
(Feb) Secondary and Post-Secondary School Organization: School Types, Programs, Subjects, Schedules
Cultural Awareness: Carnival, Cuaresma

Week 23: **Education**
(Mar) Secondary and Post-Secondary School Organization: Examinations, Grading, Diplomas
Review: Future

Week 24: **Education**
(Mar) School Life: Extracurricular Activities, Relationships, Discipline

Week 25: **Earning a Living**
(Mar) Types of Employment: Common Occupations, Summer or Part-time Employment, Volunteer Work
Review: Conditional

Week 26: **Earning a Living**
(Mar) Work Conditions: Training, Roles, Responsibilities, Benefits

Week 27: **Travel**
(Apr) Transportation, Travel Agencies
Cultural Awareness: Semana Santa

Week 28: **Travel**
(Apr) Transportation, Travel Agencies

Week 29: **Travel**
(Apr) Lodging

Week 30: **Health and Welfare**
(May) Parts of the Body: Identification and Care
Illnesses and Accidents
Cultural Awareness: Cinco de Mayo

Week 31: **Physical Environment**
(May) Physical Features

Week 32: **Physical Environment**
(May) Climate, Weather, Quality of Environment

Week 33: **Current Events**
(May) Political, Social, Economic Aspects
Cultural Aspects

Week 34: **Portfolio Presentations**
(May/June) Regents Exam Part A: Speaking

Week 35: **Regents Exam Review**
(June)

Week 36: **Regents Comprehensive Exam, Parts B, C, D:**
(June) Listening Comprehension, Reading Comprehension, Writing

7–2 *Course syllabus for Toby Brody's 8-week integrated skills course, "The Newspaper," for intermediate-advanced students in an intensive English program in the United States.* *(See page 132.)*

Syllabus		Week
Introduction:	Newspaper Scavenger Hunt	1
Focus:	Summarizing	
Tasks:	Scanning for 5Ws and H questions Predicting main ideas from headlines Reading for main ideas Answering comprehension questions Listening for main ideas—short news report Oral and written summaries	
Linguistic Focus:	Forming questions	
Culture Focus:	Asking colloquial questions (e.g., What's up?)	
Focus:	Interviewing	2
Tasks:	Predicting main ideas from headlines Skimming and scanning Reading and role-playing an interview article Interviewing students with "Interview Cards" Writing feature story based on interview Interviewing a native speaker Reporting orally on interview with native speaker	
Linguistic Focus:	Review questions Student-generated structures	
Culture Focus:	Interview a native speaker re a culture question	
Focus:	Objective reporting	3
Tasks:	Reconstructing a strip story Following and reconstructing a developing story Reading first part of an article that "jumps" and creating an ending Sequencing radio news report	
Linguistic Focus:	Transitions and adverbial connectors	
Culture Focus:	Formats of newspapers and radio broadcasts	
Focus:	Proposing solutions	4
Tasks:	Reading about and summarizing community problems Researching community problems Reporting on community problems and describing actions to be taken Creating a visual to capture a problem and its solutions Presenting a synopsis of the visual	
Linguistic Focus:	Conditionals	
Culture Focus:	Connecting community problems to local realities	

Focus: Letters—responding to editorials and seeking advice **5**

Tasks: Explaining format and purpose of editorial page
Transforming headlines into complete sentences
Summarizing editorial stance
Guessing issues readers are addressing in letters
Distinguishing fact from opinion
Predicting main ideas from headlines
Taking a stand
Responding to an editorial
Role-playing based on an advice column
Seeking and giving advice

Linguistic Focus: Modals and periphrastic modals
Culture Focus: Airing grievances and emotional baggage

Focus: Analyzing **6**

Tasks: Classifying environmental issues/problems
Making a visual of news clips depicting threats to environment
Reporting on threats and possible actions to counteract dangers
Reading and summarizing ways to reverse impact

Linguistic Focus: Student-generated structures
Culture Focus: The environment and U.S. lifestyles

Focus: Commercial and classified advertising **7**

Tasks: Matching an actual text to images in commercial ads
Listing marketing strategies in U.S. vs. home country
Making a collage to promote a service or product
Designing ads for TV, magazines, and radio
Listing and defining abbreviations in classifieds
Matching unemployed people with job opportunities
Role-playing employer/prospective employee
Comparing and contrasting features and prices of cars
Reporting results of phone inquiries to ads
Defining and practicing strategies used in responding to ads

Linguistic Focus: Imperatives and student-generated structures
Culture Focus: Marketing and the American Way

Week 8: During the final week of class, the students will be singularly busy creating their own newspaper. The project will be coordinated entirely by the students themselves. They will need to divide up responsibilities in order to work effectively. Some of the material for the newspaper will come from their written products, which have been placed in folders: other pieces can be added, as need be. Students will use Pagemaker, a program designed to configure a newspaper format. I will simply serve as a resource, as the students see fit. I am confident that eight weeks of exposure to an American newspaper would be sufficient to give them the skills to produce a homemade edition. The final product will serve as a means for me to assess whether or not the course goals have been reached.

7–3 *Course syllabus for Valarie Barnes' 4-week holiday course for young adults. (See page 134.)*

A Holiday Course

Monday	*Tuesday*	*Wednesday*	*Thursday*	*Friday*
Week One	**Theme: Shopping**			
■ Getting to know you ■ Program overview ■ Attitudes and opinions ■ Shops found downtown ■ Concentration game ■ Discussion ■ The interview ■ Downtown walkabout	■ Writing in journals ■ Walkabout follow-up ■ Song: "Big Yellow Taxi"	■ Field trip to the mall	■ Field trip follow-up ■ Discussion ■ Writing ■ Language lab ■ Panel discussion groups ■ Homework	■ Discussion groups ■ Feedback ■ Journals ■ Scrapbooks
Week Two	**Theme: Food**			
■ "This tastes ______" ■ Adjectives for foods ■ Identify the foods ■ Categories worksheet ■ "Do you like ______" ■ ABC game ■ Self-interview	■ Small group discussion ■ Interview an American ■ Discussion ■ Menus ■ Restaurant role play ■ Register ■ Vocabulary	■ Listening ■ Small group work ■ Practice ■ Error correction ■ Shops role play ■ Follow-up ■ American weights and measures ■ Language lab	■ Half-day field trip to a supermarket, a food cooperative, and a restaurant ■ Discussion ■ Synthesis activity	■ Skits ■ Feedback ■ Journals ■ Scrapbooks
Week Three	**Theme: Animals**			
■ Game ■ Brainstorming ■ Reading ■ Discussion ■ Interview preparation ■ Homework	■ Drawings ■ You become an animal ■ Process writing ■ "Talk Show" ■ Video the talk show ■ Journals	■ Field trip to the zoo	■ Field trip follow-up ■ Language lab ■ Synthesis activity ■ Homework	■ To the teacher's home ■ Murals/collages ■ Feedback ■ Journals ■ Scrapbooks

A Holiday Course

Monday	*Tuesday*	*Wednesday*	*Thursday*	*Friday*
Week Four	**Theme: Heritage**			
■ "The Old Days" ■ Pioneers ■ Pioneers of today ■ Values clarification ■ Ask an American ■ Observations	■ "Home Movies" ■ Writing ■ Journals ■ Contra/square dance	■ Field trip to historic Deerfield	■ Field trip follow-up ■ Attitudes and opinions ■ Synthesis activity ■ Journals ■ Scrapbooks ■ Homework	■ Feedback ■ Skits ■ Fun and games

7–4 *Goals and objectives for Brooks Palmer's 12-week, 48-hour, ESP course for professionals in the sciences. (See page 140.)*

Goal: Develop scientific and technical writing skills and strategies through a variety of activities moving in sequence from simple to more complex.

Objectives: Students will be able to write:

- amplified definitions
- classifications
- abstracts
- description of a mechanism
- description of a process
- "mini" research paper of 5+ pages including: introduction, materials and methods, results, and a brief description
- organize and draft a one page outline with main points and include 2–3 discussion questions
- research a topic area using at least 3–4 sources
- critique peer products in regards to content and mechanics

Goal: Develop reading skills and strategies using a wide range of reading materials including: journals, texts, technical manuals, catalogues

Objectives: Students will be able to

- skim and scan material for information
- read for meaning
- derive vocabulary meaning from context
- use a dictionary

Goal: Develop speaking and listening skills and strategies specifically through public speaking and presentation activities involving technical writing products produced in the class.

Objectives: Students will be able to:

- deliver a 15–minute oral presentation on a technical topic of student's choice
- conduct and manage a discussion (10–15 minutes) afterward, discussing the pros and cons of the topic with audience
- speak with persuasion and express opinions in their presentations
- take accurate notes and paraphrase the presentations of peers
- ask for further information, repetition, and clarification of topic, vocabulary, and technical concepts presented
- critique peer presentations discussing specifically: presentation style, use of persuasion and supporting details, synthesis, and logical presentation of information

7–5 *Focus wheel blank matrix form. (See page 143.)*

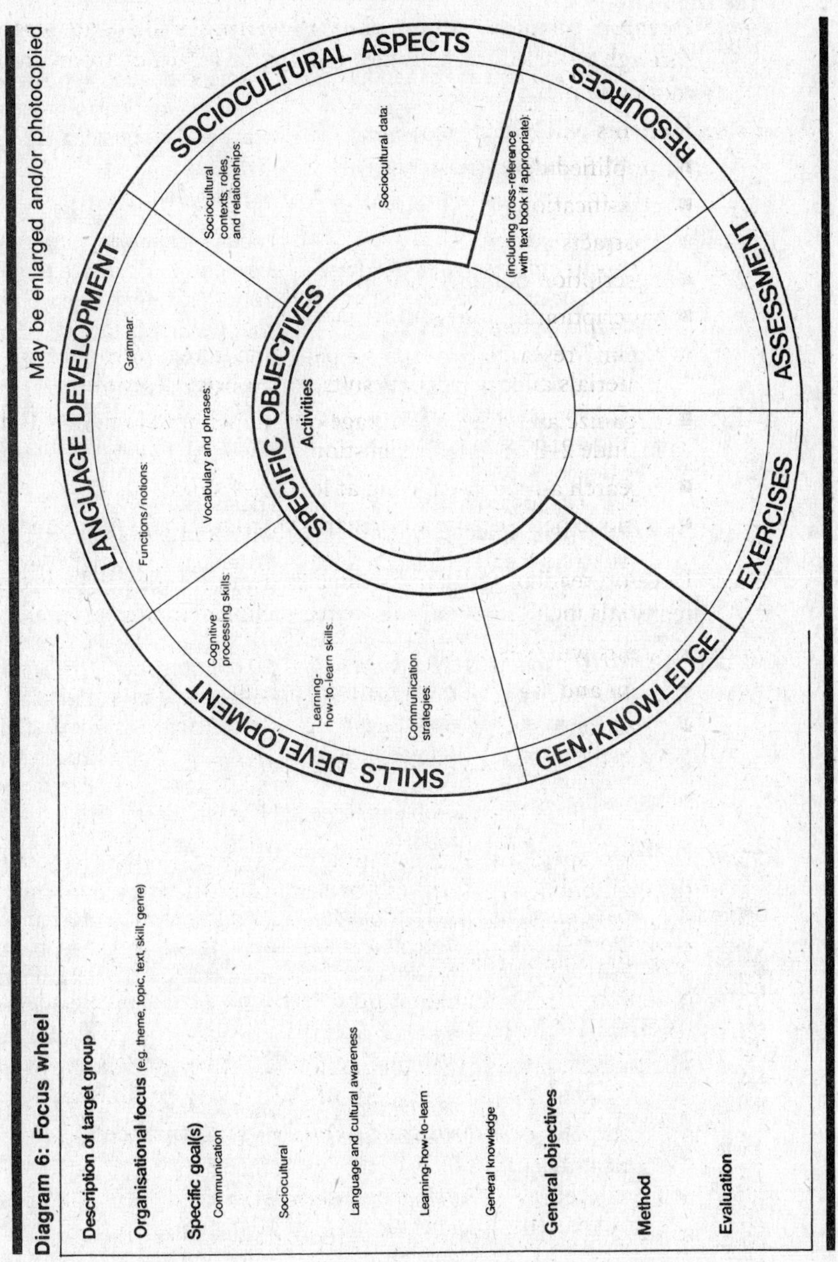

7–6 *First unit grid for Dylan Bate's course for Chinese university students who will be English teachers. (See page 146.)*

The Old Plan

Monday	*5–10 minutes* Major sentence stress: telegraph of the meaning	*20 minutes* Love in America dialogue: structures, expressions	*25 minutes* Create dialogues in pairs or small groups, perform for class, practise for speaking log *5 minutes* assignment	
Tuesday	*25 minutes* Kacuy story: schema building, stereotypes, what do you see in this picture? Focus on listening strategies: Did you understand every word? Did you have to guess the meaning? *20 minutes* Pair work: Students must describe their association for a picture to two different partners		Focus on speaking strategies How can you manage to say it better each time? How can/did your partner help you? *15 minutes* Class discussion/small group work: Morals, what are they? What is the moral of this story? Feedback: homework What strategies did you use (listening/speaking)? Were they successful? Written in logs	
Wednesday	*5–10 minutes* Pre-reading activity: schema building	*20 minutes* Code reading from Schell Romance/love Focus: Problematizing, reading strategies	*20 minutes* Responding to the reading Focus: role plays, letter writing, discussion	*15 minutes* Planning the next step: action? Feedback:
Thursday	*5–10 minutes* Word stress: verb vs. noun	*10–20 minutes* Catch up and/or writing a story from a series of pictures	*20 minutes* Working on pronunciation, major sentence stress	*10 minutes* Feedback: examining learning strategies
Friday	*10 minutes* Rhymalogues: palatization, reduced expressions	*10 minutes* Pre-feedback listing and remembering what we did and how	*20 minutes* Group work around feedback *10 minutes* Reporting to the class: What makes up a good activity?	*15 minutes* Game

7–7 *Revised unit grid for Dylan Bate's course for Chinese university students who will be English teachers. (See page 147.)*

Unit Six Topic: Love and Romance

Activity	*Listening and Speaking Skills*	*Cultural Awareness Critical Consumers*	*Learner Autonomy*
Story: Kacuy	■ Listening to story: schema building ■ Speaking: explaining your views several times	■ Sex stereotypes, thirst for love, sibling love ■ Morals (for stories)	■ L Strategies: selective listening, getting the gist ■ S Strategies: improving your speaking through peer feedback
Code Reading: Romance	■ Group work: role play, writing a letter together, discussion	■ Reading a foreigner's view of Chinese romance ■ Responding to outside perspectives	■ R Strategies: pre- and post activities ■ Planning and carrying out a plan of action ■ Writing as a way of helping thinking
Love in America	■ Dialogue: read, discuss vocabulary, expressions ■ Create own dialogues/perform	■ Discussion: love in U.S. vs. China	■ L Strategies: major sentence stress ■ Feedback
Rhyma-logues	■ Small dialogues: adjacency pairs	■ Humor (of a questionable sort)	■ L/S Strategies: authentic speech, palatization, reduced expressions
Weekly Feedback: Oral and Written	■ Reviewing the week: telling what we did and how ■ Group work: stating your view, restating others' views ■ Reporting to the whole class	■ U.S. vs. Chinese norms of feedback ■ Individual vs. group learning styles (implicit)	■ Examining differences in learning styles ■ Evaluating activities for effectiveness: what makes up a successful activity? ■ Making choices and evaluating them ■ Giving feedback
Speaking/ Listening Logs	■ Practicing and recording dialogues, songs, stories, and poems ■ Comparing self to native speaker	■ Making choices about what to adopt in the new language/ culture	■ Discriminating between global and local errors ■ Setting goals and adjusting them ■ Analyzing weakness-es and strengths, picking appropriate strategies ■ Taking risks

Chapter Eight

8-1 *Sound Ideas. (See pages 158–160.)*

Voice mail: not the answer?

by John Flinn

It's a **long shot,** but if this revolt ever succeeds, grateful telephone users may someday erect a statue to Ed Crutchfield, the man who fired the shot heard 'round the world against **voice mail.**

Joyful employees stood and applauded last month when Crutchfield, chairman of First Union Bank in Charlotte, N.C., sent out a memo ordering the bank to *"press 1 to disconnect now"* from its hated voice-mail system.

"The next time I call and get an answering machine, we're going to be minus one telephone answering machine operator," warned Crutchfield's memo.

His memo has become a rallying point of voice-mail haters, who say the computerized phone answering systems symbolize the **contempt** some businesses display for their customers and that government agencies show for the taxpayers. . . .

One reason we **chafe at** voice mail may be buried deep within the human psyche, according to new research conducted at Stanford University. The technology violates basic rules of human communication that have existed since the first cavemen **grunted at** each other, according to Clifford Nass, an assistant professor of communication at Stanford.

"When people hear a human voice, it sets off strong cues within their brain, and it sets up certain expectations," Nass said. "This is a very hard-wired, **visceral** response."

One Bay Area business is even capitalizing on our **loathing** of voice mail in its advertising campaign.

TakeCare Health Plan, the Concord-based **health maintenance** plan that covers 230,000 members in California, doesn't advertise that it has the most liberal coverage or doctors with the warmest bedside manner.

It advertises that its members don't have to suffer through voice mail when they call.

"If you have a question, press 1, now. If you would like it answered, press 2, now. If you would like to be put on hold for 10 minutes, press 3, now," the ads say, **lampooning** their competitors' **impenetrable** voice-mail systems. *"If you want a membership card, please punch in Beethoven's Fifth, now, in D minor."*

Instead of using a computer, TakeCare employs 12 human operators to handle calls from its customers on its toll-free line. On an average day, they handle 1,170 inquiries.

"Voice mail erects a wall between service industries and their customers," said Mike Massaro of Goldberg Moser O'Neill, the agency that created the campaign.

The people who make voice mail say none of this is the fault of the technology. The problem, they insist, lies with users who do a **shoddy** job of programming their systems.

"People will love it eventually," predicts Maria DeMarco, marketing director for Pacific Bell Voice Mail.

Most of the **acrimony** toward voice mail could be eliminated, says DeMarco, if system users made sure callers always had an easy way to punch out of the system and talk to a live human being.

And voice-mail supporters point out that pushing buttons or talking to a recording can't be any more irritating than listening to a busy signal or a phone ringing endlessly without being answered.

There's one person who never gets tired of hearing that **disembodied** voice say, ". . . or, press 1, for more options." That's because Joan Kenley of Oakland loves hearing her own voice.

Kenley, a former singer who has performed with Ethel Merman, is the voice of voice mail. Northern Telecom, Pacific Bell and other major system suppliers have hired her because **oscilloscope** tests show her intonations retain warmth and "smile" on a computer chip. "I'm everywhere," she says. "I'm **ubiquitous.**"

Former singer Joan Kenley is the voice of voice mail, hired by companies for the "smile" she brings to the recorded messages.

Before You Listen: Listening Passage 2

PREPARATION FOR LISTENING TO "CALL WAITING COULD COST YOU FRIENDS"

Call Waiting," according to Pacific Bell Calling Customer Information, "gives a special tone when someone calls while you are already on the phone. You can answer the second call and then return to your original call without hanging up."

Many people say that it is rude to ask someone you are talking to to hold on while you see who's on the other line.

You are going to hear a listening passage which has two parts:

a. a dialogue between two friends, Wanda and Pat. Pat is very upset. (Stop the tape when you hear the beep at the end of the dialogue so that you can answer the questions under **A** below.)

b. a conversation between interviewer Bob Edwards and newspaper columnist Judith Martin, otherwise known as "Miss Manners"®, who answers letters from readers about manners and politeness. They talk about the dialogue between Wanda and Pat, and about the subject of call waiting.

As You Listen: Listening Passage 2

LEARNING STRATEGY

Remembering New Material: Picturing scenes in your mind helps you remember and understand what you hear.

A. Close your eyes and listen to the dialogue once or twice. Then, write as many words as you can that describe the three people:

Pat is: [for example: upset, a close friend, etc.]

Wanda is:

Gary is:

With members of your class,

a. share the above descriptions and why you chose them.

b. predict what the interviewer and Miss Manners will say about Pat's and Wanda's specific situation and call waiting in general.

B. Continue listening, and then answer the following questions:

1. What bothers Miss Manners the most about call waiting?
2. According to Miss Manners, what is a better way for a caller to find out that you are already on the phone?
3. Did Pat really jump off a bridge? How do you know?
4. What did Miss Manners mean when she asserted that "if it's a genuine emergency, it is one of these 'drop everything and attend to your friend' situations"?

In the cartoon below, the man has just called "911," the emergency number used throughout the United States. To his surprise, he hears a recording of a "voice-mail menu."

1. Why do you think this is called a "menu"?
2. Notice the musical notes at the end of the recording. And notice that the man sarcastically says, "Oh, great. Muzak." Can you guess what "Muzak" is and where people usually hear it played?
3. What is absurd about the situation portrayed in this cartoon?
4. Have you ever heard of or had to use a voice-mail menu? If so, how do you feel about it?

BIZARRO By DAN PIRARO

....THANK YOU FOR CALLING "911." IF YOU WISH TO REPORT A FIRE, PUSH "ONE".... IF YOU WISH TO REQUEST AN AMBULANCE, PUSH "TWO".....IF YOU ARE BEING ROBBED, PUSH "THREE"......IF YOU ARE BEING ATTACKED, OR ARE NOT CALLING FROM A TOUCH-TONE PHONE, PUSH "ZERO", OR STAY ON THE LINE AND AN OPERATOR WILL BE WITH YOU IN A MOMENT......
—OH GREAT. MUZAK.
PIRARO 11-23

Source: The "BIZARRO" cartoon by Dan Piraro is reprinted by permission of Chronicle Features, San Francisco, California

8–2 *Handout on clarifying and paraphrasing (Monday, II) for Cyndy Thatcher-Fettig's speaking and listening course.* *(See page 158.)*

Communication Skills

Technique 4–Clarifying/Paraphrasing

Often we are not sure exactly what the speaker wants to say. In this unit we are going to learn how to ask for clarification, how to restate, and how to paraphrase.

Key phrases

Asking for clarification:

What do you mean?
I'm not sure what you mean.
Sorry, but I don't understand what you mean.
Could you explain what you mean by . . . ?
Are you saying that . . . ?
I'm not sure I follow you. Did you say that . . . ?

Clarifying or restating:

I mean . . .
In other words . . .
The point I'm trying to make is . . .

Paraphrasing:

Joe said that . . .
What Mary means is . . .
I believe Dan's point is . . .
I think Ann feels . . . Isn't that right?
Let me see if I understood. You said . . .

Checking for understanding:

Do you see/know what I mean?
Is that clear?
Do you understand?

Activity

Discuss the following topics with your partner. Make sure to use the expressions for clarifying, paraphrasing, and restating.

1. Explain how you feel about telling a white lie.
2. Explain the advantages and disadvantages of living with someone before marriage.
3. Explain how you feel about hunting for pleasure or hunting for food.
4. Explain how you feel about welfare.

8–3 *Blank handout for practical situations (Wednesday, II) for Cyndy Thatcher-Fettig's speaking and listening course. (See page 159.)*

Practical Situations

Telephoning

Calling	Receiving
	In:
	In but not available:
	Out:

Leaving messages	*Taking messages*

Saying good-bye	Hanging up

Wrong number

If receiver is you

On another line

Receiver	Caller one	Caller two

Answering machines

Machine greeting	Leaving messages on machines

8–4 *Example materials for Cyndy Thatcher-Fettig's speaking and listening course: simulation roles, role-play cards, situations (Tuesday, III simulation; Thursday, III role-play cards; Friday, II telephone situations).* *(See pages 159–160.)*

Example Materials

I. Roles for the simulation activity on Tuesday (adapted from Sound Ideas):

A particular language school has had an influx of calls lately and the one receptionist has not been able to handle all of the calls. The question being raised in this meeting is: Should the school hire an additional receptionist or should they get voice-mail?

President: You have called this meeting in order to listen to everyone's view-point

Manager: You want to hire another telephone receptionist to take all of the phone calls.

Sales manager: You are against voice-mail. You think that personal sales is an asset to your institute.

Financial analyst: Your funds are low and although the company can afford to hire another person, you think that voice-mail is more economical.

Receptionist: You think that getting voice-mail should help in the influx of calls.

Teacher: You are against voice-mail, you think it is too impersonal.

II. Cue cards for role-play activity on Thursday:

Caller:

- Call Joe.
- You are going to be late in picking him up.

Receiver:

- Joe is in the shower.
- Take a message.

III. Case situations for warm-up activity on Friday:

- You want to call the cable company and ask them how to get cable installed in your house.

- A long-distance telephone company keeps on calling you to change your long-distance carrier.

8–5 *Handout for practical situations: getting information on the phone (Friday, III) for Cyndy Thatcher-Fettig's speaking and listening course.* *(See page 160.)*

Practical Situations

Getting Information on the Phone

Asking a complicated question is difficult. Asking it on the phone is even more difficult. The following phrases will help you when you are calling to get information.

Key Phrases

I'm calling to find out . . .
I'd like to ask you about . . .
Could you tell me . . .
I'm calling about . . .
I was wondering if you could tell me . . .
I wonder if you could help me . . .

With your partner, match each of the following situations (1–6) with the appropriate response (a–f) and then role-play them.

1. You are calling the theater to find out what time tonight's performance starts.
2. You are calling the post office to find out how to send a package to your country so that it arrives in time for Christmas.
3. You are calling the airline to find out the earliest flight from Tokyo to Hong Kong next month.
4. You are calling your doctor's office to make an appointment with Dr. Crawford.
5. You are phoning your local paper to find out how to place an advertisement—you want to sell a pair of skis.
6. You are calling a language school to find out how much their evening courses cost.

a. By surface before November 1st. By air before December 3rd.
b. It has been canceled.
c. Ads must be placed by 4:30 p.m. on Wednesday.
   Pay cash at the office or credit card by phone.
d. Two evenings/three hours per evening/$180 per term.
e. He is on vacation for a month/his assistant is Dr. Mills.
f. 6:30 a.m., then 10:30 a.m., 3:30 p.m., 7:00 p.m.

Homework

Brainstorm places to call and make one phone call to get information.

8-6 *Goals and partial objectives for Cyndy Thatcher-Fettig's speaking and listening course.* *(See page 160.)*

Cyndy has five goals for her course.

By the end of the course the students will have:

1. developed the oral and listening language skills they need to perform independently in an academic setting.
2. developed the functional and notional skills they need to perform independently in United States daily life.
3. developed and be able to employ communication strategies to independently participate in discussions and conversations.
4. developed an awareness of the cultural and sociolinguistic factors related to academic and daily life situations in the United States.
5. had practice and experience in academic and United States daily life situations to feel competent to handle situations outside of the ESL class confidently.

Objectives for Goal #2

Students will be able to:

a. express needs for services in which they will be engaged.
b. use formulaic expressions (formal and informal) related to each functional situation.
c. listen to, respond to, and formulate questions.
d. pronounce the formulaic expressions with the appropriate stress and intonation.
e. behave in culturally appropriate ways in United States daily life situations, being aware of paralinguistic, extralinguistic, and sociolinguistic factors.

8.8 *Study Cyndy's unit on telephone technology. What relationship do you see between the unit and Goal #2 and its objectives?*

8–7 *Example letters for Chris Conley's course for intermediate adult learners in a community adult education program in the United States. (See pages 161–163.)*

May 7, 1997

Jan Clark
Hanaford's Supermarket
123 Elm St.
Boston, MA 98765

Dear Ms. Clark:

We are writing to you today to invite you as a guest speaker to the XYZ Institute. We are interested in having a presentation about the history of your store. Our class is interested in the businesses of our neighborhood.

Our institute teaches English, computers, and has job training to help people to get a better job. We are a class of 15 students studying English at XYZ Institute. We are interested in your business since it is in our community and we shop there every day.

We hope that you will accept our invitation and speak to our class. We would be very happy to hear your presentation about Hanaford's Supermarket. Our phone number is 123-4567. We will call you in a few days to ask you about your decision. Thank you very much.

Sincerely,

The students at XYZ Institute and their teacher, Chris Conley

5-7-97

Dear Jan,

How are you doing? I hope you are doing well. Are you busy at work these days? It seems to be a busy season for you.

I have a question for you. Could you come to our class and give us a presentation about your company's employee training program? My class and I have been studying about an issue that relates to employee—customer relations. We would be interested to hear from an employer about your company's training. If you could give me a call, I would appreciate it. My number is 123-4567.

Thank you for your time. Keep working hard. Please say hello to your husband for me.

Bye,

Chris

Mr. and Mrs. Dennis L. Danielson
and
Mr. and Mrs. Donald R. Torgerson
invite you to share in the joy
of the marriage uniting their children
Michele Marie
and
Anthony Carl
on Saturday, the thirty-first day of May
Nineteen hundred and ninety-seven
at four o'clock in the afternoon
Glenwood Lutheran Church
206 Minnesota Avenue East
Glenwood, Minnesota

Reception and Dance
immediately following ceremony
Lakeside Ballroom

The School for International Training
cordially invites you to attend our reception at the
31st Annual TESOL Convention

Friday March 14, 1997

7:30 – 9:30 P.M.

The Indian Room
at the Sheraton World Resort
10100 International Drive,
Orlando, Florida

Hors d'Oeuvres • Cash Bar

Chapter Nine

9–1 *Two pages from Unit 13 of* Intercom 2000, *Book 1.*
(See page 189.)

UNIT 13

COMMUNICATION
Talking about the past • Talking about the seasons and the weather • Expressing likes and dislikes • Asking for and giving reasons

GRAMMAR
Past tense of *be* • Adverbs of frequency after *be* • Preposition *in* + the seasons and months • *Like* + noun; *like to* + verb • Direct object pronoun: *it* • Questions with *why*; answers with *because*

Introducing Toshio Ito

Toshio Ito is a flight attendant for World Airlines. Toshio likes his job because he likes to travel and he likes to work with people. Last month he was in South America. He was in Brazil and Colombia. Last week he was in Hong Kong and Tokyo. Right now he is in Winfield at the home of his friends, the Logans.

SAM: How was the flight, Toshio?
TOSHIO: Difficult. The weather was bad, and we were late getting into San Francisco. I'm sure the passengers weren't happy about that flight!
LISA: Mr. Ito, do you like your job?
TOSHIO: Sure, Lisa. Today was just a bad day.
LISA: Why do you like it?
TOSHIO: I like to work with people, and I like to travel.
LISA: What's your favorite place?
TOSHIO: That's a hard question. I like South America. I go to Colombia and Brazil a lot. The people are very nice, and I like the weather there. It's always warm. Of course, I like the United States too. New York is nice in the summer, but I don't like it in the winter.
LISA: Why not?
TOSHIO: It's too cold. I hate cold weather.
LISA: I love winter. I love to ice skate.
TOSHIO: A lot of my friends like to skate too, Lisa, but not me.

2 Practice

Name	Yesterday	Last week	Last month
Toshio	Winfield	Hong Kong,Tokyo	Brazil, Colombia
Nhu Trinh	New York	California	Hong Kong,Tokyo
the Logans	Winfield	Winfield	New York City
the Youngs	Winfield	Boston	New York City

Look at the chart. Make statements about where the people were. Another student will accept or correct the statement.

The Logans / New York City / last month
A: The Logans were in New York City last month.
B: That's right.

Toshio / Hong Kong / yesterday
A: Toshio was in Hong Kong yesterday.
B: No. He was in Winfield.

1. Nhu Trinh / Boston / yesterday
2. The Logans / Winfield / last week
3. Toshio / Hong Kong / last month
4. The Youngs / Winfield / last week
5. Toshio / South America / last month
6. The Logans / Hong Kong / yesterday
7. Nhu Trinh / California / yesterday
8. The Logans / New York City / last month
9. Toshio / Brazil / last week
10. The Youngs / Boston / yesterday

3 Interaction

Find out where five of your classmates were yesterday and last week. Report to the class.

A: I was ________ ________. What about you?
B: I was ________ .

9–2 *Introductory pages preceding Unit 1 of* East West Basics. *(See page 193.)*

CLASSROOM LANGUAGE

SPORTS
Golf
Tennis
Baseball
Volleyball

Practice the conversation.

Listen.

Write.

Read.

Open your book.

Close your book.

Make a list.

Interview your classmates.

Pair work.

Group work.

Class activity.

Role play.

1

USEFUL EXPRESSIONS

How do you say [cat] in English?
Cat.

How do you say ___ in English?

How do you spell cat?
C-A-T.

How do you spell ___?

How do you say this word?
Skydiving.

How do you say this word?

What does "skydiving" mean?

What does ___ mean?

What kind of music do you like?
Please speak more slowly.
Sorry. What kind of music do you like?
I like pop music.

Please speak more slowly.

What's your age?
I'm sorry. I don't understand.
How old are you?
Oh. I'm seventeen.

I'm sorry. I don't understand.

2

9–3 *Unit 1 of* East West Basics. *(See pages 193–196.)*

UNIT 1

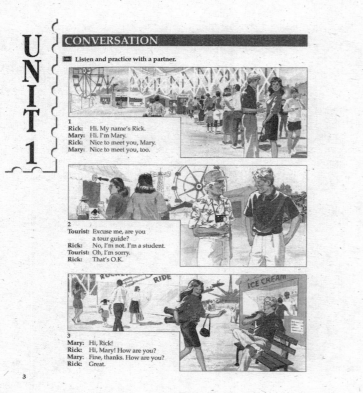

CONVERSATION

Listen and practice with a partner.

1
Rick: Hi. My name's Rick.
Mary: Hi. I'm Mary.
Rick: Nice to meet you, Mary.
Mary: Nice to meet you, too.

2
Tourist: Excuse me, are you a tour guide?
Rick: No, I'm not. I'm a student.
Tourist: Oh, I'm sorry.
Rick: That's O.K.

3
Mary: Hi, Rick!
Rick: Hi, Mary! How are you?
Mary: Fine, thanks. How are you?
Rick: Great.

3

SPEAKING

1 Introducing yourself: *Hi. My name's...*

I am Judy Stone.	**I'm** Judy Stone.
My name is Mike Miller.	**My name's** Mike Miller.

I am → I'm
My name is → My name's

1. *Pair work.* Practice the conversation.

Mike: Hi. My name's Mike Miller.
Judy: Hi, Mike. I'm Judy Stone.
Mike: Nice to meet you, Judy.
Judy: Nice to meet you, too.

Now practice the conversation again. Use your own name.

2. *Class activity.* Meet five classmates.

2 Greeting someone: *How are you?*

How are you?	Fine. O.K. Pretty good. Not bad. Great!

1. *Pair work.* Practice the conversation.

Carlos: Hi, Kazuko.
Kazuko: Hi, Carlos. How are you?
Carlos: Fine, thanks. How are you?
Kazuko: Great!

Now practice the conversation again. Use your own name.

2. *Class activity.* Greet five classmates.

4

3 Identifying someone: *Excuse me, are you...?*

Are you Tom Cruise?	Yes, I am.
	No, I'm not.

1. *Pair work.* **Practice the conversation.**

    A: Excuse me, are you Julia Roberts?
    B: No, I'm not. I'm Mary Hall.
    A: Oh, I'm sorry.
    B: That's O.K.

    Now practice the conversation again.
    Student B: Use your own name.

2. *Pair work.* **Practice the conversation.**

    A: Excuse me, are you Tom Cruise?
    B: Yes, I am.
    A: Hi. My name's Rick Long.
    B: Nice to meet you, Rick.
    A: Nice to meet you, too.

    Now practice the conversation again.
    Student A: Use your own name.
    Student B: You are Tom Cruise or Julia Roberts.

3. *Class activity.*

1. Write your name on three pieces of paper.
2. Put the pieces of paper into a box.
3. Choose three new names from the box.
4. Find the three classmates.

5

4 Vocabulary: *Jobs*

1. *Pair work.* **Match the words with the pictures. Then practice saying the words.**

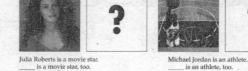

h 1. an artist
___ 2. an athlete
___ 3. a businessman
___ 4. a doctor
___ 5. an engineer
___ 6. a movie star
___ 7. a reporter
___ 8. a singer
___ 9. a teacher

Use **a** before consonants. → **a** movie star
Use **an** before vowels. → **an** athlete

2. *Group work.* **Complete the sentences about famous people.**

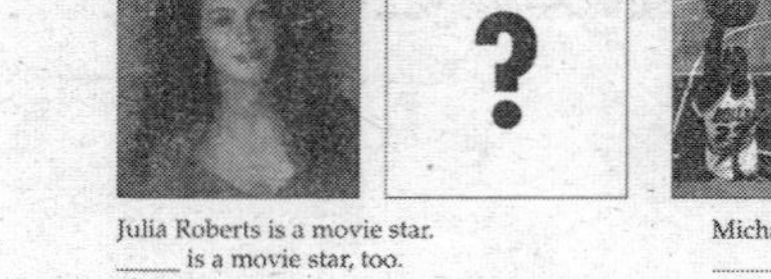

Julia Roberts is a movie star.
_____ is a movie star, too.

Michael Jordan is an athlete.
_____ is an athlete, too.

Now make sentences about other famous people.

6

LISTENING

1 Listen and match the conversations to the pictures.

1. ____
2. ____
3. ____
4. ____

2 Listen and choose the correct answer. Circle *a* or *b*.

1. (a.) Hi. My name's Mary.
   b. No, I'm not.
2. a. Oh, I'm sorry.
   b. Nice to meet you, Rick.
3. a. Fine, thanks.
   b. Hi, Mary.
4. a. My name's Rick.
   b. Fine, thanks.
5. a. Yes, I am.
   b. That's O.K.
6. a. That's O.K.
   b. Nice to meet you.

3 Listen and answer the questions.

1. ________________
2. ________________
3. ________________
4. ________________

7

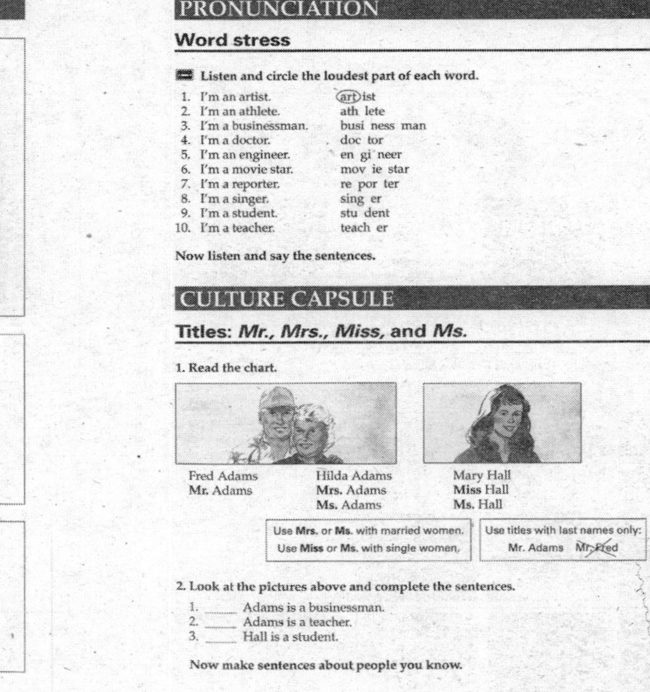

PRONUNCIATION

Word stress

Listen and circle the loudest part of each word.

1. I'm an artist.	(art) ist
2. I'm an athlete.	ath lete
3. I'm a businessman.	busi ness man
4. I'm a doctor.	doc tor
5. I'm an engineer.	en gi neer
6. I'm a movie star.	mov ie star
7. I'm a reporter.	re por ter
8. I'm a singer.	sing er
9. I'm a student.	stu dent
10. I'm a teacher.	teach er

Now listen and say the sentences.

CULTURE CAPSULE

Titles: *Mr., Mrs., Miss,* and *Ms.*

1. Read the chart.

Fred Adams	Hilda Adams	Mary Hall
Mr. Adams	**Mrs.** Adams	**Miss** Hall
	Ms. Adams	**Ms.** Hall

Use **Mrs.** or **Ms.** with married women.
Use **Miss** or **Ms.** with single women.

Use titles with last names only:
Mr. Adams ~~Mr. Fred~~

Put It Together. Unit 1 Extra practice on page 88.

2. Look at the pictures above and complete the sentences.

1. ____ Adams is a businessman.
2. ____ Adams is a teacher.
3. ____ Hall is a student.

Now make sentences about people you know.

8

LANGUAGE CHECKLIST

UNIT 1

Grammar Points

Present tense of *BE*

Statements			Contractions
I	am	→	I'm
You	are	→	You're
It	is	→	It's
My name	is	→	My name's

Yes-no questions

Are you a tour guide?

Short answers

Yes, I am.
No, I'm not.

Information questions

How are you?

Short answers

Fine.

Indefinite articles A/AN

I'm an artist.
(Use *an* before vowel sounds.)
I'm a businessman.
(Use *a* before consonant sounds.)

New Words

Jobs

artist
athlete
businessman
doctor
engineer
movie star
reporter
singer
student
teacher

Useful Expressions

Introductions

Hi. I'm ______.
Hi. My name's ______.
Nice to meet you.

Greetings

Hi.
How are you?
Fine, thanks.
Great!

Apologizing

I'm sorry.
That's O.K.

Other expressions

Excuse me. Are you ______?
I'm a student.

87

Game: *Are you...?*

1. *Pair work.* Write names of famous people under each job.

athlete	businessman
movie star	artist
reporter	singer

2. *Pair work.* Practice the conversation.

A: Are you a singer?
B: No, I'm not.
A: Are you a movie star?
B: Yes, I am.
A: Are you Julia Roberts?
B: Yes, I am.

Now practice the conversation again.

Student A: Choose a name from the list above.

Student B: Guess your partner's name.

3. *Class activity.* Choose another name from your list. Then talk to other classmates and guess their jobs and names.

Are you...?

88

9–4 *Unit 6 of* New Interchange 3. *(See page 196.)*

CONVERSATION

A Listen and practice.

Clerk: Can I help you?
Helen: Yes, I'd like to return this jacket.
Clerk: Is there something the matter with it?
Helen: Yes. I didn't notice when I bought it, but there are a few problems. First, it has a tear in the lining.
Clerk: Hmm. Actually, it's torn in several places.
Helen: And some of the buttons are very loose. This one came off, in fact. And there's a stain on the collar.
Clerk: I'm really sorry about this. Would you like to exchange it for another one?
Helen: Well, to be honest, I don't think this jacket is very well made. I'd rather get a refund.
Clerk: I understand. Do you have the receipt?

B ***Class activity*** Have you ever returned anything to a store? Why? How did the store respond?

GRAMMAR FOCUS

Need *with passive infinitives and gerunds*

Need + *passive infinitive*	**Need + *gerund***
The refrigerator **needs to be fixed**.	It **needs fixing**.
The temperature control **needs to be checked**.	It **needs checking**.

A What needs to be done in this apartment? Write statements about these items using *need* with passive infinitives or gerunds.

1. the walls (paint)
2. the carpet (shampoo)
3. the windows (wash)
4. the door (repair)
5. the lamp shade (replace)
6. the wastebasket (empty)

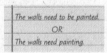

The walls need to be painted.
OR
The walls need painting.

B ***Pair work*** Think of five improvements you would like to make in your home. Which improvements will you most likely make? Which won't you make?

"First of all, the carpet in the living room needs to be replaced. I can't afford it right now, though, so I'll probably do that next year. . . ."

READING

Consumer Affairs

How to Complain to – and About – a Business

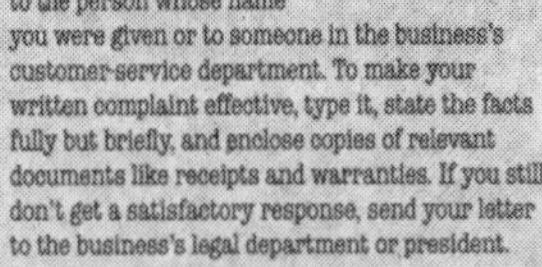

Do you know how to complain to a business?

Dear Annabelle,
My new car has a problem: Every few hundred miles, more oil needs to be added. I think this means something is broken. Each time I take the car into the dealer, though, the service people insist that nothing needs fixing. What can I do?

– Broken Down in Detroit

Dear Broken Down,
I don't know much about cars, but I can diagnose your problem: You're dealing with an unresponsive business. Fortunately, there are many things you can do:

1. For starters, complain to the business, in person or by phone. Explain the problem in a way that is firm but not rude. If you don't seem to be getting anywhere, give up – for the moment. Find out who you're talking to and who you should talk to next. Make notes of what's been said.
2. Next, complain in writing to the person whose name you were given or to someone in the business's customer-service department. To make your written complaint effective, type it, state the facts fully but briefly, and enclose copies of relevant documents like receipts and warranties. If you still don't get a satisfactory response, send your letter to the business's legal department or president.
3. If no one within the company has helped you, it's time to take your complaint to people outside the company. Check your phone book for the numbers of the Better Business Bureau and local consumer groups. Find out whether your local newspaper or radio station has a consumer hotline.

This might sound like a lot of work, but it's worth it. As a consumer, you have certain rights. Stand up for them!

– Annabelle

A Read the column. Based on the advice in the letter, explain what each of these consumers did wrong. Then say what each should have done.

1. When Mira's new TV didn't work, she went back to the store to complain. The salesperson she spoke to didn't seem to care, so Mira began yelling at him. She kept yelling, even when he turned to help another customer.
2. Ed couldn't get his new computer to work. Feeling angry and frustrated, he immediately began looking for consumer groups to complain to.
3. When Alex couldn't get any help by complaining on the phone, he sent the customer-service department a ten-page handwritten letter that explained his problem fully.

B ***Group work*** Talk about these questions.

1. Which of this advice have you used or would you use? Why?
2. What else can you do when you have a complaint about a business?
3. Are there organizations in your country that help people when they have complaints? What are they?

WRITING *Letters of complaint*

A Choose one of these situations and write a letter describing the problem and what needs to be done.

There are several things that need fixing in your apartment.

Dear Mrs. Anderson,
I'm a tenant in Apartment . . . .
I'd like to point out a few things that need fixing. First, in the kitchen . . . .

You bought an appliance that doesn't work. You took it back, but the clerk refused to exchange it.

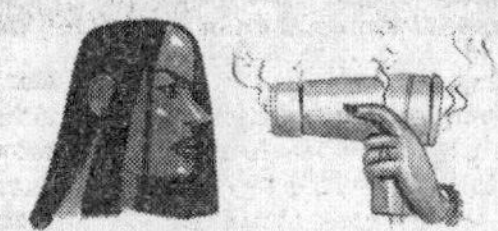

To Whom It May Concern:
Several weeks ago, I bought a hair dryer in your store. After using it just two times, it started to . . . .

B ***Class activity*** Pass your letters around the class. Who has the most unusual problem?

PRONUNCIATION *Contrastive stress*

A Listen and practice. Notice how the second speaker stresses the words he is contrasting.

A: Are you calling about the bedroom **fán**?
B: No, I'm calling about the **kítchen** fan.

A: Are you calling about the bedroom **wíndow**?
B: No, the bedroom **dóor**.

B Mark the words that have contrastive stress in these conversations. Listen and check. Then practice the sentences.

1. A: Did you need two lightbulbs?
   B: No, I asked for three lightbulbs.
2. A: Does your television need to be repaired?
   B: No, my telephone needs to be repaired.

SNAPSHOT

Source: U.S. Department of Commerce and Consumer Protection Office

Talk about these questions.
Have you ever complained about any of these types of businesses?
What are three other businesses or things people often complain about?
Have you ever wanted to complain about something, but didn't? What was it?

3 GRAMMAR FOCUS

Describing problems

With past participles as adjectives	*With nouns*
The jacket lining is **torn**.	It has **a tear** in it./There's **a hole** in it.
The collar of the jacket is **stained**.	It has **a stain** on the collar.
The car is **damaged** in the back.	It has **some damage** in the back.
The furniture is **scratched**.	There are **a lot of scratches** on it.
The glass is **cracked**.	There's **a crack** in it.
The pipe is **leaking**.*	It has **a leak** in it.

***This is an exception: is leaking is a present continuous form.**

For a list of irregular past participles, see the appendix at the back of the book.

A Here are some comments made by customers in a restaurant. Write sentences in two different ways using forms of the word in parentheses. Then compare with a partner.

1. This tablecloth isn't very clean. Look, it . . . . (stain)
2. Let's ask for another water pitcher. This one . . . . (leak)
3. The chairs look pretty worn. The wood . . . , too. (scratch)
4. The waiter needs a new shirt. The one he's wearing . . . . (tear)
5. I'm sorry. Could you bring me another glass? This one . . . . (chip)

B ***Pair work*** Describe two problems with each thing, using past participle, verb, or noun forms of the words below or other words of your own.

A: The vase is chipped.
B: Yes. And it has a crack on the side.

break
burn
chip
crack
dent
leak
loose
scratch
stain
tear

1. a vase 2. a fountain pen 3. a CD
4. a pair of sunglasses 5. a pair of jeans 6. a shirt

C ***Group work*** Look around your classroom. How many problems can you describe?

A: The carpet is a little worn.
B: Yes. And the windows are a bit dirty.
C: Look over there. The curtains . . . .

35

ROLE PLAY *What's the problem?*

Student A: You are returning an item to a store. Decide what the item is and explain why you are returning it.

Student B: You are a salesperson. A customer is returning an item to the store. Ask these questions:

What exactly is the problem? Can you show it to me?
When did you buy the item? Was it like this when you bought it?
Do you have the receipt? Would you like a refund or a store credit?

CONVERSATION

A Listen and practice.

Ms. Lock: Hello?
Mr. Burr: Hello, Ms. Lock. This is Jack Burr.
Ms. Lock: Uh, Mr. Burr . . . in Apartment 205?
Mr. Burr: No, in Apartment 305.
Ms. Lock: Oh, yes. What can I do for you? Does your refrigerator need fixing again?
Mr. Burr: No, it's the oven this time.
Ms. Lock: Oh, so what's wrong with it?
Mr. Burr: Well, I think the temperature control needs to be checked. Everything I try to cook gets burned.
Ms. Lock: Really? OK, I'll have someone look at it right away.
Mr. Burr: Thanks a lot, Ms. Lock.
Ms. Lock: Uh, by the way, Mr. Burr, are you sure it's the oven and not your cooking?

WORD POWER *Appliances*

A Find a suitable sentence in column B to describe a problem with each appliance in column A. Then compare with a partner.

A	*B*
1. air conditioner	a. The water won't drain, and my clothes are left soaking.
2. central heating	b. I put it on high, but it doesn't cool down the room.
3. electric blanket	c. I sometimes smell gas even when I'm not cooking.
4. food processor	d. I turn it on, but it doesn't heat up.
5. iron	e. I can't get a dial tone.
6. stove	f. It gets too hot and burns my clothes.
7. telephone	g. My apartment is freezing cold in the morning.
8. washing machine	h. The blades are dull, so it doesn't chop vegetables very well.

B ***Pair work*** Describe other things that can go wrong with some of the appliances in part A.

LISTENING *Repair jobs*

Listen to three repair people talking about their jobs. Complete the chart.

	What does this person repair?	What is the typical problem?
1. Joe		
2. Louise		
3. Sam		

LISTENING *Fair exchange?*

Listen to three customers returning items they purchased. Complete the chart.

Item	Problem	Will the store exchange it? Yes	No
1.		☐	☐
2.		☐	☐
3.		☐	☐

9–5 *Mary Patten's mind map for* Crosscurrents 2, *Unit 2, on theme of male and female. (See page 200.)*

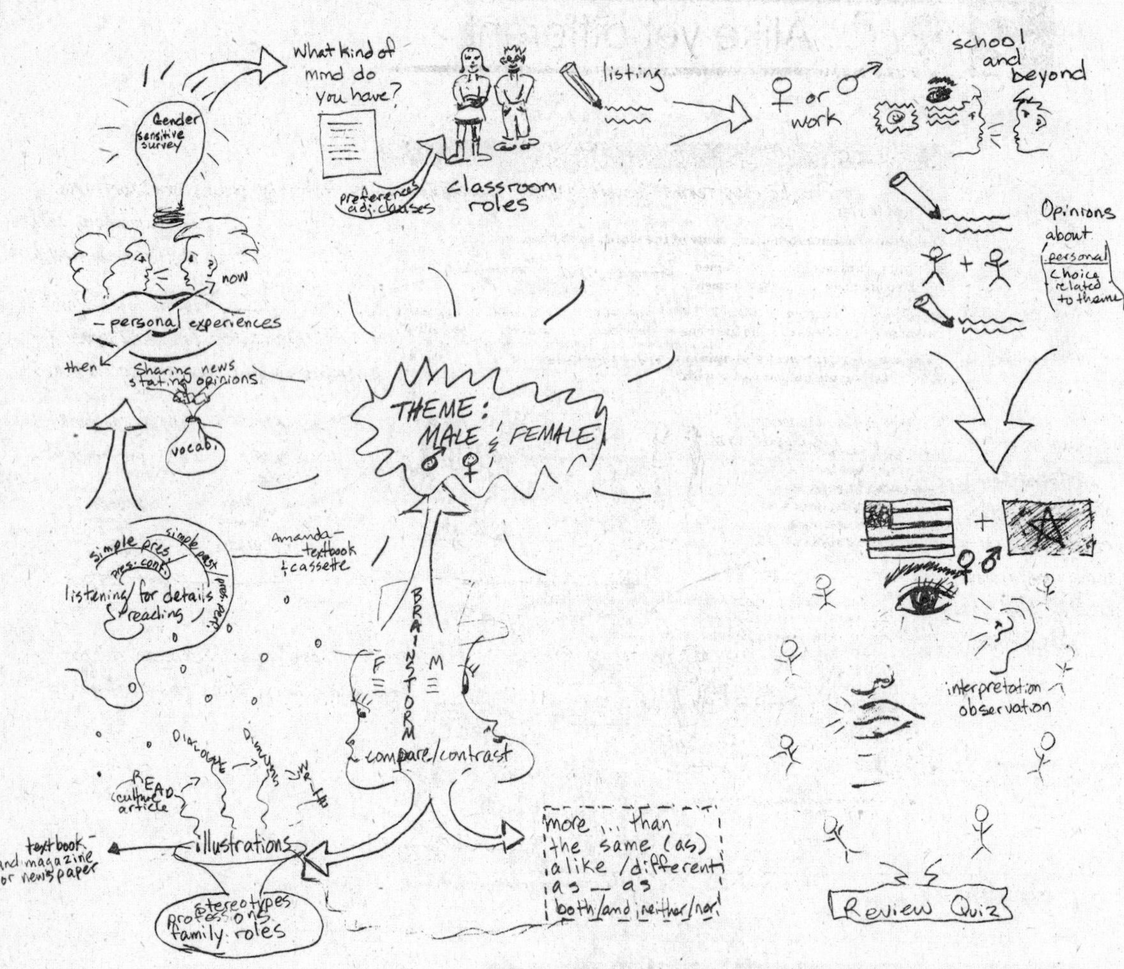

9–6 *Mary Patten's notes for page 1 of* Crosscurrents 2, *Unit 2.*
(See page 200.)

UNIT

♀♂ : Alike yet different

Speak out

Pre: Discuss terms: generalization, stereotype, roles → brainstorm portrayal of men, women, and children in media → review vocab. for #1

1 Talk it over

Complete the sentences using some of the words in the list.

Women are more ____ than men. ← *expand*
Men are more ____ than women.

competitive	cautious	logical	possessive	emotional	aggressive
considerate	intuitive	industrious	generous	relaxed	sensitive

Compare your sentences and opinions with a classmate. Which statements do you agree with?

brainstorm phrases/vocab. for comparing and contrasting on board

expand #1 with these phrases and vocab. — make list on board

Men	*Women*
as generous	*as*

How do these reflect Moroccan culture? American culture? Why do you think so?

2 Talk about... Cartoons *and illustrations*

Look at these cartoons. Describe what is happening in each one. What generalizations do they show about men, women, and children?

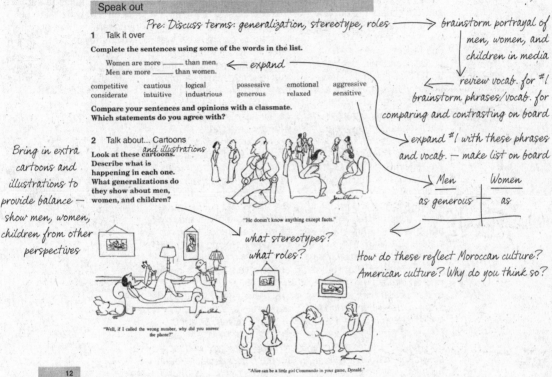

Bring in extra cartoons and illustrations to provide balance — show men, women, children from other perspectives

what stereotypes? what roles?

"He doesn't know anything except facts."

"Well, if I called the wrong number, why did you answer the phone?"

"Alice can be a little *girl* Commando in your game, Donald."

12

9–7 *Mary Patten's sequence for* Crosscurrents 2, *Unit 2, on theme of male and female.* *(See page 200.)*

Activity Sequencing: Unit 2 (Culture and Community Aspects)

Day 1	Day 2	Day 3
Discuss the meanings/concepts of the words *generalization, stereotype,* and *roles* with students to build/activate schema about how men, women, and children are portrayed through various media. Cartoons and illustrations: Discuss information provided by the visuals and brainstorm generalizations that can be made from them, which ones portray stereotypes. Discuss (in pairs, then as a whole class) which ones are reflective of Moroccan culture, of the students as individuals, as men, women, and children, and why. Which ones do they think are reflective of American culture and why? Reading on *Culture* from *Lonely Planet* (1993) *to provide an opportunity for them to go through the process of taking their background knowledge and using it as they read through a passage and apply the topic to themselves, on various levels, from general to specific.* Students brainstorm important aspects of M. culture that foreign visitors should be aware of, note those they feel are most important from their own points of view, skim the reading, noting similarities and differences to what they said—dialogue with a partner about findings, read to find roles or groups they identify with, discuss findings and thoughts with small group. HW: freewriting about anything concerning the topics covered in class, to bring to the next class.	Students share and respond to freewritings with partners—find main ideas and brainstorm examples to support them, and write them on a separate sheet of paper, which they can look back at later in the unit. Pre-listening: talk about and describe family members and their roles and discuss how a family is a micro community—*this is to build student awareness of overlapping communities and how each individual may take on different roles in different communities.* Post-listening community questions and culture questions—who took on the role of the cook in the listening passage? Why do you think it was a shared role? What about in your culture? In your family? Why? Freewriting: 5 minutes—about role(s) students play in their families, or other members of their families, *to generate ideas and incorporate personal background.* Discuss in small groups about their roles, then create a mini role play (2–3 minutes) around one theme (such as cooking, driving, etc.) and each member of the group plays a different role. *This is to help develop roles within the groups as well as to reflect personal, individual roles from their family lives—thus building an overlap of communities.* HW: freewriting about class topics, relation to real life.	Students share and respond to freewritings with partners—find main ideas and brainstorm examples to support them, and write them on a separate sheet of paper, which they can look back at later in the unit.

Activity Sequencing: Unit 2 (Culture and Community Aspects)

Day 5	Day 6	Day 8
Classroom roles: brainstorm what they are—identification. Students identify which ones they take on, when, why—in pairs. In small groups, discuss which they value more/less, why? As a whole class, discuss opinions. Talk about how many roles make up the class community, and what happens when various roles are missing—flux of the group. Pictures and questions: Boys' Work or Girls' Work—students are divided into small groups with mix of ages and sexes, and asked to divide into roles (secretary, time keeper, etc.) and talk about at least 4 questions from each category and be ready to report their findings to the class. *This allows students to be conscious of the roles they are playing and to possibly experiment with one they are not used to, and to see how they work together to build group cohesiveness.* HW: freewriting (as in previous days, to be shared at the beginning of the next class).	Working with writing partners, students review brainstorming ideas and examples about the topics presented during the unit and try to find one main idea that they want to write a paragraph about. Students help each other identify any supporting ideas or examples that can be included or considered. *This aims at unifying the unit theme and reviewing the daily presentations and helping students connect their individual backgrounds to their learning process.* HW: write first draft.	Interpretation and observation: Students and I brainstorm generalizations chart about Moroccan and American men and women. Discuss whether generalizations are always appropriate and/or accurate. Talk about the terms *interpretation* and *observation.* Look at chart and try to identify interpretations and observations (if none of these are on chart, ask students to try to give some, or provide an example first) and look at the differences between them and why it is important to distinguish between them. In small groups, students look at making generalizations, interpretations, and observations about the unit theme, as it relates to them (roles they play, community, cultural aspects), and write down one statement for each term, to present to the class. *This aims at incorporating all the material covered in the unit, and allowing students to personalize it.*

Chapter Ten

10–1 *Error correction symbols handout for David Thomson's 4-week course, "Teaching Writing Using Computers." (See page 217.)*

Error Correction Symbols

Symbol	*Kind of Error*	*Example of error*	*Corrected Sentence*
1. wf	word form	He is strangely.	He is strange.
2. co	collocation/ co-occurence	She is polite at strangers.	She is polite to strangers.
3. sva	subject-verb agreement	He go to the movies.	He goes to the movies.
4. vt	verb tense	She go yesterday.	She went yesterday.
5. aux	auxiliary verb	He don't going.	He isn't going.
6. mod	modal	You should be right.	You may be right.
7. vbal	verbal	I enjoy to eat ice cream.	I enjoy eating ice cream.
8. #	number (singulars/plurals)	He has many friend.	He has many friends.
9. wo	word order	She is late never.	She is never late.
10. prep	preposition	It is at my pocket.	It is in my pocket.
11. sp	spelling	I like his stile.	I like his style.
12. p̸ or p	punctuation	She works, very hard	She works very hard.
13. ww	wrong word	He is Susan.	She is Susan.
14. inc	incomplete sentence	Because they are old.	They have less energy because they are old.
15. RO	run-on sentence	I like ice cream it tastes good.	I like ice cream. It tastes good.
16. ^	insert	She used live in Boston.	She used to live in Boston.
17. /	omit	I am going to there.	I am going there.
18. c or c̸	capitalization	he is my Friend.	He is my friend.
19. pp	paragraph		
20. ???	Meaning is unclear; I do not understand.		

10–2 *Self-rating forms for David Thomson's 4-week course, "Teaching Writing Using Computers."* *(See page 217.)*

Types of Writing

1. Social Correspondence

| ________ | ________ | ________ | ________ | ________
poor fair good very good excellent

Strategies: ____

2. Summaries

| ________ | ________ | ________ | ________ | ________
poor fair good very good excellent

Strategies: ____

2. Short Narratives (factual topics)

| ________ | ________ | ________ | ________ | ________
poor fair good very good excellent

Strategies: ____

2. Descriptions (factual topics)

| ________ | ________ | ________ | ________ | ________
poor fair good very good excellent

Strategies: ____

Writing Evaluation Forms

I. Content/Organization

A. Introduction/Thesis Statement

I __________ I __________ I __________ I __________ I __________
poor fair good very good excellent

Strategies: ____

____

EXCELLENT: The writing has an introduction that clearly frames and establishes the purpose of the paper, and gets the reader's attention. For multi-paragraph assignments, a clear thesis statement has been written to inform the reader of the gist (perhaps point of view, theme, primary point of argument, etc.) of the paper.

B. Topic Sentence(s)/Supporting Details

I __________ I __________ I __________ I __________ I __________
poor fair good very good excellent

Strategies: ____

____

EXCELLENT: Each paragraph has a clearly stated topic sentence that is followed by supporting information, details, facts, or opinions. The writer's ideas and/or opinions are well developed and supported.

C. Logical Sequencing/Connection of Ideas and Information / Cohesion

I __________ I __________ I __________ I __________ I __________
poor fair good very good excellent

Strategies: ____

____

EXCELLENT: The writing is well organized at all levels. Information flows in a logical sequence (from general to specific, from most important to least important, chronologically, etc.). Information in the paragraph is directly related to the topic sentence. Appropriate transition words are used throughout. The writer effectively uses pronouns and other referential links.

D. Conclusion

I __________ I __________ I __________ I __________ I __________
poor fair good very good excellent

Strategies: ____

____

EXCELLENT: The main points of the writing assignment have been briefly reiterated or summarized in a conclusion.

II. Vocabulary/Word Choice

A. Range/Variety

I ____________ I ____________ I ____________ I ____________ I ____________
poor fair good very good excellent

Strategies: ____

____

EXCELLENT: A mix of words appropriate for the assignment has been used throughout. The writer uses words confidently and correctly to describe and inform, and is able to effectively use idiomatic expressions. The writer has not had to rely on a dictionary or translation; the words used in the writing are suitable for the purpose.

B. Word Form

I ____________ I ____________ I ____________ I ____________ I ____________
poor fair good very good excellent

Strategies: ____

____

EXCELLENT: Writer consistently uses the correct form of words, i.e., the adjectival form when appropriate, the noun form when appropriate, etc.

C. Collocation/Co-occurrence

I ____________ I ____________ I ____________ I ____________ I ____________
poor fair good very good excellent

Strategies: ____

____

EXCELLENT: The writer uses phrasal verbs, adjective + preposition, verb + preposition, verb + noun, etc. combinations in correct forms.

III. Language Use

A. Subject Verb Agreement

I ____________ I ____________ I ____________ I ____________ I ____________
poor fair good very good excellent

Strategies: ____

____

EXCELLENT: There are few if any subject/verb agreement errors.

B. Verb Tense/Aspect

I ____________ I ____________ I ____________ I ____________ I ____________
poor fair good very good excellent

Strategies: ____

____

EXCELLENT: The writer uses correct verb tense and aspect throughout the assignment.

C. Singular/Plural (#)

| ______ | | ______ | | ______ | | ______ | | ______
poor | fair | good | very good | excellent

Strategies: ______

______

EXCELLENT: There are few, if any, errors with regard to the use of singulars and plurals (number).

D. Word Order

| ______ | | ______ | | ______ | | ______ | | ______
poor | fair | good | very good | excellent

Strategies: ______

______

EXCELLENT: Writer shows good ability to structure sentences; has a tacit understanding of phrase structure rules.

E. Prepositions

| ______ | | ______ | | ______ | | ______ | | ______
poor | fair | good | very good | excellent

Strategies: ______

______

EXCELLENT: The writer has made few errors that distract from intended meaning.

IV. Mechanics

A. Spelling

| ______ | | ______ | | ______ | | ______ | | ______
poor | fair | good | very good | excellent

Strategies: ______

______

EXCELLENT: The spelling checker has been used effectively, so there are no spelling errors.

B. Punctuation

| ______ | | ______ | | ______ | | ______ | | ______
poor | fair | good | very good | excellent

Strategies: ______

______

EXCELLENT: There are few errors that distract from the intended meaning.

10–3 *End-of-course evaluation for Sally Cavanough's EAP writing course.* *(See page 226.)*

End-of Course-Evaluation

Mark each of the following statements concerning evaluation on a scale from disagree to agree.

The Course

1. The content of the course was appropriate to my needs.
   disagree 1 2 3 4 5 agree

2. The skills taught in the course were appropriate to my needs.
   disagree 1 2 3 4 5 agree

3. There were no cultural misunderstandings.
   disagree 1 2 3 4 5 agree

4. All instructions were clear.
   disagree 1 2 3 4 5 agree

5. Materials and learning activities were appropriate.
   disagree 1 2 3 4 5 agree

6. The class atmosphere was positive.
   disagree 1 2 3 4 5 agree

7. The pacing of lessons was appropriate.
   disagree 1 2 3 4 5 agree

8. There was enough variety in the lessons.
   disagree 1 2 3 4 5 agree

9. Error correction and feedback were appropriate.
   disagree 1 2 3 4 5 agree

Grading

10. My overall understanding of the class assessment plan was clear from the beginning of the course.
    disagree 1 2 3 4 5 agree

11. The grades that I received assessed my work fairly.
    disagree 1 2 3 4 5 agree

12. I understood my teachers' method of grading my work.
    disagree 1 2 3 4 5 agree

13. I prefer to participate when the teacher makes the grading criteria for the written assignments, e.g., the essay on poverty.

    disagree 1 2 3 4 5 agree

14. I prefer it when the teacher uses outside grading criteria for the written assignments, e.g., the AIDS report, Capital Punishment.

    disagree 1 2 3 4 5 agree

15. I would have liked to participate when the teacher decided the overall class grading system at the beginning of the course.

    disagree 1 2 3 4 5 agree

Teaching

16. The teachers taught us what we needed most.

    disagree 1 2 3 4 5 agree

17. The teachers were well prepared for class.

    disagree 1 2 3 4 5 agree

18. The teachers treated me fairly.

    disagree 1 2 3 4 5 agree

19. General class management was good.

    disagree 1 2 3 4 5 agree

20. The teachers were responsive to my needs.

    disagree 1 2 3 4 5 agree

Self-Assessment

21. I tried to improve my research skills by spending time in the library looking around, borrowing books, and asking questions.

    disagree 1 2 3 4 5 agree

22. I tried to improve my vocabulary skills by using a monolingual English dictionary.

    disagree 1 2 3 4 5 agree

23. I tried to improve my writing skills by keeping a record of my mistakes in a notebook.

    disagree 1 2 3 4 5 agree

24. I tried to improve my word-processing skills by practicing a lot and asking questions.

    disagree 1 2 3 4 5 agree

25. I tried to improve my word-processing skills by keeping a record of all the new commands that I learnt in a notebook.

    disagree 1 2 3 4 5 agree

26. I tried to improve my essay writing by asking one of my teachers for help writing an outline.

disagree 1 2 3 4 5 agree

27. I tried to improve my essay writing by focusing carefully on the introduction and asking for feedback if necessary.

disagree 1 2 3 4 5 agree

28. I tried to prepare myself for my further studies by contacting and getting information from the department that I will be studying in.

disagree 1 2 3 4 5 agree

29. I tried to prepare myself for my further studies by asking my department for a list of readings/textbooks that I could begin reading.

disagree 1 2 3 4 5 agree

30. I tried to prepare myself for my further studies by asking my department what referencing style they expect in student essays.

disagree 1 2 3 4 5 agree

31. I carefully organised my notes and course handouts in a 3-ring A4 binder (folder).

disagree 1 2 3 4 5 agree

10–4 *Criteria for comparison and contrast essay in Sally Cavanough's EAP writing course.* *(See page 227.)*

E7 Written Assignment 1: Comparison and Contrast Essay

Due: Monday, Oct. 24 (Week 3)

Topic: Compare studying in Australian universities to studying in universities in your country.

Length: 750 words

Grade: 15 marks
You must get 60% to pass.

A 14–15

B 12–13

C 9–11

Requirements: You must meet the requirements below. If you do not, you may have to resubmit your essay.

1. answer the essay question;
2. include 3 references (supplied by your teachers) which you must cite according to the Style Manual, and format correctly in a List of References at the end of your essay;
3. include a cover page and a list of references;
4. double space your text;
5. use standard A4 paper;
6. if you write by hand: use a pen and write neatly, write on one side of the paper;
7. if you type, take special care with formatting and spacing;
8. write no less than the required word limit, and not too much more;
9. paraphrase, do not plagiarise;
10. do not use abbreviations—spell everything out, for example, don't/do not; e.g.,/for example.
11. You must get 60% to pass.

Criteria: Your essay will be graded according to the criteria below:

Organization The essay displays a logical organisational structure which includes:

1. Introduction
   thesis statement
   general statement
2. Body
   similarities
   differences
3. Conclusion
   summarises main points
   includes final comments

Paragraphs display a logical organisation structure which includes: topic sentences, supporting sentences, concluding sentences.

The writing is well organised for the message to be followed throughout.

Content Both similarities and differences are clearly presented and well developed.

Tone and style are appropriate for the task.

Facts and informed judgements are based on valid sources, for example, first hand experience and referenced material.

Form Vocabulary is wide and used appropriately.

There is a good variety of sentence structures used which are generally accurate and appropriate.

While errors may occur, they are generally minor.

Errors in spelling are few.

Punctuation errors are few.

Comparison and contrast linking words are used appropriately.

10–5 *Criteria for argument essay developed in Sally Cavanough's EAP writing course.* *(See page 228.)*

Written Assignment 2: Argument Essay

Due: Monday, Week 6

Topic: Your own topic related to population control

Length: 750 words

Grade: 20 marks
You must get 60% to pass.
A 18–20
B 15–17
C 12–14

Requirements: You must meet the requirements below. If you do not, you may have to resubmit your essay.

1. answer your essay question drawing from your reading;
2. include 5 references (supplied by your teachers) which you must cite according to the Style Manual, and format correctly in a List of References at the end of your essay;
3. include no more than 2 direct quotes with a maximum of three lines; the rest of your citations must be indirect quotes;
4. include a cover page and a list of references;
5. double space your text;
6. use standard A4 paper;
7. if you write by hand: use a pen and write neatly, write on one side of the paper;
8. if you type, take special care with formatting and spacing;
9. write no less than the required word limit, and not too much more;
10. paraphrase, do not plagiarise;
11. do not use abbreviations—spell everything out, for example, don't/do not; e.g.,/for example.
12. You must get 60% to pass.

Criteria: Your essay will be graded according to the criteria below:

Organization The writing displays a logical organisation which enables the reader to follow the message easily.

The essay has the following:

An introduction, which:

1. links the topic to a recent event;
2. defines the theme with a question that sets out the problem behind the topic;
3. gives a statement of why some people disagree with the writer;
4. gives a main idea statement (MIS) that sets out your opinion on the topic.

Supporting arguments, each of which has:

1. a restatement of the MIS, e.g., the first reason;
2. a counter argument, an opposing view that adds weight to your argument;
3. supporting evidence, an example that proves your support is valid;

A conclusion, which gives a solution to the problem that you introduced in your introduction.

Content Both sides of the question are clearly presented and well developed.

Ideas are relevant and well supported.

The argument follows a clear and logical progression.

Abundant examples are used.

Arguments are presented in an interesting way.

Form A wide range of vocabulary is used.

There are few errors in spelling, punctuation, word choice, and grammar.

A wide range of sentence structures is used.

There is good use of agreement and disagreement structures used in support and counter-argument statements.

References

Apple, M. 1986. *Teachers and texts: A political economy of class and gender relations in education.* New York: Routledge.

Asher, J. 1982. *Learning another language through actions: The complete teacher guidebook* (expanded 2nd ed.). Los Gatos, CA: Sky Oaks Productions.

Auerbach, E. 1992. *Making meaning making change: Participatory curriculum development for adult ESL literacy.* McHenry, IL: Delta Systems.

Auerbach, E. 1993. Putting the P back in participatory. *TESOL Quarterly* 27 (3): 543–545.

Auerbach, E., and D. Burgess. 1987. The hidden curriculum of survival ESL. In I. Shor (ed.), *Freire for the classroom.* Portsmouth, NH: Boynton/Cook. Originally published in *TESOL Quarterly* 19 (3): 475–495, 1985.

Auerbach, E., and L. McGrail. 1991. Rosa's challenge: Connecting classroom and community contexts. In S. Benesch (ed.), *ESL in America: Myths and possibilities.* Portsmouth, NH: Boynton/Cook.

Auerbach, E., and N. Wallerstein. 1987. *ESL for action: Problem-posing at work.* Reading, MA: Addison-Wesley.

Bailey, K. 1998. *Learning about language assessment: Dilemmas, decisions, and directions.* Boston: Heinle & Heinle.

Benesch, S. 1996. Needs analysis and curriculum development in EAP: An example of a critical approach. *TESOL Quarterly* 30 (4): 723–938.

Berwick, R. 1989. Needs assessment in language programming: From theory to practice. In R. K. Johnson (ed.), *The second language curriculum.* Cambridge, UK: Cambridge University Press, 48–62.

Blyth, Maria del Carmen. 1996. Designing an EAP course for postgraduate students in Ecuador. In K. Graves (ed.), *Teachers as course developers.* New York: Cambridge University Press.

Bravo ASL! Curriculum 1996. Sign Enhancers, Inc.

Breen, M. 1989. Contemporary paradigms in syllabus design. *Language Teaching* 20 (2–3): 81–92, 157–174.

Brindley, G. 1989. The role of needs analysis in adult ESL programme design. In R. K. Johnson (ed.), *The second language curriculum.* Cambridge, UK: Cambridge University Press, 63–78.

Brinton, D. M., M. A. Snow, and M. B. Wesche. 1989. *Content-based second language instruction.* Rowley, MA: Newbury House.

Brown, H. D. 1994. *Teaching by principles.* Englewood Cliffs, NJ: Prentice Hall Regents.

Brown, J. D. 1995. *Elements of language curriculum: A systematic approach to program development.* Boston: Heinle & Heinle.

Brown, J. D. 1998. (ed.). *New ways of classroom assessment.* Alexandria, VA: TESOL.

Burnaby, B. 1989. Parameters for projects under the settlement language training program. Toronto, Ontario: TESL Canada Federation. (EDRS No. 318 286)

Canale, M., and M. Swain. 1980. Theoretical bases of communicative approaches to second language teaching and testing. *Applied Linguistics* 1: 1–47.

Cavanough, S. 1995. Learner-centered assessment for the classroom teacher. Unpublished Master's thesis, University of Melbourne, Melbourne, Australia.

Chamot, A. U., I. Rainey de Diaz, J. Baker de Gonzalez, and R. Yorkey. 1991. *Intercom 2000 Book 1*. Boston: Heinle & Heinle.

Clark, C., and P. Peterson. 1986. Teachers' thought processes. In M. Wittrock (ed.), *Handbook of research on teaching* (3rd ed.). New York: Macmillan Publishing, 255–297.

Clark, E. T. 1997. *Designing and implementing an integrated curriculum*. Holistic Education Press.

Crookes, G., and S. Gass (eds.). 1993. *Tasks in a pedagogical context: Integrating theory and practice*. Clevedon, Avon: Multilingual Matters.

Curran, C. 1976. *Counseling-learning in second languages*. Apple River, IL: Apple River Press.

Day, R. 1993. *New ways in teaching reading*. Alexandria, VA: TESOL.

Dixon, C. 1990. *The language experience approach to reading and writing*. Hayward, CA: Alemany Press.

Elbow, P. 1986. *Embracing contraries*. Oxford, UK: Oxford University Press.

Erickson, F. 1986. Qualitative methods in research on teaching. In M. Wittrock (ed.), *Handbook of research on teaching* (3rd ed.). New York: Macmillan Publishing, 119–161.

Fairclough, N. 1992. *Critical language awareness*. London: Longman.

Fantini, A. 1995. At the heart of things: CISV's educational purpose. *Interspectives: A Journal on Transcultural and Educational Perspectives* (vol. 13), CISV International, Newcastle, England.

Feez, S. 1998. *Text-based syllabus design*. Sydney: National Centre for English Language Teaching and Research.

Fisher, P. 1996. Designing a seventh-grade social studies course for ESL students at an international school. In K. Graves (ed.), *Teachers as course developers*. New York: Cambridge University Press.

Fisk Ong, M., K. Harrington, and D. Occhiuzzo, 1995. *Crosscurrents 1*. London: Longman.

Fragiadakis, H., and V. Maurer. 1994. *Sound ideas: Advanced listening and speaking*. Boston: Heinle & Heinle.

Freeman, D. 1998. *Doing teacher research: From inquiry to understanding*. Boston: Heinle & Heinle.

Freire, P. 1973. *Education for critical consciousness*. New York: Seabury Press.

Fujiwara, B. 1996. Planning an advanced listening comprehension elective for Japanese college students. In K. Graves (ed.), *Teachers as course developers*. New York: Cambridge University Press.

Gardner, H. 1983. *Frames of mind: The theory of multiple intelligences*. New York: Basic Books.

Gee, J. 1990. *Social linguistics and literacies: Ideology in discourses.* Philadelphia: Falmer Press.

Genesee, F., and J. Upshur. 1996. *Classroom-based evaluation in second language education.* New York: Cambridge University Press.

Gorsuch, G. 1991. Helping students create their own learning goals. *Language Teacher* 15 (12): 3, 9.

Grady, K. 1997. Critically reading an ESL text. *TESOL Journal* 6 (4): 7–10.

Grant, C., and S. Shank. 1993. Discovering and responding to learner needs: Module for ESL teacher training. Available through ERIC (EDRS No. ED 367 196).

Grant, N. 1987. *Making the most of your textbook.* London: Longman.

Graves, K. (ed.). 1996. *Teachers as course developers.* New York: Cambridge University Press.

Graves, K. 1993. Self tests. In D. Freeman, and S. Cornwall (eds.), *New ways in teacher education.* Alexandria, VA: TESOL.

Graves, K., and D. P. Rein. 1988. *East West.* New York: Oxford University Press.

Graves, K., and A. Rice. 1994. *East West Basics.* New York: Oxford University Press.

Gronlund, N. E. 1985. *Stating objectives for classroom instruction* (3rd ed.). New York: Macmillan.

Halliday, M. 1994. *An introduction to functional grammar* (2nd ed.). London: Edward Arnold.

Hawkins, D. 1967. *The informed vision: Essays on learning and human nature.* Agathon Press.

Heaton, J. B. 1990. *Classroom testing.* London: Longman.

Hull, L. 1996. A curriculum framework for corporate language programs. In K. Graves (ed.), *Teachers as course developers.* New York: Cambridge University Press.

Huizenga, J., and G. Weinstein-Shr. 1994. *Collaborations.* Boston: Heinle & Heinle.

Hutchinson, T., and A. Waters. 1987. *English for specific purposes: A learning-centred approach.* Cambridge, UK: Cambridge University Press.

Johnson, K. 1999. *Understanding language teaching: Reasoning in action.* Boston: Heinle & Heinle.

Johnson, R. K. 1989. A decision-making framework for the coherent language curriculum. In R. K. Johnson (ed.), *The second language curriculum.* Cambridge, UK: Cambridge University Press, 1–23.

Kolb, D. A. 1984. *Experiential learning.* Englewood Cliffs, NJ: Prentice Hall.

Krashen, S., and R. Terrell. 1983. *The natural approach.* Hayward, CA: Alemany Press.

Larsen-Freeman, D. 1991. Teaching Grammar. In M. Celce-Murcia (ed.), *Teaching English as a second or foreign language* (2nd ed.). Boston: Heinle & Heinle.

Larsen-Freeman, D. 1997. Chaos/complexity: Science and second language acquisition. *Applied Linguistics* 18 (2): 141–165.

Lortie, D. 1975. *Schoolteacher: A sociological study.* Chicago: University of Chicago Press.

Mager, R. R. 1962. *Preparing instructional objectives.* Belmont, CA: Fearon Publishers.

Markee, N. 1997. *Managing curricular innovation.* Cambridge, UK: Cambridge University Press.

Master, Peter A. 1986. *Science, medicine, and technology: English grammar and technical writing*. Englewood Cliffs, NJ: Prentice Hall.

Matthews, A., M. Spratt, and L. Dangerfield. 1985. *At the Chalkface*. London: Edward Arnold.

Munby, J. 1978. *Communicative syllabus design*. Cambridge, UK: Cambridge University Press.

Nover, S. 1997. An overview of language planning, deaf education, and bilingual education. Presentation at Austine School for the Deaf, Brattleboro, Vermont.

Nunan, D. 1988. *Syllabus design*. Oxford, UK: Oxford University Press.

Nunan, D. 1989. *Designing tasks for the communicative classroom*. Cambridge, UK: Cambridge University Press.

Omaggio Hadley, A. 1993. *Teaching language in context* (2nd ed.). Boston: Heinle & Heinle.

O'Malley, M., and A. U. Chamot. 1990. *Learning strategies in second language acquisition*. New York: Cambridge University Press.

Oxford, R. 1990. *Language learning strategies: What every teacher should know*. Rowley, MA: Newbury House.

Perkins, D. 1995. *Smart schools: From training memories to educating minds*. New York: Free Press.

Peyton, J. K., and L. Reed (eds.). 1990. *Dialogue journal writing with nonnative English speakers*. Alexandria, VA: TESOL.

Pinheiro Franco, M. E. 1996. Designing a writing component for teen courses at a Brazilian language institute. In K. Graves (ed.), *Teachers as course developers*. New York: Cambridge University Press.

Rardin, J., and D. Tranel. 1988. *Education in a new dimension: The counseling-learning approach to community language learning*. East Dubuque, IL: Counseling-Learning Publications.

Richards, J. C. 1990. *The language teaching matrix*. Cambridge, UK: Cambridge University Press.

Richards, J. C., J. Hull, and S. Proctor. 1991. *Interchange 3*. New York: Cambridge University Press.

Rigg, P. 1989. Language experience approach: Reading naturally. In *When they don't all speak English: Integrating the ESL student into the regular classroom*. Chicago: National Council of Teachers of English.

Saphier, J., and R. Gower. 1987. *The skillful teacher: Building your teaching skills*. Carlisle, MA: Research for Better Teaching, Inc.

Savage, L. 1993. Literacy through a competency-based educational approach. In J. A. Crandall and J. K. Peyton (eds.), *Approaches to adult ESL literacy instruction*. Washington, DC and Henry, IL: Center for Applied Linguistics and Delta Systems.

Shannon, P. 1987. Commercial reading materials, a technological ideology and the deskilling of teachers. *The Elementary School Journal* 87 (3): pages.

Shulman, L. 1987. Knowledge and teaching: Foundations of the new reform. *Harvard Education Review* 57 (1): 1–22.

Snow, M. A., M. Met, and F. Genesee. 1989. A conceptual framework for the integration of language and content in second/foreign language instruction. *TESOL Quarterly* 23 (quarter): 201–217.